SAP PRESS e-books

Print or e-book, Kindle or iPad, workplace or airplane: Choose where and how to read your SAP PRESS books! You can now get all our titles as e-books, too:

- By download and online access
- For all popular devices
- And, of course, DRM-free

Convinced? Then go to www.sap-press.com and get your e-book today.

SAP S/4HANA® Cloud

 **PRESS**

SAP PRESS is a joint initiative of SAP and Rheinwerk Publishing. The know-how offered by SAP specialists combined with the expertise of Rheinwerk Publishing offers the reader expert books in the field. SAP PRESS features first-hand information and expert advice, and provides useful skills for professional decision-making.

SAP PRESS offers a variety of books on technical and business-related topics for the SAP user. For further information, please visit our website: *www.sap-press.com*.

Bardhan, Baumgartl, Chaadaev, Choi, Dudgeon, Lahiri, Meijerink, Worsley-Tonks
SAP S/4HANA: An Introduction (2nd Edition)
2018, approx. 550 pp., hardcover and e-book
www.sap-press.com/4499

Bhattacharjee, Monti, Perel, Vazquez
Logistics with SAP S/4HANA: An Introduction
2018, approx. 500 pp., hardcover and e-book
www.sap-press.com/4485

Singh, Feurer, Ruebsam
SAP Hybris: Commerce, Marketing, Sales, Service, and Revenue with SAP
2017, 329 pages, hardcover and e-book
www.sap-press.com/4394

Silvia, Frye, Berg
SAP HANA: An Introduction (4th Edition)
2017, 549 pages, hardcover and e-book
www.sap-press.com/4160

Michael Jolton, Yosh Eisbart

SAP S/4HANA® Cloud

Use Cases, Functionality, and Extensibility

Rheinwerk
Publishing

Editor Meagan White
Acquisitions Editor Emily Nicholls
Copyeditor Melinda Rankin
Cover Design Graham Geary
Photo Credit iStockphoto.com/185126130/© hudiemm
Layout Design Vera Brauner
Production Marissa Fritz
Typesetting III-satz, Husby (Germany)
Printed and bound in the United States of America, on paper from sustainable sources

ISBN 978-1-4932-1595-9
© 2017 by Rheinwerk Publishing, Inc., Boston (MA)
1st edition 2017

Library of Congress Cataloging in Publication Control Number: 2017028734

Contents at a Glance

PART I   Getting Started

1   The Basics: What Is SAP S/4HANA Cloud? 27

2   Customer Use Cases: Who Should Use SAP S/4HANA Cloud? 49

3   Implementation: How Do You Set Up SAP S/4HANA Cloud? 79

4   Costs: How Much Will SAP S/4HANA Cloud Cost? 111

5   Maintenance: How Do You Maintain SAP S/4HANA Cloud? 125

PART II   Business Processes

6   Product Functionality: What Processes Does SAP S/4HANA
     Cloud Perform? 147

7   Embedded Analytics: What Can SAP S/4HANA Cloud Teach You
     About Your Business? 239

PART III   Next Steps

8   Integrations: Can You Connect SAP S/4HANA Cloud with Other
     Applications? 267

9   Extensibility: How Can You Personalize SAP S/4HANA Cloud? 287

10   Roadmap: Where Do We Go from Here? 309

Dear Reader,

Publishing a "cloud" book can be a challenge. Because release dates for new software versions are so close together, up-to-date information is more valuable than ever—but even harder to pin down. And when the SAP product in question is brand new? Just imagine the editorial obstacles.

Luckily, we had an all-star team for this book. Our expert authors, Michael Jolton and Yosh Eisbart, brought to this project what every twenty-first-century company wants from its software provider: expertise, adaptability, and forward thinking. As their editor, I can honestly say that it has been a joy to work with both MJ and Yosh. These two overcame the challenge of writing on this dynamic product (we had to cut a whole chapter halfway through the project because SAP S/4HANA Cloud no longer has "editions"!) and nimbly delivered new material on an aggressive schedule. The outcome is a compact volume of fantastic work—as you'll soon see.

What did you think about *SAP S/4HANA Cloud: Use Cases, Functionality, and Extensibility*? Your comments and suggestions are the most useful tools to help us make our books the best they can be. Please feel free to contact me and share any praise or criticism you may have.

Thank you for purchasing a book from SAP PRESS!

Meagan White
Editor, SAP PRESS

meaganw@rheinwerk-publishing.com
www.sap-press.com
Rheinwerk Publishing · Boston, MA

Contents

Foreword from SAP 13

Foreword by Geoffrey Scott 15

Preface 17

PART I   Getting Started

1   The Basics: What Is SAP S/4HANA Cloud?   27

1.1	**Overview**	28
1.2	**Cloud ERP and the Two-Tier Model**	33
1.3	**Preconfigured End-to-End Business Processes**	35
1.4	**ERP Cloud Building Blocks**	38
	1.4.1 Software as a Service	38
	1.4.2 Platform as a Service	40
	1.4.3 Infrastructure as a Service	40
1.5	**Ongoing Support**	41
	1.5.1 SAP Production Support Models	41
	1.5.2 Business Analyst	42
	1.5.3 Extensibility Support	43
1.6	**Summary**	47

2   Customer Use Cases: Who Should Use SAP S/4HANA Cloud?   49

2.1	**ERP in the Cloud**	50
	2.1.1 Minimal IT Spend	51
	2.1.2 International Businesses	52
	2.1.3 Outsourced IT	54
	2.1.4 Faster Upgrade Cycles	55

2.2	**Preconfigured ERP**		55
	2.2.1	SAP Best Practices	56
	2.2.2	Standard Business Practice-Driven Model	59
	2.2.3	The Fit-to-Standard Approach	62
2.3	**Two-Tiered ERP Model**		64
	2.3.1	Two-Tiered Approach: Maturity Level	66
	2.3.2	Federated Manufacturing Model	67
	2.3.3	Holding Company Model	70
	2.3.4	Start-ups and Mergers and Acquisitions	72
2.4	**Localization**		77
2.5	**Summary**		78

3   Implementation: How Do You Set Up SAP S/4HANA Cloud?

			79
3.1	**SAP S/4HANA Cloud Best Practices**		79
	3.1.1	Navigating	80
	3.1.2	Content	83
3.2	**SAP Activate**		86
	3.2.1	Discover	89
	3.2.2	Prepare	90
	3.2.3	Explore	95
	3.2.4	Realize	102
	3.2.5	Deploy	106
	3.2.6	Run	108
3.3	**Team Requirements and Timing**		108
3.4	**Summary**		110

4   Costs: How Much Will SAP S/4HANA Cloud Cost?

			111
4.1	**Subscription Price Structure**		112
	4.1.1	Simplifying the SAP S/4HANA Cloud Licensing Model	113

4.1.2   Current Pricing 113

4.2   SAP's Cloud Extension Model 114

4.3   Implementation Cost Components 115

4.4   Estimating Implementation Costs 119
        4.4.1   Fit-to-Standard Process 119
        4.4.2   Cost Estimation Process 119

4.5   End User Support via SAP Application Management Services 121

4.6   Summary 123

5   Maintenance: How Do You Maintain SAP S/4HANA Cloud?   125

5.1   Quarterly Release Management 126
        5.1.1   Communicating with Users 127
        5.1.2   SAP Communications 132
        5.1.3   Enabling New Releases 134

5.2   Report Development 136

5.3   Tile Customization 139

5.4   Integration Management 143

5.5   End User Support via Application Management Services 143

5.6   Summary 144

PART II   Business Processes

6   Product Functionality: What Processes Does SAP S/4HANA Cloud Perform?   147

6.1   The Big Picture 148

6.2   Streamlined Procure-to-Pay 150
        6.2.1   Procurement Master Data 150

6.2.2	Supplier Management	151
6.2.3	Operational Purchasing	156
6.2.4	Contract Management and Collaborative Sourcing	166
6.2.5	Inventory Management	168
6.2.6	Invoice and Payables Management	173
6.2.7	Procurement Analytics	175

6.3 Accelerated Plan-to-Product ... 178

6.3.1	Basic Production Planning	179
6.3.2	Basic Production Processing	182
6.3.3	Inventory Management	190
6.3.4	Maintenance Management	190
6.3.5	Project Control and Product Development	192

6.4 Optimized Order-to-Cash ... 193

6.4.1	Order-to-Cash Scope Items Covered in Other Functional Groupings	193
6.4.2	Order and Contracts Management	194

6.5 Project Services ... 210

6.5.1	Project Management	210
6.5.2	Contract-to-Cash	215
6.5.3	Time and Expense Management	216

6.6 Core Finance ... 218

6.6.1	Accounting and Closing Operations	218
6.6.2	Statutory Reporting	229
6.6.3	Treasury and Financial Risk Management	232
6.6.4	Receivables Management	233

6.7 HR Connectivity ... 234

6.8 Data Management ... 234

6.8.1	Basic Data Integration	235
6.8.2	Master Data Maintenance	235
6.8.3	Master Data Management	236

6.9 Functionality in New Releases ... 236

6.10 Summary ... 238

7   Embedded Analytics: What Can SAP S/4HANA Cloud Teach You About Your Business?   239

7.1	SAP Fiori UX Overview	240
7.2	Tiles	244
	7.2.1 SAP Smart Business Tiles	244
	7.2.2 Custom Tiles	247
7.3	Standard Graphical Reports	251
7.4	Standard Overview Apps	255
7.5	Multidimensional Analytics	256
7.6	Customized Queries	260
7.7	Summary	263

PART III   Next Steps

8   Integrations: Can You Connect SAP S/4HANA Cloud with Other Applications?   267

8.1	Built-in Integrations	268
8.2	Custom Integrations	274
	8.2.1 SAP Cloud Platform	274
	8.2.2 Development Process and Components	276
	8.2.3 APIs	281
	8.2.4 Electronic Data Interchange	285
8.3	Summary	286

9 Extensibility: How Can You Personalize SAP S/4HANA Cloud? 287

9.1 In-App Extensibility 288

    9.1.1 In-App Extensibility Authorization 288

    9.1.2 Locating Extensible Apps 288

    9.1.3 Changing, Adding, and Deleting Fields and Groups on a Screen 290

    9.1.4 Adding Logic 296

    9.1.5 Adding Business Objects 299

    9.1.6 Adding CDS Views 303

9.2 Side-by-Side Extensions Using SAP Cloud Platform 306

9.3 Customer-Developed Extensions via SAP S/4HANA Cloud SDK 308

9.4 Summary 308

10 Roadmap: Where Do We Go from Here? 309

10.1 Current Roadmap 310

    10.1.1 The Importance of the Roadmap 311

    10.1.2 Upcoming Functionalities 312

10.2 Recent Innovations and How They Might Affect the Roadmap 316

    10.2.1 Master Data 317

    10.2.2 Extensibility 317

10.3 Where to Find Roadmap Updates 319

10.4 Summary: What a Long, Strange Trip It's Been 319

Conclusion 321

The Authors 325

Index 327

Foreword from SAP

Businesses must run differently in the digital age. Customers demand service anywhere, any time, on any device. Enterprise processes have to change with the availability of real-time data that enables competitive advantage. The cloud is the key enabler—it matches the modern business need for innovation and speed of service and is the only delivery system for enterprise resource planning (ERP) capable of helping an organization to run ahead. Businesses that don't adopt public cloud services won't just be at a disadvantage—they'll become cautionary case studies in business history.

While the first generation of cloud ERP was focused on speed of adoption, the new generation of cloud ERP is intelligent. Through artificial intelligence (AI), it learns, anticipates, and is one step ahead, offering unrivalled agility in business operations and instant business value. SAP is the leader in intelligent cloud ERP through its significant investment in SAP S/4HANA Cloud.

The business case for intelligent cloud ERP is strong. Businesses can offer their talent a digital age user experience, driving higher rates of adoption and productivity. Total cost of ownership (TCO) can be reduced as the need for expensive architecture decreases. Crucially, businesses can adopt SAP S/4HANA Cloud rapidly, transforming into a fully digital operation and seeing near instant value.

Implementation is a clear measure of speed to value. In traditional deployments, CIOs are responsible for tremendous overhead in provisioning, application management, middleware, and maintaining IT support systems, not to mention ongoing security. For SAP S/4HANA Cloud, you need only two things: a browser and your company's data. No servers, no front-end rollout, no monolithic change management are necessary.

This new model speeds that time to value. SAP S/4HANA Cloud averages 14-16 weeks from order to full implementation and that time will decrease with further automation. SAP provides quarterly updates to continuously expand the innovative potential of this intelligent cloud ERP.

What could you do accomplish if you focused on delivering business value instead of keeping the lights on?

The future of software is in applications that learn from your business, provide information in context, and offer real-time analytics on streaming data. The future of enterprise software is in artificial intelligence and machine learning.

To date, in all ERP, there's only one product that has machine learning live: SAP S/4HANA Cloud. SAP CoPilot, a truly intelligent digital assistant, provides in-context alerts that help every one of your users take daily actions to increase productivity. Machine learning can also greatly reduce manual tasks—such as automatically matching payments against invoices—freeing up time for the talent in your organization to focus on innovation. SAP S/4HANA Cloud currently has over 30 machine learning-powered scenarios live or in the works to aid productivity and simplify processes, which we'll continue to roll out on our quarterly update schedule.

Not every business may be ready to go all in on the cloud. However most business leaders I speak to plan starting or extending their cloud journey today. Together with our partners we are engaged in countless conversations of this kind every day, working to find the best possible solution for each business need.

SAP is migrating businesses to the cloud and one of our key partners is NIMBL. As an experienced and recognized SAP ecosystem thought leader with countless successful initiatives to their name, NIMBL fully understands the potential of cloud ERP and the business benefits for customers. NIMBL was one of the first companies to embrace SAP S/4HANA Cloud, becoming an official Lighthouse Partner in 2016. NIMBL knows what it takes to implement SAP S/4HANA Cloud. This experience ensures customers are in the best possible position to find a solution that fits their needs.

We've seen first-hand how NIMBL has harnessed the benefits of Cloud that drive true business transformation. That energy and experience have been captured in this comprehensive book on SAP S/4HANA Cloud. We're excited to work with NIMBL on this project—and we look forward to bringing the full benefits of our partnership to life on many customer projects in the future.

Melissa Di Donato
Chief Revenue Officer, SAP S/4HANA Cloud
August 2017

Foreword by Geoffrey Scott

Browse any technology or media website today and it won't take long for you to come across a reference to *the cloud*. In fact, do a basic Google search for "Cloud" and you will see nearly two billion results returned. That's a lot of results for what seems like a simple word. Clearly there's a lot going on underneath.

For some, the cloud is where they host their computing infrastructure. For others, it represents the ability to construct applications using various virtual platforms. However, for the purposes of this book, it means accessing enterprise resource planning (ERP) software that is managed, hosted, and maintained by someone else in the cloud. What a great and novel idea!

Since the early 1990s, when ERP software applications first came into focus, they have required big servers running in organization-owned data centers, managed by teams of people, and customizable to the needs of the organization running it. For small and medium-sized businesses, the cost of operating this landscape has been prohibitive, and as a result they have found solutions elsewhere.

For those able to afford an ERP platform, progress has been steady over the decades. Perhaps their server infrastructure is now running on the cloud or their support teams have been reconfigured with offshore, nearshore, and onshore resources, but the core ERP software architecture remained largely the same. That all changed when SAP announced the SAP HANA database and SAP S/4HANA in 2010 and 2015, respectively. Since then, change has accelerated rapidly.

These new flagship ERP products from SAP offer new opportunities to simplify, modernize, and reduce the cost the operations of the core ERP. With SAP S/4HANA, SAP introduced both on-premise and cloud versions of the product.

This cloud version, aptly named SAP S/4HANA Cloud, holds great promise for organizations, perhaps like yours, who heretofore have been unable to implement a full-scale ERP platform. The investment may have been outside your reach, or perhaps you're a subsidiary of a larger organization where the implementation and integration cost is prohibitive, or you're located in another country where regulations and practices differ significantly from the home country organization. Whatever the reason, there is now a solution from SAP that warrants your close attention and inspection.

Looking at the opportunities SAP S/4HANA Cloud affords only through a cost lens fails to uncover the full picture. What should also be considered are the opportunities for innovation that this platform offers. The clear advantage of cloud applications, and especially SAP S/4HANA Cloud, is the ability to incorporate software upgrades and innovations simply. The pace of innovation in cloud applications is moving much faster than what can be achieved with internally developed innovations. Your organization's ability to not only adapt to but also to leverage these innovations more rapidly than others could be the very competitive edge that you need to thrive in today's digital world.

The pages that follow will help you determine if SAP S/4HANA Cloud is right for your organization. You will learn how to plan, purchase, implement, and integrate this software. Even more importantly, you will gain a better understanding of how you can leverage analytics to gain the crucial insights that separate your organization from the rest.

The team at NIMBL has done an outstanding job presenting this information to you so that you are well equipped when it comes to making important decisions about your ERP strategy. NIMBL has been a long-time partner with SAP as well as the Americas' SAP Users' Group (ASUG). Personally, I have engaged them in projects and have been extremely satisfied with the results.

This book is an essential start to your journey of understanding SAP S/4HANA Cloud. We also encourage you to check out ASUG, a central community for helping you and your organization succeed with SAP technologies. For more than twenty-five years, ASUG has been the core of education, networking and influence for SAP customers. We are excited to welcome those who are joining the SAP community for the first time through an investment in SAP S/4HANA Cloud! As you proceed along this journey we want to hear your story. We encourage you to share it with all of us so that we can all gain from your knowledge and experience. This is the true gift of any community, and most especially of ASUG.

Read on! As you read I welcome you to connect with me, ASUG, and these outstanding authors to share your thoughts, opportunities, and challenges overcome with this software. We are here to help!

Geoffrey Scott
CEO, Americas' SAP Users' Group
August 2017

Preface

The massive stadium seating room at the Orange County Convention Center was packed to the gills. The Orlando, Florida, audience was abuzz with excitement, patiently waiting for the keynote address at the world's largest and most important SAP conference in the world: the 2015 SAPPHIRE and America's SAP User Group (ASUG) Annual Conference. It was and is common knowledge that new SAP products and innovations are debuted at SAPPHIRE. The date was May 6, 2015, the time 9 a.m. Eastern. The audience: SAP customers across North America and around the world, vendors, SAP leadership, industry analysts, and partners reaching all four corners of the globe. The atmosphere: part information technology conference, part circus.

Juxtaposed against the thrill in the air, the stage was dark. The aesthetics were clean lines and stark German simplicity, indicative of the SAP brand. Moving gracefully across the stage—almost floating—Bernd Leukert, executive SAP board member and long-time SAP products innovation leader, made the announcement: "SAP S/4HANA is now available in the cloud." The audience erupted in applause.

This proclamation changed the face of enterprise resource planning (ERP) software as a service (SaaS).

Apologies for the dramatics, but we believe that SAP S/4HANA Cloud will be a game changer for the ERP market. Obviously, we're a bit biased; our consulting company, NIMBL, is an SAP consulting firm and SAP S/4HANA Cloud lighthouse partner. However, we do believe for a multitude of reasons, being as objective as possible, that SAP S/4HANA Cloud will change how businesses both large and small implement, deploy, and look at ERP software.

Simply put, SAP S/4HANA Cloud is SAP's SaaS solution for rapid, cost effective, out-of-the-box cloud-based ERP.

Objective of This Book

The SAP S/4HANA Cloud world is unfolding before our eyes. Within the SAP world, I can't remember a more exciting time. Now, a new SAP ERP SaaS product, tectonic platform shifts towards cloud services, unprecedented user adoption, a wide-open partner ecosystem, unprecedented SAP transparency, and true SAP partnership embracement have converged and all aligned in the customer's favor. NIMBL has embraced the SAP S/4HANA Cloud message for all these reasons, coupled with the fact that we truly believe in the game-changing opportunity for this software.

Thus, when the opportunity arose for NIMBL (*www.benimbl.com*) to write the first SAP PRESS book on SAP S/4HANA Cloud, it was one of those once-in-a-lifetime moments—truly. As many of you already know, we believe strongly in thought leadership through education. By presenting at seminars and SAP conferences across the globe on a wide range of SAP topics, NIMBL's thought leaders share their knowledge and experience. We believe in the power of blogging, vlogging, speaking, writing, and presenting to our fellow SAP-philes in the hopes of sharing knowledge and greater SAP ecosystem collaboration.

To be able to present on new and older SAP technologies and subjects, our team must stay abreast of the latest and greatest info, often learning as we go and frequently staying one step ahead of the field. This held true for this book and this topic.

As a quickly evolving software, SAP S/4HANA Cloud pivoted even as we were writing. It kept us on our toes. Not only did the speed of innovation require us to become experts in the product quickly, but perhaps more importantly it gave us a greater appreciation for the product. With so much energy, buzz, and investment around SAP's newest flagship SaaS ERP product, we wanted to write a resource book that captured SAP S/4HANA Cloud objectively, not from a sales perspective. (Ironically, during the short writing timeframe [only three months] of this book, several key components changed, including some fundamental building blocks, such as SAP S/4HANA Cloud's pricing construct and concept of editions.)

Simply put, the intention and objective of this book is to provide a valuable, high-level resource guide for understanding SAP S/4HANA Cloud. This product's quarterly innovation release schedules make it simply impossible to write a book that will always remain current.

However, in our opinion, if this SAP S/4HANA Cloud book effectively provides the following information, we'll consider it a success:

- A foundational product understanding
- SAP S/4HANA Cloud's use cases
- High-level understanding of SAP S/4HANA Cloud business functionality
- How to expand SAP S/4HANA Cloud's functionality
- Implementation effort required for SAP S/4HANA Cloud
- Support needs of SAP S/4HANA Cloud

Target Audience of This Book

This book's intended audience is individuals and companies unfamiliar with SAP S/4HANA Cloud and its potential use. SAP S/4HANA Cloud is a very new product; coupled with the tremendous amount of confusion in the marketplace regarding the countless SAP acronyms, concepts, products, and platforms, it can be confused with other SAP platforms. For example, people frequently assume that SAP S/4HANA Cloud is part of SAP HANA Enterprise Cloud!

As an ever-evolving and developing SAP innovation, SAP S/4HANA Cloud and its nuances are constantly changing. Thus, this book is *not* intended to be an in-depth how-to manual depicting step-by-step configuration documentation.

Instead, this book is geared toward the following types of readers:

- Interested parties unfamiliar with SAP S/4HANA Cloud
- Companies exploring SAP S/4HANA Cloud as a potential ERP solution
- Organizations looking to build the business case for SAP S/4HANA Cloud

SAP S/4HANA Cloud presents an interesting and exciting new opportunity for companies looking to deploy a best-of-breed, lightweight ERP solution rapidly for a fraction of the on-premise cost. This book is geared toward understanding the potential value of SAP S/4HANA Cloud specific to a business and toward empowering the reader to build a viable business case for its deployment.

How to Read This Book

The book has been designed and written in a purposeful manner. Broken down into three distinct sections or parts, each chapter builds upon previously discussed concepts to flesh out the greater SAP S/4HANA Cloud story.

The book certainly can be utilized as a resource book in which specific topics can be referenced on an as-needed basis, but our intent was for it to be read end-to-end. Furthermore, as you'll see from the part titles, the idea is that the parts become progressively deeper and more complex as the book continues.

Regardless of reading style preference, a reader should be able to derive value from either reading approach—selective or end to end.

Ahead, you'll find an overview of the content covered in each part and how the parts tie together holistically across the entire fabric of the book.

Part I: Getting Started, or SAP S/4HANA Cloud 101

Part I begins the SAP S/4HANA Cloud discussion by laying a solid foundation for the basics. In **Chapter 1**, we discuss, from user and customer perspectives, what's included with SAP S/4HANA Cloud and basic industry concepts embedded with SAP S/4HANA Cloud as part of its fundamental design. Concepts such as infrastructure as a service (IaaS), software as a service, and other prevalent industry software models are described and dissected. These important technical precepts are essential for understanding cloud software in general and SAP S/4HANA Cloud.

In **Chapter 2**, we begin to dig deeper into the right businesses to implement SAP S/4HANA Cloud, essentially making a business case for best-suited product application. We discuss several of the most widely used organizational scenarios, including the two-tiered SAP ERP model along with the midmarket (and start-up) single cloud ERP example. This chapter specifically is important because being able to effectively articulate the business rationale for deploying SAP is perhaps the most important step in product selection. (No business case justification means no SAP S/4HANA Cloud deployment.)

Continuing to **Chapter 3**, we break down the SAP Activate implementation approach and phases specific to deploying SAP S/4HANA Cloud. The SAP S/4HANA Cloud suite of accelerators also exists as an important component within SAP S/4HANA Cloud implementations. This chapter is an excellent resource guide for exploring and performing the process of rolling out SAP S/4HANA Cloud.

Chapter 4 tackles the ever-important discussion of cost—that is, how much it might cost to implement SAP S/4HANA Cloud. Cost components such as software, implementation, and long-term support are all important decision-making factors related to whether a business should and can invest in a new software product. Although nailing down specific costs are difficult for implementing any software, this chapter attempts to provide a framework or reference point for understanding the approximate costs for successfully deploying SAP S/4HANA Cloud, from product selection to total cost of ownership.

Rounding out Part I, **Chapter 5** delves into the postimplementation stage and highlights the activities, requirements, and effort associated with effectively maintaining SAP S/4HANA Cloud in a manner that maximizes the product's value. Important product concepts such as the quarterly release schedule, tile customization, and report development all are explored. Maintaining your productive SAP S/4HANA Cloud system in the best possible way promotes not only successful user adoption but also maximization of your SAP S/4HANA Cloud investment.

Part II: Business Processes, or SAP S/4HANA Cloud 201

Moving deeper into the product, Part II focuses a great deal on some of the specifics of SAP S/4HANA Cloud, focusing on product functionality and analytics. Although this evolving product is constantly innovating, the basic business process framework, approach, and functionality have gelled and will most likely continue to exist as the foundation for future SAP S/4HANA Cloud innovation.

Chapter 6 documents SAP S/4HANA Cloud's business functionality and corresponding capabilities. This chapter is a cornerstone of the book. For those interested in learning how SAP S/4HANA Cloud addresses a given business process, such as core finance or procure-to-pay, this chapter is an excellent reference guide and resource—especially for those new to SAP S/4HANA Cloud.

SAP S/4HANA Cloud features built-in analytics capabilities, and **Chapter 7** discusses this important topic. Real-time analytical features within SAP S/4HANA Cloud provide an immediate opportunity for users to act based on SAP S/4HANA Cloud data. Graphical reporting, key performance indicators (KPIs), and other analytical features are explored for the SAP S/4HANA Cloud audience.

Part III: Next Steps, or SAP S/4HANA Cloud 301

Wrapping up the book, Part III continues to build on the natural evolution of the product through extensibility and future innovation. **Chapter 8** explores the world of SAP S/4HANA Cloud integration via out-of-the-box SAP S/4HANA Cloud business extension functionality. The wealth of SAP's prebuilt SAP-product-to-SAP-product integrations (built-in integrations) adds value as part of the greater SAP S/4HANA Cloud platform. Furthermore, custom integrations provide another extensibility alternative with SAP Cloud Platform and SAP Business API Hub. In short, the integration feature within SAP S/4HANA Cloud provides additional reach, whether custom-specific or predelivered by SAP.

Chapter 9 continues to explore how SAP S/4HANA Cloud can be customized from an end user perspective without modifying any core SAP S/4HANA Cloud code. The two methods for SAP S/4HANA Cloud extensibility are in-app and side-by-side. In Chapter 9, both extensibility methods are featured, providing an understanding of the personalization functionality that exists for making SAP S/4HANA Cloud your own.

Finally, wrapping up Part III, **Chapter 10** explores the SAP S/4HANA Cloud roadmap and, more importantly, provide valuable information on where to find resources related to SAP S/4HANA Cloud innovation and future releases. As the product continues to grow in functionality and scope, understanding how the mothership (SAP) plans to roll out new features and the corresponding timeframe is paramount.

Acknowledgments

When I wrote my first (and only other) SAP PRESS book in 2009, it was a very different time. My business partner, Michael Pytel, and I had literally just started NIMBL, and I just had my first child. Fast-forward to today: My wonderful family has grown to four beautiful children, and NIMBL has grown to over 100 folks strong and is known across North America as a trusted SAP partner.

As the saying goes: "It takes a village"—and this saying holds true when writing a book as well. Thus, I would like to thank the many people who contributed.

First, I'd like to thank the SAP team for their amazing support in teaching us about SAP S/4HANA Cloud. Brent Reed, SAP S/4HANA Cloud's North American vice president, and his leadership team, including Jason Hardy and Michael Foley, have been tremendous in providing us access to this innovative product and great program. Steve Strawbridge has been a long-time trusted colleague and is very much responsible for introducing NIMBL and I to SAP S/4HANA Cloud. Thank you, my friends, for being so open to the potential of SAP S/4HANA Cloud—and the warts.

I would like to thank my coauthor Michael Jolton (or MJ). As NIMBL's vice president of delivery and key catalyst in helping NIMBL mature its delivery organization, MJ often is tasked with driving NIMBL's strategic initiatives. Building an SAP S/4HANA Cloud practice from scratch has been one of the most important strategic initiatives in NIMBL's history. MJ has embraced this challenge with vigor, passion, and ownership. NIMBL is where it is today in its SAP S/4HANA Cloud practice squarely because of his effort and commitment. Thank you so much, MJ, for everything!

When building a business with a partner, the marriage analogy isn't strong enough. My business partner Michael Pytel and I have been together as a couple since 2005, before the concept of NIMBL ever existed. Over the last 13 years, we have matured, fought, laughed, struggled, persevered, and learned from each other as only two strong-willed and strong-minded business partners can do and understand. I am truly grateful for my relationship with Michael and can say in all honesty that our connection is stronger today than it has ever been. Thank you, Michael.

Finally, I would like to thank my incredible wife Orly. Orly has always been the rock of my life and the foundation of our family. Nothing is more important to me than my family. Orly consistently brings me back to this. All the long hours, sweat, stress, frustration, ups and downs, and so on for NIMBL have been aimed at creating opportunities for our family—and much of this burden falls on Orly, who continues to create the best environment for me and our children. I am truly blessed to have such an amazing, supportive partner, who teaches me constantly how to evolve and focus on that which is important. Thank you, baby, for you and everything you do.

For those interested in connecting, it would be my pleasure. My email is *yosheisbart@benimbl.com* and my twitter handle is *@yosheisbart*.

Thank you for taking the time to read this book. All the best.

—Yosh Eisbart

For my part, I want to first thank the owners of NIMBL, Michael and Yosh, for allowing me to work on this book and be part of such a dynamic company. It's a great honor to be asked to join such an undertaking. I have been around business systems for more years than I care to remember, and I truly believe that SAP S/4HANA Cloud is a revolutionary development that changes the ERP game. I also want to echo Yosh's sentiments regarding the support received from the NIMBL and SAP teams. I work with the best in the business and am proud to come to work every day. On a personal note, I want to thank my partner in life and all that it brings, Lisa. Thank you for your support through late nights and early mornings. Finally, I would like to thank the lights in my eyes, my children: Jared, Adam, and Ryan. My sun will always rise and set with you fine young men.

Like Yosh, I am always happy to connect. My email is *michael.jolton@benimbl.com* and my twitter handle is *@michaeljolton*.

I hope you enjoy the book.

—Michael Jolton

On with the Show

SAP S/4HANA Cloud truly is an innovative SAP product and is being positioned as a game changer within the SAP and greater ERP SaaS worlds. Capturing all the nuances of SAP S/4HANA Cloud in a static book is impossible. However, providing a solid foundation for those interested in exploring more and building the business case for SAP S/4HANA Cloud implementation is achievable—even for an ever-evolving SAP SaaS product.

With that said, let's get to it!

PART I

Getting Started

By now, the concept and value proposition of ERP products is ubiquitous. The value proposition of cloud-based software is also widely accepted. Bringing these two concepts together and adding preconfiguration with SAP Best Practices introduces a new dimension that dramatically changes the ERP landscape. This new combination, when implemented with the newly released SAP Activate methodology, completely changes how ERP applications are implemented and maintained. The first part of this book provides an overview of what SAP S/4HANA Cloud is and who it's for (no single solution will fit the needs of every company). In addition, it will address how SAP S/4HANA Cloud is implemented, what it costs, and how much effort is required to maintain it as an ongoing business application. These are the types of questions that need to be answered prior to digging deeper into the application's capabilities.

Chapter 1
The Basics:
What Is SAP S/4HANA Cloud?

With the SAP S/4HANA, cloud edition, we are delivering on our promise to give complete choice to customers for adopting the next-generation business suite.
—Bernd Leukert, member of the Executive Board, Products & Innovation, SAP SE

In this chapter, we'll provide a high-level overview of some of the basics of SAP S/4HANA Cloud from a prospective·buyer's perspective. The goal of this chapter is to summarize the salient components of SAP S/4HANA Cloud in terms of functionality, platform, infrastructure, and postproduction support at a thousand-foot level. Knowing the basics behind SAP S/4HANA Cloud helps organizations understand how the product fits a customer's specific ERP needs and whether additional exploration is necessary.

Before we begin, we'll highlight the importance of speaking the challenging language known as SAPanese in the following box.

The Ancient Language of SAPanese

For those new to the world of SAP, SAPanese (i.e., the global language of SAP-speak) can be foreign and intimidating, without question. With terms, versions, modules, products, and acronyms rolling off the tongue effortlessly from seasoned SAP professionals, following conversations—especially those technical in nature—can become difficult quickly without a solid foundation. Thus, we've done our best throughout this book to translate all SAPanese by spelling out and explaining terms that might not be self-evident. With a bit of practice, you too can speak SAPanese fluently.

1.1   Overview

SAP S/4HANA Cloud is SAP's newest and most innovative software as a service (SaaS) ERP product. Although SAP has built and invested in previous small to midsize business ERP products (such as SAP Business One and SAP Business ByDesign), none of the earlier offerings have had as much investment, energy, or SAP executive sponsorship as SAP S/4HANA Cloud.

Why is SAP investing in cloud ERP? It's not change for the sake of change. Instead, cloud provides the perfect platform to drive speed and deliver results. Businesses are going to realize it's not a matter of if, but how they start with cloud ERP.

New digital technologies and capabilities are disrupting business models across entire sectors. SAP has identified a need for cloud ERP that's easy to use, packed with latest technologies, such as SAP CoPilot and machine learning, comes with a UI tailored to every person in an organization, and underpinned by powerful business capabilities. The idea is to combine SAP's end-to-end processes with the speed of cloud delivery to power digital transformation and agility. This approach to intelligent cloud ERP provides users with software that is easy to use and provides contextual experiences and interactions to help users be more efficient—freeing up resources for innovation—while at the same time helping them make better strategic decisions.

Figure 1.1 shows how SAP distinguishes internally among SAP products targeting the small to midsize market based on user count.

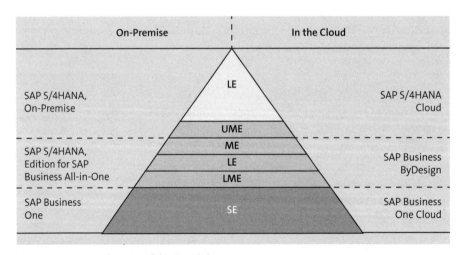

Figure 1.1 ERP Product Portfolio Breakdown

Built on the same code base as SAP's flagship enterprise-level business software (on-premise SAP S/4HANA), SAP S/4HANA Cloud provides functionality very like its sibling's. However, the there are some very important differences between the two products. In turn, who should implement which product (as discussed in Chapter 2) is likewise quite different.

Before we dig much deeper into what exactly SAP S/4HANA Cloud is, a cheat sheet of key facts about the software will provide a good starting point (see the following box).

SAP S/4HANA Cloud Fact Sheet

Note the following ten key facts about SAP S/4HANA Cloud:

1. **Software subscription pricing is per user, per month.**
   SAP S/4HANA Cloud's software pricing structure mirrors the standard cloud pricing construct of a monthly cost per user. The on-premise pricing construct of and initial upfront cost per user along with annual maintenance fees is no longer applicable to this cloud product. The barrier for entry (i.e., the cost of the software) is much lower than for on-premise ERP from SAP. This new enterprise-level ERP pricing structure enables mid-sized businesses with $20 million in annual revenue or more as well as smaller, but fast-growing business to implement SAP S/4HANA Cloud as their business software backbone.

2. **Implementing is measured in weeks, not years.**
   As a generalization, the implementation time to deploy SAP S/4HANA Cloud is measured in weeks, as opposed to the months (or even years) needed to implement other ERP products from SAP on-premise. Because of the intuitive and contextualized browser-based UI, users can also start with far less training. This rapid implementation schedule is no coincidence; SAP has adopted the greater cloud software model of accelerated plug-and-play deployment. The hurdle of expensive implementation timelines and costs is no longer applicable here. Again, this rapid ERP SaaS deployment schedule from SAP now provides options previously unavailable for companies with less than $250 million in annual revenue (a loose benchmark metric used within the SAP world).

3. **SAP Best Practice configuration is ready out of the box.**
   One of the value propositions of SAP S/4HANA Cloud is that configuration options are more limited on purpose. Based on designing the product via SAP Best Practices, SAP S/4HANA Cloud's tight control over configuration options deliberately drives customers towards standard deployment. Wizard-based configuration based on SAP Best Practices greatly accelerates SAP S/4HANA Cloud's initial set-up timelines

---

and ongoing postproduction support needs. By using their decades of experience with industries and steering customers toward the most efficient processes for standard functions, SAP is helping customers focus their energy instead on growing capabilities that differentiate them in the market.

4. **Postproduction can be self-supported.**
   Speaking of standard deployment, and because of the out-of-the-box implementation model, postproduction support requirements are nominal if not nonexistent. No longer are organizations required to either build robust SAP support teams or engage vendors to keep their SAP systems running effectively and current. In turn, SAP S/4HANA Cloud provides low total cost of ownership (TCO). SAP S/4HANA Cloud's postproduction support essentially becomes a business-driven business-analyst model in which superusers are empowered to support the system from a business functional perspective instead of the traditional SAP technical upkeep driven by configuration and development requirements. Large SAP support staffs are no longer required! (There is one exception related to extensibility, which is discussed in Chapter 9.)

5. **Innovation is fast and quarterly.**
   SAP S/4HANA Cloud's innovation strategy is vastly different than that for SAP's on-premise ERP model. Again, this is intentional and meant to drive more customers towards cloud. SAP S/4HANA Cloud innovation cycles are quarterly (i.e., SAP pushes out new functionality to its clients every 90 days), whereas SAP's ERP on-premise functionality enhancements are delivered on a yearly schedule. One of the advantages of this innovation model/schedule is that new SAP S/4HANA Cloud functionality is automatically delivered. This means customers get access to the latest technologies, such as machine learning capabilities, with every regular update cycle. One of the potential disadvantages of this model is that new functionality deployment is no longer optional but mandatory.

6. **SAP S/4HANA Cloud isn't the right fit for everyone.**
   One of the advantages of SAP S/4HANA Cloud is the simplicity of its implementation, based on its SAP Best Practices–driven functionality. For organizations that can leverage standard business processes (which includes most organizations), SAP S/4HANA Cloud can be a great fit; however, for businesses requiring industry-specific functionality, it might not be. At the time of writing, SAP S/4HANA Cloud supports industry-specific functionality for professional services and component manufacturing. Support for several industries such as oil & gas, chemicals specialty, public sector, telco, banking, and consumer products is on its way, with more industries will following in 2018.

7. **SAP S/4HANA isn't just for smaller companies.**

One of the biggest growing SAP S/4HANA Cloud use cases is (drum roll, please) for large enterprise organizations. Although SaaS utilization in general is wide and ubiquitous within the start-up and midmarket sectors—therefore providing a great use case for SAP S/4HANA Cloud—large enterprise companies (businesses loosely defined as having annual revenues/turnover exceeding $1 billion) also are embracing SAP S/4HANA Cloud within a two-tier ERP architecture. Attracted by the cost, speed, and necessary functionality for smaller divisions, large enterprises are deploying SAP S/4HANA Cloud for subsidiaries, smaller divisions, satellite offices, and the like and then integrating SAP S/4HANA Cloud with their primary SAP ERP installations (SAP ERP or SAP S/4HANA). This model is a two-tier federated strategy. It gives the smaller division/entity more agility and speed while maintaining total integration with the systems of record in the rest of the organization. More information about this hybrid ERP approach will be discussed later in this chapter.

8. **SAP's investment in SAP S/4HANA is mind-blowing.**

In more than 22 years, we've never before seen this much investment of resources, executive leadership, marketing, salesforce, and development into a single product. The effort, energy, investment in resources, etc. alone being displayed by SAP as an organization proves SAP S/4HANA Cloud's significance as a flagship product. Clearly, SAP sees intelligent cloud ERP as the future of ERP for digital business because of the way it combines speed and results—speed in deployment and user adoption, results in faster time-to-value and continuously expanding capabilities with new releases.

9. **SAP S/4HANA Cloud is from the same code line as on-premise SAP S/4HANA.**

SAP S/4HANA Cloud's code base foundation is the same as that of the on-premise version. Why does this matter? It means that SAP S/4HANA Cloud possesses much of the same functionality as SAP's flagship on-premise version. Unlike previous (and current) SAP midmarket ERP solutions, such as SAP Business All-in-One, SAP Business One, and SAP Business ByDesign, SAP S/4HANA Cloud is in sync with the enterprise version.

10. **SAP S/4HANA Cloud is extensible.**

For some customers, SAP S/4HANA Cloud might not be sufficient to cover all needed business functions. SAP understands this, and so SAP S/4HANA Cloud has been designed as a digital core, enabling additional desired functionality to be added through extensibility via SAP Cloud Platform. Extensibility includes native integration with other SAP products such as SAP SuccessFactors for human resources, integration with third-party applications, or customer-specific functionality created via SAP Cloud Platform, the system integration is there to extend core SAP S/4HANA Cloud's business functionality. SAP is also rolling out a new model of customer collaboration: the SAP S/4HANA Cloud software development kit (SDK). The SDK will enable customers to build out new industry-specific capabilities and use the SAP App Center as a go-to-market platform.

These ten key facts about SAP S/4HANA Cloud make a compelling case for organizations both familiar with and foreign to SAP ERP to look at this solution for running their business.

SAP is strategically positioning SAP S/4HANA Cloud as the nexus of SAP's digital cloud core. Wall Street values cloud revenue at higher multiples than traditional, on-premise-driven revenue, and SAP is following suit by moving more and more functionality to the cloud. Large acquisitions over the last decade, including SAP Hybris, SAP Fieldglass, SAP Ariba, Concur, and SAP SuccessFactors, have clearly sent messages to the market that SAP is invested and will grow investment in the cloud.

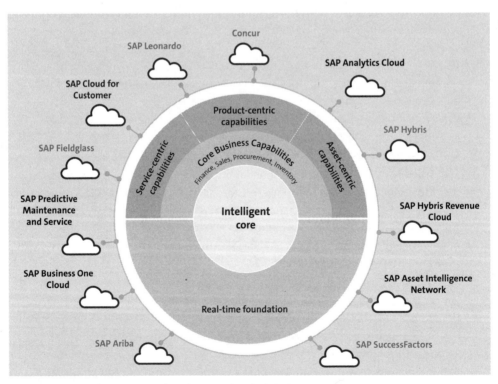

Figure 1.2 S/4HANA Cloud as the SAP Cloud Digital Core

As shown in Figure 1.2, SAP S/4HANA Cloud sits in the middle, the nexus for all SAP Cloud Platform products, which are specialized for distinct business process domains. This modular plug-and-play approach from SAP presents the consumer with an understanding that various business processes can be tackled by connecting and integrating multiple SAP products and non-SAP applications (including custom apps).

1.2   Cloud ERP and the Two-Tier Model

For many businesses already running SAP, hybrid deployment of SAP S/4HANA Cloud is the most likely first step to see what the cloud ERP platform has to offer. One reason is that it would be hard for most mid- to large-size companies to justify completely replacing a functioning on-premises system with a cloud-based SaaS platform all at once. Another reason is that the benefits of intelligent cloud ERP are most keenly felt in specific parts of a large organization: divisions, subsidiaries, acquired companies, satellite offices, etc. These businesses want to configure their systems as needed, and extend capabilities via the SAP Cloud Platform. They need a deployment model that reduces complexity and total cost of ownership. The subsidiaries or branches also want to maintain the agility to support new business models alongside the company's traditional operations. While all these features make SAP S/4HANA Cloud a compelling choice for the satellites, large businesses already running SAP are most likely to want to maintain a single technical vendor even if smaller subsidiaries deploy differently.

Because SAP S/4HANA Cloud shares a code line with SAP S/4HANA, integration is easier than in any other multi-vendor set-up—and because the SAP S/4HANA Cloud system has the same data model and user experience—smaller branches or divisions of large organizations can adopt the faster innovation cycle of the cloud platform without learning a new system or isolating themselves from the parent company's processes. Headquarters gains faster enterprise-wide consolidations and close. IT and business leaders can rest easy knowing there will be operational consistency across subsidiaries and divisions.

There are multiple scenarios for two-tier ERP, ranging from the incremental to the truly transformational. All have a place as companies pursue digital transformation and try to gain the greatest value from what SaaS ERP has to offer. Following are four examples of common scenarios:

- **Scenario 1: Rapid adoption**

  One of the more incremental paths to digital transformation is also fast to adopt. When headquarters is running SAP ERP, the subsidiary can deploy S/4HANA Cloud and reap all the benefits of innovation at the edge without disrupting the core. This would be a typical hybrid use case in scenarios such as establishing a new line of business, or migrating a new acquisition from a legacy system to an SAP platform. The subsidiary gets the benefits of innovation—AI, machine learning, advanced analytics—and maintains integration with the center. The downside is that headquarters doesn't gain the benefits as well.

- **Scenario 2: Best of both worlds**

  When headquarters is running SAP Business Suite powered by SAP HANA or SAP HANA Enterprise Cloud and the subsidiary deploys SAP S/4HANA Cloud, both entities benefit. SAP Business Suite on SAP HANA and SAP HANA Enterprise Cloud speed processes with SAP HANA and there's some simplification of data integration from SAP S/4HANA Cloud at the subsidiary site. This approach maintains the option for headquarters to run systems on-premises (SAP Business Suite on SAP HANA) or in a managed cloud (SAP HANA Enterprise Cloud) and keeps the full functionality of industry-specific solutions such as IS-Oil and IS-Retail if your business demands it.

- **Scenario 3: Greater flexibility**

  When headquarters is running SAP S/4HANA and the subsidiary S/4HANA Cloud, things get really interesting. Headquarters users gain upgraded processes that drive efficiency and value, and the SAP Fiori UX that speeds adoption and enhances daily productivity with in-context insights for users across the organization. With HQ running SAP S/4HANA, it will also have greater flexibility in customization; usually for better when it means differentiating services, sometimes for worse when it comes to maintenance and upgrades.

- **Scenario 4: Transformation enabler**

  When headquarters runs SAP S/4HANA Cloud, private option and the subsidiary runs SAP S/4HANA Cloud, there is real potential for transformation across the organization. Consider this the best of both worlds, cloud and on-premises, where the center and edges of the business gain access to new capabilities and faster innovation in tandem. In this model, headquarters can also fully outsource infrastructure management to stay focused on optimizing the business. Plus, HQ gets access to the per-user pricing and instant access to innovation through quarterly updates, two real strengths of SAP S/4HANA Cloud.

1.3   Preconfigured End-to-End Business Processes

One of the biggest critiques of implementing traditional SAP ERP since the days of SAP R/3 (including on-premise SAP S/4HANA) has centered on the time required for implementation. As the idiom says, time is money. Within the SAP construct, longer implementation times translate into higher internal or external resource deployment. What can be done to gain speed? SAP S/4HANA Cloud offers several ways to hit the accelerator. It's faster to deploy (weeks, not months or years), reducing overhead and the uncertainty and inefficiencies of transition periods. The intuitive, contextualized UI provides faster uptake by users across the organization with less training. It is also faster to upgrade, with regular quarterly updates that provide steady, incremental improvements as well as access to truly innovative technologies such as machine learning. All this leads to faster business results.

One of the major advantages of the SAP S/4HANA Cloud functionality footprint is its focus on core business functionality. Fundamental core business processes specific to finance, order-to-cash, procure-to-pay, plan-to-product, and human resources are all included as part of SAP S/4HANA Cloud. See Figure 1.3 for a high-level overview of SAP S/4HANA Cloud's core business processes.

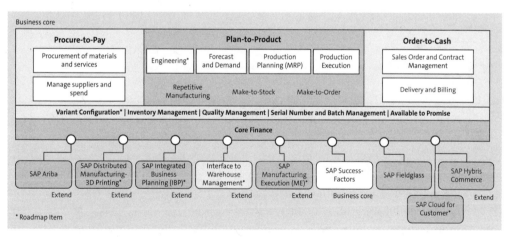

Figure 1.3 SAP S/4HANA Cloud's Core Business Processes

Another major advantage of SAP S/4HANA Cloud is its intentional design governing how to implement the product. SAP S/4HANA Cloud is built as minimally configurable business software, which also leads to minimal implementation costs. As a multitenant cloud-based product, SAP S/4HANA Cloud has blueprinted a robust, generic business platform leveraging SAP Best Practices for fundamental, mission-critical business processes mandatory for running an organization. Basic core processes such as asset management, finance, manufacturing, and so on are delivered preconfigured in a model SAP calls fit-to-standard, which is based on decades of experience and the company's unique knowledge of effective and efficient core business processes. This approach is a major break from the complex, customized ERP implementations of years past.

As you can see in Figure 1.4, within the manufacturing solution scope, a series of best practices exist out of the box for the easy deployment of preconfigured business functionality.

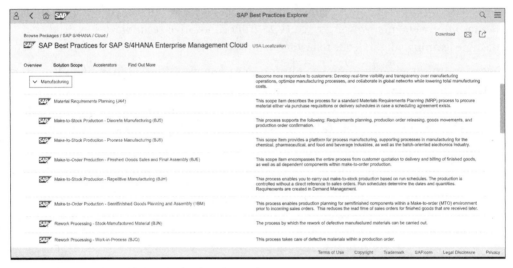

Figure 1.4 SAP S/4HANA Cloud Best Practices

In fact, digging even a little bit deeper, you can see the depth and wealth of business best practices baked into SAP S/4HANA Cloud. For example, within the manufacturing solution scope within the *make-to-order production—finished goods sales and final assembly (BJE)* functionality, a detailed process model breaks the end-to-end process into easily understandable responsibilities and tasks sorted by business user (see Figure 1.5).

Once broken down into business user functions (i.e., internal sales representative, billing clerk, etc.), the business process flow shows the interdependencies and responsibilities across a given preconfigured business process. These process flows translate into preconfigured configurations specific to the role, function, and responsibilities of each user in the system.

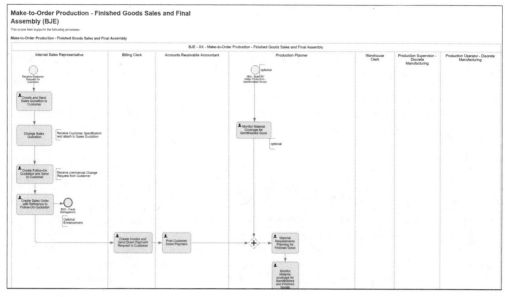

Figure 1.5 Example SAP S/4HANA Cloud Preconfigured Best Practices Process Flow

SAP S/4HANA Cloud provides preconfigured best practices, but how do these translate into ready-for-use functionality? As part of SAP S/4HANA Cloud, the user answers a series of questions as part of initial setup. No longer are you required to spend hours or days within a conference room determining your business requirements. Unlike SAP S/4HANA (on premise), which exposes the traditional SAP IMG low-level configuration interface to the customer, SAP S/4HANA Cloud uses two methods of configuration, as follows:

- Self-service configuration UIs (SSCUIs) which provide a selection of settings to adjust system behavior to power users
- Expert configuration for low-level adjustments to the system that can be requested by the customer from the service center

Customization, long requirements-gathering workshops, and IMG and/or SPRO configuration are things of the past.

SAP Confidential

The role of the SAP consulting partner will change drastically due to the way SAP is building SAP S/4HANA Cloud. Generating revenue through long implementations for this product will no longer be an option, and services integrators (SIs) will need to adapt.

1.4   ERP Cloud Building Blocks

From an architecture perspective, it's important to understand how SAP S/4HANA Cloud is designed. Understanding the basics of SaaS, platform as a service (PaaS), and infrastructure as a service (IaaS) will provide the logical framework necessary to understand how to deploy SAP S/4HANA Cloud and to support the product after go-live. Figure 1.6 breaks down the various aspects of cloud software deployment within the SAP S/4HANA Cloud world.

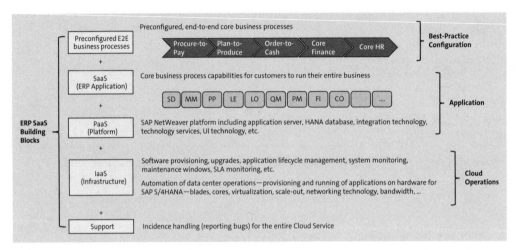

Figure 1.6 ERP Cloud Building Blocks

In the following sections, we'll discuss the ERP cloud building blocks in greater detail, including their purpose, functionality, and impact on SAP S/4HANA Cloud.

1.4.1   Software as a Service

Although SaaS has been around as a concept within the information technology (IT) world since the 1990s (and arguably before), SAP begun to build SaaS products only in the last few years. Two important examples are SAP S/4HANA Cloud and SAP Cloud Platform.

Simply put, SaaS products are multitenant software products residing within the cloud. (*Multitenant* refers to software architecture designed to be used by multiple users at the same time without impacting other concurrent users.) One of the beauties of multitenant software is speed to market. For example, within the multitenant software world, enhancements to software can be rapidly applied for all users with minimal disruption. SAP takes advantage of this capability by offering quarterly updates and pushing out new features, such as value-driving applications using machine learning. Whether via bug fixes or product enhancements, SaaS offerings provide the luxury of proactive improvement for all users.

SAP S/4HANA Cloud is founded on SaaS-based architecture with SAP HANA at its core. This software delivery platform is far from mind-blowing outside of the SAP world, but nonetheless its structural design is newer for SAP-built products (as opposed to the numerous recent SAP SaaS acquisitions).

One of the advantages of SaaS architecture specifically for SAP S/4HANA Cloud is its ability to rapidly innovate. The SAP S/4HANA Cloud innovation cycle is like that of no other SAP product within the portfolio with its quarterly innovation cycles pushed to the end user. This is particularly valuable when it comes to delivering solutions based on fast-changing technologies such as machine learning and AI, powered by SAP Leonardo. With machine learning, SAP has stated its aim to design software that learns from its users and can predict what information they need based on context. It will be difficult for on-premises deployments to compete in this space for quite a while as their update cycle is on the order of years. Quarterly updates with machine learning and real-time analytics capabilities can power functions such as transaction fraud detection, assessing job applicants, smarter procurement, and more. Figure 1.7 illustrates SAP S/4HANA Cloud's quarterly innovation schedule.

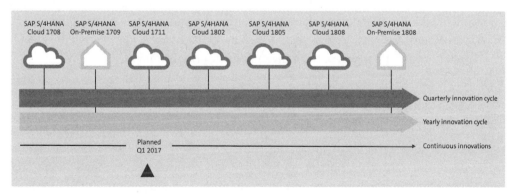

Figure 1.7 SAP S/4HANA Cloud's Quarterly Innovation Cycle

Another distinct positive associated with SaaS-architected products is end user cost. Because software companies invest in research and development, as well as product design, code construction, testing, and support, leveraging a single code base (i.e., one program design, delivery, and support) provides cost-efficiency savings, which are passed on to the customer. In short, SaaS saves customers money. The potential for direct cost savings are multiplied many-fold by better time-to-value with faster deployment, faster user adoption, and faster upgrade cycles.

Furthermore, to make SAP S/4HANA Cloud even more interesting, its code base is built on the same code line as the on-premise version. Again, greater SAP efficiencies equate to lower subscription costs, which in turn drive licensing costs down.

1.4.2   Platform as a Service

PaaS is the next technology support layer down from SaaS. Simply put, PaaS provides the appropriate technology platform necessary for software residence as well as the layer that enables you to develop and run extension on SAP S/4HANA Cloud. Specifically, for SAP S/4HANA Cloud, SAP HANA is the database, which is part of the SAP Cloud Platform which itself is the PaaS, while the application layer of SAP S/4HANA Cloud is written in ABAP and SAPUI5.

For the end consumer, the PaaS layer is invisible and a nonfactor, but this critical component of the SAP S/4HANA Cloud stack can't be underestimated. Not only does PaaS provide the foundation for business-critical applications and associated extensions, but it also eliminates yet another cost for the consumer. Without PaaS, the software layer would have no ability to exist. Although PaaS isn't truly a free component with the ERP cloud model (because the cost is ultimately passed down to the consumer), the cost can be spread across multiple customers leveraging the greater platform, in turn lowering the individual usage per customer.

1.4.3   Infrastructure as a Service

IaaS is another critical layer within the ERP cloud delivery mechanism. IaaS exists as the "iron" (i.e., hardware for servers, storage, networking, etc.) and supporting services responsible for hosting all software and platform requirements. Additional components within IaaS include services involved in supporting all the hardware. Because SAP S/4HANA Cloud resides off-premise from customers in centralized data-centers, fundamental data center infrastructure and support services are required, such as facilities like buildings, cooling and heating, and so on. All of this is hidden from the end consumer, just like PaaS.

SAP S/4HANA Cloud's infrastructure resides within SAP HANA Enterprise Cloud, which is hosted either directly by SAP or through one of SAP's trusted strategic suppliers, such as SAP hosting specialists like Freudenberg IT (FIT), IBM, and others.

Another component within IaaS is the managed services that support the iron. Although these services are different from application management services (AMS), they provide critical infrastructure-related support to the database and operating system.

1.5 Ongoing Support

One of the most exciting components of the SAP S/4HANA Cloud model is its impact on postproduction support requirements. Because the software is controlled centrally by SAP, the primary support needed for organizations is a business function as opposed to a traditional SAP technical role. Figure 1.8 illustrates the typical SAP S/4HANA Cloud production support model.

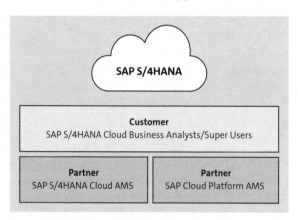

Figure 1.8 SAP S/4HANA Cloud Ongoing Support Model

SAP production support models are typically delivered via several well-established mechanisms. We'll highlight some of the most common components of these models next.

1.5.1 SAP Production Support Models

In the traditional SAP ERP post-go-live model for SAP enterprise platforms such as SAP ERP or on-premise SAP S/4HANA, organizations must address how to most effectively support their SAP landscape.

The most common models include the following:

- *Internal*: Internalizes all SAP production support functions via full-time employees to cover all necessary skillsets
- *External*: Partners with an SAP vendor for SAP application management services for skillset support
- *Hybrid*: Leverages a hybrid approach in which a subset of a customer's SAP production support needs are handled internally (perhaps by business-facing SAP analysts and SAP architects) and supplemented by an external SAP application management services partner

SAP Production Support Model Fact Sheet

Note the following key facts about common SAP production support models:

1. **Businesses are moving more and more towards highly outsourced SAP models.**
   As businesses are being asked to drive costs down across their organizations, IT departments are looking for ways to be more creative and cost-competitive in supporting business software. Within the SAP world, this reality and opportunity is no different. As such, CIOs are frequently looking towards SAP outsourcing and SAP application management services mechanisms to either augment or completely outsource their SAP production support needs. The options for quality external SAP production support are abundant. The alternatives are plentiful and different depending upon the objectives driving the decision (i.e., pure cost savings, flexibility, geographic preference, etc.).

2. **Most midmarket organizations can't afford large internal SAP production support staffing.**
   For those businesses that have deployed traditional SAP ERP installations, such as SAP ERP 6.0, supporting even the basic core functionality (e.g., financials, manufacturing, and sales and distribution) requires a team of SAP experts. At a minimum, SAP production support teams consist of three (superhuman) people who can cover the breadth of SAP functional and SAP technical needs. Many midmarket IT organizations simply can't afford this expense and, therefore, look externally for SAP application management services providers that specialize in these services.

1.5.2 Business Analyst

With the SAP S/4HANA Cloud revolution, the role of the SAP business analyst changes dramatically. In traditional SAP ERP environments, the SAP business analyst acts as a bridge between the business and IT. In the new world of SAP S/4HANA Cloud, the business analyst *is* IT.

SAP S/4HANA Cloud business analysts now sit at the center of the SAP landscape, supporting the business based on a deep knowledge of how SAP S/4HANA Cloud services the organization. Because configuration capabilities and development options are tremendously limited, the old-school requirements of deep SAP technical knowledge no longer apply. Skills such as implementation guide (IMG) configuration, transaction code knowledge, ABAP programming, SAP Basis magic, and so on, aren't required for ongoing support and aren't available for end user modifications.

Therefore, the role of the SAP S/4HANA Cloud business analyst is crucial for successful ongoing production support.

1.5.3   Extensibility Support

Although many an SAP S/4HANA Cloud customer could easily survive without any additional support outside of the business analyst role, one major exception exists. If an organization has extended SAP S/4HANA Cloud to other software products, there's the potential that additional resources might be needed.

For example, if a business is using SAP S/4HANA Cloud as its digital business core with integrations with other software, such as SAP Hybris, it's quite possible that an SAP Hybris support resource is needed as part of the overall SAP support. Furthermore, if an organization has developed a customer-specific application via SAP Cloud Platform, this technical support requirement, such as a skilled SAP Cloud Platform consultant is most likely needed.

With SAP S/4HANA Cloud as the digital core, greater functionality can be extended via three primary extensibility methods, as follows:

1. **User interface (UI) adaptation**
   UI adaptation allows a user to modify or personalize a given screen for his or her own user experience without modifying any underlying configuration. The UI modification is tied specifically to the user profile. Figure 1.9 shows an example of adding an additional field within a given screen.

2. **In-application (in-app) extensibility**
   In-app extensibility is a more in-depth modification of SAP S/4HANA Cloud, but it's not customization. Some examples of in-app extensibility include adding custom forms, fields, reports, or process logic. Adding in-app extensibility requires more SAP S/4HANA Cloud understanding and potential coding experience. Figure 1.10 shows an example of in-app extensibility, adding custom logic.

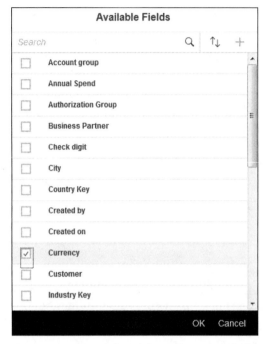

Figure 1.9 User Interface Adaptation Extensibility Example

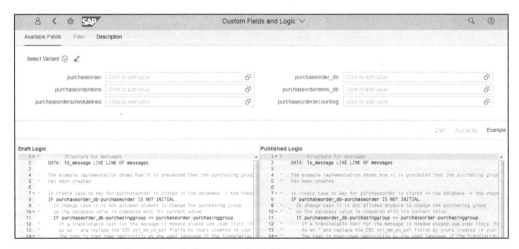

Figure 1.10 In-App Extensibility Example, Adding Custom Logic

3. **Side-by-side extensibility**

The final form of SAP S/4HANA Cloud extensibility is the side-by-side form. This extensibility is supported via the development of functionality with SAP Cloud Platform. Custom cloud platform application construction and integrating SAP S/4HANA Cloud with other software (whether SAP or non-SAP) are available methods for SAP S/4HANA Cloud functionality enhancement. Furthermore, SAP S/4HANA Cloud currently has over 40 out-of-the-box, side-by-side extensibility hooks (or whitelisted APIs) available for integration for common information transfer. These whitelisted APIs are available at *www.api.sap.com*, as shown in Figure 1.11.

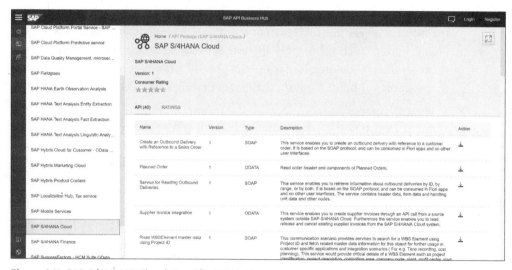

Figure 1.11 SAP S/4HANA Cloud-Specific API Listing

Beyond this, the SAP S/4HANA Cloud SDK (in beta release) enables users to develop their own application extending SAP S/4HANA by providing all the necessary libraries and project templates to get going quickly. These extensions can even be leveraged into commercial offerings for businesses facing similar challenges. More information on the SAP S/4HANA Cloud SDK is at *https://www.sap.com/developer/topics/s4hana-cloud-sdk.html*.

An additional option for SAP S/4HANA Cloud ongoing support is SAP application management services. Depending on how an organization implements, leverages, and supports SAP S/4HANA Cloud, the business analyst function might not be enough. SAP application management services can act as a supplement for SAP S/4HANA Cloud-deployed environments for myriad reasons. The following are several common engagement scenarios:

- **SAP Cloud Platform**
  If a company has implemented or requires an integration between SAP S/4HANA Cloud and other business software, then SAP application management services services could be involved for support and ongoing enhancements. This is probably more applicable for customer-specific SAP Cloud Platform-developed applications than for common SAP-to-SAP integrations (i.e., SAP S/4HANA Cloud to SAP SuccessFactors).

- **Bandwidth**
  If a business is very thin on IT staff or wants to complement internal SAP S/4HANA Cloud support, such as business analysts, leveraging an SAP application management services model might make sense. Specific examples could pertain to vacation support, off-hours support, challenges finding local talent, and so on.

- **TCO**
  Sometimes, external application management services are simply less expensive than internal options. In expensive cities such as San Francisco, London, New York, or Sydney, the cost of talent coupled with fierce competition makes it tremendously challenging to find quality and cost-effective internal resources. Long-term support cost is an important, frequently overlooked component of implementing any ERP offering. Expensive TCO can be crushing.

- **Continuity vs. turnover**
  Another key factor involved in potentially leveraging SAP S/4HANA Cloud application management services is IT continuity for the business. Constant turnover is not only disruptive and frustrating but costly. Leveraging an SAP S/4HANA Cloud application management services provider eliminates that factor completely; the application management services provider's role is to offer consistency, responsiveness, and quality delivery, all based on quantifiable service levels.

- **Strategic vs. tactical**
  Leveraging SAP S/4HANA Cloud application management services enables an IT organization to utilize its internal resources for more strategic purposes, as opposed to tactical activities. Many companies have concluded that the most bang for their buck in employee investment is not to be found in commoditized activities, but in actions that drive top-line revenue growth or bottom-line cost savings. SAP S/4HANA Cloud application management services is a commoditized service.

1.6 Summary

Hopefully, this chapter provided a clear overview of *what* SAP S/4HANA Cloud is at a high level. SAP S/4HANA Cloud is a powerful tool that can provide best-in-class core business functionality. Understanding its basic features and functions allows us to progress further into a meaningful discussion.

In the next chapter, we'll dig into the *who* of SAP S/4HANA Cloud: Who can potentially derive value from SAP S/4HANA Cloud? In our discussions, we'll include some customer use cases.

Let's get to it.

Chapter 2

Customer Use Cases: Who Should Use SAP S/4HANA Cloud?

SAP S/4HANA Cloud's use case within the market ranges from start-ups to Fortune 1000. This exciting new cloud SaaS ERP [offering] is changing the game.

—Brent Reed, SAP S/4HANA Cloud National COO

In the previous chapter, we introduced SAP S/4HANA Cloud. We explored the product's functionality at a high level, its positioning within the SAP ERP landscape, why cloud as a platform makes sense, and what it takes to support SAP S/4HANA Cloud in postproduction. Hopefully, you established a sound understanding of what SAP S/4HANA Cloud is; now, we'll begin to discuss who the potential candidates are for SAP S/4HANA Cloud.

In this chapter, we'll delve deeper into which organizations—both big and small—are best positioned to make the most out of SAP S/4HANA Cloud and drive the biggest return on investment (ROI). Regardless of how robust a given software package is; how much potential it has to positively impact your business; and the myriad features and functions it possesses, deciding to ultimately implement that software for your company is not solely based on those factors.

Behind the Curtain: Who's It For?

At first glance, you might believe that SAP S/4HANA Cloud is meant for only a specific subset of customers. In fact, the messaging directly from the mothership indicates that SAP S/4HANA Cloud is best positioned for customers with more than 1,500 users. However, the action on the street is different; organizations with employee bases of as few as 20 full-time employees are purchasing the software. The primary reason in our opinion for this positioning is the "crowded" set of SAP software already positioned within the small to midsize market (SME), loosely defined as companies with annual revenue or turnover of less than $1 billion. With SAP Business ByDesign and SAP Business One marketed as solutions for this stratosphere, SAP's attempt to position another product within this realm could cause confusion. However, we believe that SAP's positioning of SAP S/4HANA Cloud will gel quickly as the product matures and other products are pastured.

SAP S/4HANA Cloud is SAP's strategic SaaS ERP product and is being positioned as the primary ERP for organizations not looking for on-premise solutions. In the following section, we'll examine the most viable candidates to use SAP S/4HANA Cloud as a core IT solution that can deliver meaningful business value.

2.1   ERP in the Cloud

Everything is moving to the cloud. In a recent IT analyst report (*http://www.gartner.com/newsroom/id/3616417*), Gartner—one of the industry's most highly respected researching bellwethers—predicts that worldwide public cloud services adoption will grow by 18 percent in 2017 alone. Cloud adoption is no longer foreign to business and decision makers; conversely, cloud services are a major driver for companies. Table 2.1 summarizes Gartner's worldwide public cloud services forecast.

	2016	2017	2018	2019	2020
Cloud business process services	40,812	43,772	47,556	51,652	56,176
Cloud application infrastructure services (PaaS)	7,169	8,851	10,616	12.580	14,798
Cloud application services (SaaS)	38,567	46,331	55,143	64,870	75,734
Cloud management and security services	7,150	8,767	10,427	12,159	14,004
Cloud system infrastructure services (IaaS)	25,290	34,603	45,559	57,897	71,552
Cloud advertising	90,257	104,516	118,520	133,566	151,091
Total market	209,244	246,841	287,820	332,723	383,355

Table 2.1 Gartner Study: Worldwide Public Cloud Services Forecast (in Millions of Dollars)

SAP's business model and its strategic direction is either to build new cloud software natively or purchase best-of-breed complementary products and integrate them into the SAP product portfolio. From the building perspective, SAP Cloud Platform (formerly called SAP HANA Cloud Platform) is creating an entire blossoming ecosystem for new SAP cloud development. (For more information, check out SAP Startup Focus at *http://startups.sap.com/*.) From a buying perspective, SAP has been acquiring best-of-breed software market leaders such as Concur (for time and expenses), Hybris (for e-commerce), SuccessFactors (for human resources), and several others—all focused on bolstering its cloud offerings.

For customers looking to embrace ERP in the cloud, SAP S/4HANA Cloud is a viable solution. There are myriad reasons that cloud-based ERP products work well for businesses. In the following sections, we'll dig into some of the specific reasons that an organization focused on cloud would be interested in SAP S/4HANA Cloud.

2.1.1 Minimal IT Spend

SAP S/4HANA Cloud provides tremendous benefits for organizations focused on minimizing costs as part of an ERP deployment. From software purchase through long-term support, SAP S/4HANA Cloud lowers an organization's spending and investment in software systems and support. With previous SAP options for robust ERP software deployment, companies needed to deploy significant capital across myriad areas, including upfront software purchase; necessary infrastructure, such as servers, operating systems, database, and the like; small armies of human capital, whether internal (full-time employees) or external (third-party consultants); and postproduction IT mechanisms to support the installed ERP system.

With the advent of ERP SaaS and SAP S/4HANA Cloud, most of these expenses are eliminated or greatly reduced. Thus, for organizations driven by cost savings first and foremost, SAP S/4HANA Cloud solves many problems.

Table 2.2 describes the different cost savings opportunities made available by implementing SAP S/4HANA Cloud.

Cost Component	Cost Savings Opportunity
Software	SaaS-based pricing allows for payment per user, per month.
Infrastructure	No infrastructure costs are required to be paid separately. Infrastructure costs are embedded into the overall payment per user, per month pricing.

Table 2.2 Cost Savings Opportunities When Deploying SAP S/4HANA Cloud

Cost Component	Cost Savings Opportunity
Implementation	SAP S/4HANA Cloud implementation timeframes are drastically shorter than those of traditional SAP ERP projects. A general rule of thumb is that the implementation cost is between one and two times the cost of the annual software. For example, if an SAP S/4HANA Cloud subscription costs $100,000 per year, then the estimated implementation cost should be between $100,000 and $200,000.
Postproduction support	In the past, the support needs of an SAP production environment were massive. Even for a small SAP ERP deployment, the SAP production support team needed to include at least three people. With an additional 30 percent burden, the internal support cost would be expensive. The same holds true for leveraging third-party SAP production support services. However, with SAP S/4HANA Cloud, postproduction support is essentially nonexistent, because the software is directly supported by SAP; also, because configuration is minimal, any "config" changes can be handled by strong business users. (The one noteworthy exception relates to any extensibility scenarios, such as SAP Cloud Platform development, for which some technical knowledge will be required.)

Table 2.2 Cost Savings Opportunities When Deploying SAP S/4HANA Cloud (Cont.)

Therefore, the cost to deploy SAP S/4HANA Cloud is very reasonable, relatively speaking, enabling even organizations with small ERP deployment budgets to be able to afford the initial implementation and long-term product sustainability.

2.1.2   International Businesses

SAP S/4HANA Cloud is a viable solution for international businesses. Organizations with business units, satellite offices, acquisitions, remote plants, workplaces with poor connectivity, and so on spread throughout disparate regions across the globe make a strong case for implementing SAP S/4HANA Cloud.

In previous SAP ERP releases, such as SAP R/2, SAP R/3, and SAP ERP, companies looking for a holistic SAP-deployed platform were left with several choices for how to create an integrated perspective, as follows:

- Deploy SAP ERP at all locations, regardless of the size of deployment.
- Leverage another software tool and interface.
- "Integrate" manually (e.g., via manual upload of Excel spreadsheets).

With SAP S/4HANA Cloud, companies now can truly integrate disparate business units via a multipronged SAP approach by leveraging SAP S/4HANA Cloud within the distributed regions and on-premise SAP S/4HANA for the corporate headquarters.

In addition, SAP S/4HANA Cloud can be leveraged for multinational organizations as the *only* SAP ERP platform, depending on the functionality required for the greater business. If core SAP ERP functionality tackles a large percentage of the business requirements, then SAP S/4HANA Cloud can be deployed if the specific localizations (language, country, and legal requirements) have been deployed as part of the solution set. (At the time of writing, SAP currently supports 21 countries and is continuing to increase this number.)

Behind the Curtain: Magic Number

To determine if SAP S/4HANA Cloud is the right solution for an organization, we typically recommend an out-of-the-box functionality fit of approximately 80 percent—meaning that if an organization's business requirements are 80 percent handled appropriately though base configuration and product functionality, the organization passes the litmus test for implementation. Although this is just an approximation, in our experience it's a great barometer. The other 20 percent of an organization's requirements typically can be handled through either organizational change management or integration with other complementary products (whether SAP or non-SAP) via SAP Cloud Platform or API direct point-to-point integration.

Another potential SAP S/4HANA Cloud application for international businesses is the opportunity to standardize processes across multiple regions. For geographically dispersed organizations, maintaining consistent operational processes and procedures can be challenging. After coupling multinational remote locations with complex ERP business software, many organizations are left with misaligned methods for standard ways of doing business.

When leveraging SAP S/4HANA Cloud as a cloud-based ERP offering with minimal configuration options, the end user (and business) is provided with only a limited number of ways of performing a task. This might also hold true for standard templatized SAP implementations, the mere fact that SAP S/4HANA Cloud is a SaaS product creates not only an organizational foundation but also a corporate mandate and governance. Simply put, the psychology associated with SAP ERP SaaS specifically makes governance stronger.

2.1.3 Outsourced IT

As part of the quest to reduce overall organizational costs, most organizations are look-ing for ways to reduce IT expenses. In the 2000s, with the surge in managed hosting, businesses began to dip their toes into the water of outsourced infrastructure provid-ers and services. Today, hosting is a commodity and ubiquitous. If organizations aren't exploring hosting, they're missing a tremendous cost savings opportunity.

Similarly, within the SAP world, organizations are looking for ways to minimize SAP production support costs while maintaining a strategic business-facing workforce. With SAP S/4HANA Cloud, the argument for templatized ERP grows even stronger.

SAP S/4HANA Cloud, with its multitenant, cloud-based, SAP-supported software, re-quires little configuration knowledge. This model is vastly different than that of SAP S/4HANA or previous SAP ERP versions such as SAP R/3, SAP ERP 5.0, and SAP ERP 6.0. For previous SAP ERP platforms, numerous skillsets, knowledge pockets, technical skills, and corresponding workforces were required to effectively support a diverse and complex, highly configurable on-premise solution. Even in the most "basic" of previous SAP ERP landscapes, typically a minimum workforce of four skillsets would be required for basic support. Staple SAP skillsets such as ABAP (SAP development), SAP Basis (SAP administration), security (SAP role compliance and risk mitigation), and a minimum of at least one SAP functional area (such as finance, manufacturing, or sales) were necessary competencies. Although not all these skillsets necessarily required a full-time resource, they still needed to be supported via a combination of human beings.

Another fascinating fact emerging within the IT world and specifically the higher end of business software (including SAP, of course) is the rise of the contingent workforce. With trends continuing to move towards independent contracting and contingent labor, hiring qualified employees and finding available, full-time SAP talent is becom-ing more and more difficult.

The new emerging workforce grounded in the generation known as generation Y or millennials (loosely defined as people born between the 1980s and early 2000s) val-ues different ideals than previous generations. No longer are money and stability the primary motivating factors for employment for this new workforce. Different values have risen up the list of priorities. Autonomy, work/life balance, and contribution to the community are a few of the values deemed most important for the emerging worker. Thus, businesses are becoming acutely aware of the challenges involved in sourcing their IT and SAP talent. This trend will only grow, making it tremendously challenging to internalize SAP support staff.

For an organization that understands the following points, the argument for moving towards SAP S/4HANA Cloud is strong:

- **Workforce shift**
  The workforce is headed in droves towards contingent labor employment.

- **Internalizing SAP costs**
  Attempting to internalize an SAP production support staff to cover the skillsets needed for basic SAP ERP is expensive.

- **Millennial values**
  Generation Y doesn't hold the same core values as previous generations, such as job security and stability, financial wealth, and health insurance.

- **Scarcity of resources**
  Fewer young professionals are moving towards SAP as a career choice for myriad reasons, including the availability of more exciting technologies.

These are all moot points when implementing SAP S/4HANA Cloud. Because SAP S/4HANA Cloud is designed to minimize SAP implementation requirements and postproduction support essentially can be eliminated, the case for low-cost SAP S/4HANA Cloud's value is strengthened.

2.1.4   Faster Upgrade Cycles

Unlike traditional deployment timelines and upgrade cycles for on-premise ERP, SAP S/4HANA Cloud is designed to continuously upgrade features and capabilities for users. SAP has committed to a quarterly release cycle that pushes out new functionality to users. Some of these improvements may be prosaic and standard for ERP upgrades, albeit delivered faster and with less disruption than usual. In other cases, the rapid update cycle will provide users with genuinely new capabilities, such as in the emerging fields of machine learning, predictive analytics, and artificial intelligence applied to real-world business scenarios.

2.2   Preconfigured ERP

As mentioned previously, SAP S/4HANA Cloud is built on a foundation of SAP Best Practices. These SAP Best Practices have been developed and cultivated over 25 years as an evolution from earlier SAP Best Practices to those meant for SAP S/4HANA Cloud customers.

> **Industry Fit**
>
> During the writing of this book, SAP changed the construct of the SAP S/4HANA Cloud industry fit. Previously, SAP S/4HANA Cloud comprised multiple editions, including SAP S/4HANA Cloud Manufacturing, SAP S/4HANA Cloud Professional Services, SAP S/4HANA Cloud Marketing, SAP S/4HANA Cloud Finance, and SAP S/4HANA Cloud Enterprise Management. This has all changed. Now, SAP S/4HANA Cloud is simply known as SAP S/4HANA Cloud. Although the industry version nomenclature may have changed, the specific business process functionality hasn't been eliminated but has been integrated into the single SAP S/4HANA Cloud product. SAP has hinted that it might increase the industry-specific functionality as the product matures.

In the following sections, we'll look at some of features and use cases of a preconfigured ERP product, focusing on SAP S/4HANA Cloud.

2.2.1   SAP Best Practices

As part of the SAP Best Practices accelerator initiatives, SAP has provided a series of SAP Best Practices via SAP Best Practices Explorer, which categorizes results across multiple products, lines of business, industries, technologies, and other SAP building blocks (it includes much more than just SAP Best Practices for SAP S/4HANA Cloud!).

However, for SAP S/4HANA Cloud specifically, SAP provides a level-based dive into the specific solution by functional area. SAP Best Practices Explorer can be found on the web at *https://rapid.sap.com/bp/*. Figure 2.1 shows the current high-level solution packages breakdown.

These SAP Best Practices have been constructed and delivered for several key reasons, such as the following:

- **Accelerated deployment**
  SAP Best Practices provide a proven and trusted method for accelerating the implementation of SAP S/4HANA Cloud. These tried and true configuration methods enable SAP S/4HANA Cloud customers to leverage prepackaged designs for implementation.

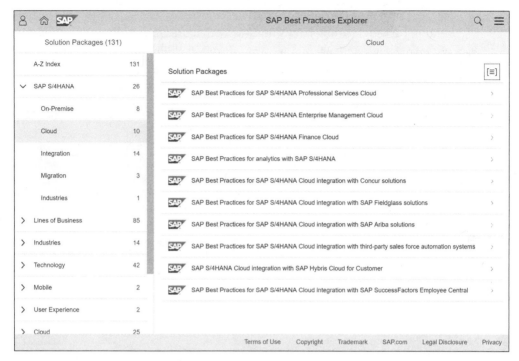

Figure 2.1 SAP Best Practices Explorer by Solution Package

- **Delivering business value**
  SAP differentiates its offering from other ERP platforms through a focus on *business value* as opposed to technical value. SAP Best Practices have nothing to do with technical value. It's true that the configuration is technical and packaged for underlying SAP S/4HANA Cloud technical deployment, but SAP Best Practices are business processes constructed through a business process lens. Figure 2.2 shows an example of SAP Best Practices' business value for, in this case, the financial functions of accounts payable.

- **Providing a foundation for those without one**
  This value-add function is especially important for newer, rapidly growing companies and for divestitures. Although many SAP S/4HANA Cloud customers are and will be those with years of experience and knowledge, many organizations implementing SAP S/4HANA Cloud will be newer businesses, potentially without any established business practices. SAP Best Practices provide an excellent foundation

for these scenarios. Common examples of companies that fit this scenario include venture-backed start-ups, family businesses that use QuickBooks as their financial system of record, and mergers and acquisitions; including divestitures) businesses that previously had structured business processes as part of the larger organization but now have few to none as standalone entities.

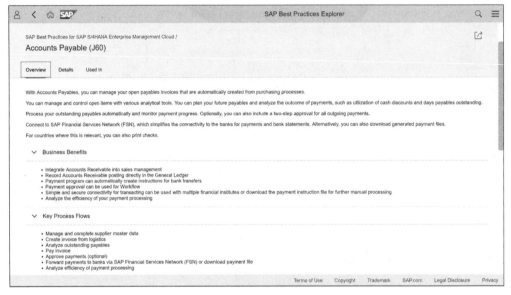

Figure 2.2 SAP Best Practices, Enterprise Management Accounts Payable

- **Reference point**
  Even for business that are mature and have well-established business processes, SAP Best Practices exist as an excellent business process reference point. SAP Best Practices are a construction of 25-plus years of experience, knowledge, learning, correction, and evolution. This extensive treasure trove of knowledge can be a wonderful reference point to see how SAP recommends performing a given business process flow.

- **Quicker time to value**
  One of the strongest reasons that SAP designed and delivered SAP Best Practices was to provide SAP S/4HANA customers with the ability to realize quicker time to value. Previous SAP ERP on-premise solutions required implementation timelines factored in months (and years) as opposed to weeks. With SAP S/4HANA Cloud, implementations can be spun up in rapid cycles. This accelerated speed of rollout

provides much faster value to the business, enabling companies to realize faster ROI.

For organizations looking for preconfigured business process functionality out of the box, SAP S/4HANA Cloud can provide a fantastic solution and accelerator.

Behind the Curtain: Preconfigured SAP Best Practices Home Run

SAPPHIRE is SAP's largest customer convention, and during SAPPHIRE 2017, we met with a tremendously innovative self-driving car start-up that's a spin-off of a global household name tech company. In the face-to-face meeting, we discussed SAP S/4HANA Cloud's preconfigured SAP Best Practices, offered as part of the package. The customer could not have been more excited. We explained that if they chose to leverage their existing business processes, they would need to work closely with the SAP Best Practices to ensure their fit-to-standard process would closely align. The customer's response was golden: "We have no business processes," the chief financial officer stated. "We will gladly embrace SAP Best Practices. This will make our lives so much easier."

The luxury of SAP Best Practices empowers SAP S/4HANA Cloud customers with a vetted set of business functionality capable of laying a solid ERP foundation. The need to develop/blueprint business processes no longer exists. SAP S/4HANA Cloud provides this feature both as a product offering for rapid deployment and for minimizing (self-servingly) production support, both from software and application managed services perspectives.

2.2.2   Standard Business Practice-Driven Model

Many organizations struggle with IT systems. The concept of ERP systems was to consolidate business functions within a single business software platform. As time progressed and ERP (and SAP) grew, the "simplicity" of consolidated business functions began to grow more and more complicated. Heavy, customer-specific customization began to emerge, attempting to fill in the gaps that SAP theoretically was unable to support. This proliferation of customization created webs of code and custom objects, which further complicated SAP landscapes. Couple the customization challenge with heavy integration, and you can find yourself in a gooey mess difficult to move through.

The challenge of customization simply doesn't exist within SAP S/4HANA Cloud. Standard SAP Best Practices-driven functionality and implementation methods provide the necessary framework for implementing SAP S/4HANA Cloud out of the box. Furthermore, SAP S/4HANA Cloud doesn't provide the ability to change SAP code. Because of the SaaS-based architecture and multitenant design, source code customization isn't possible. Thus, even the temptation to make "minor" software customizations can't be indulged, in turn eliminating the possibility of any pain point.

Beyond the inability to modify source code within SAP S/4HANA Cloud, the method or methodology for implementing SAP S/4HANA Cloud also provides a solid framework for standard business practice-driven delivery. The SAP S/4HANA Cloud implementation approach is known as *SAP Activate*.

Let's dig a bit deeper into this important SAP S/4HANA Cloud concept. Some of the common questions and answers about SAP Activate are as follows:

- **What is SAP Activate?**
  SAP Activate is more than an implementation methodology. SAP Activate is an implementation framework comprised of preconfigured SAP Best Practices, project delivery accelerators, implementation tools, and a more agile-focused project-delivery approach. Although not exclusive to SAP S/4HANA Cloud or its implementation, SAP Activate is SAP's recommended approach for SAP S/4HANA Cloud projects.

- **Why create a new SAP delivery methodology?**
  Over the years, SAP has developed and promoted multiple project deployment methodologies and approaches to assist organizations in best practice implementation rollouts. Without question, the most recognized SAP project methodology prior to SAP Activate was Accelerated SAP (ASAP). ASAP was originally designed to for implementing on-premise SAP software via a traditional "waterfall" approach. With the surge of SAP cloud products, SAP Activate was developed as a more iterative deployment strategy for cloud, on-premise, hybrid, and mobile projects.

- **What are the primary components of SAP Activate?**
  As a framework, versus a methodology only, SAP Activate provides multiple complementary components aimed at collaboratively driving successful SAP projects. Some of the fundamental components include the following:

  - *SAP Best Practices:* Described in Section 2.2.1, SAP Best Practices are extensive knowledge pools for how to most effectively implement SAP products based on years of industry, successful implementation, and technical expertise. These

SAP Best Practices packages provide consultative guidance on deployment, including business functionality deployment.

– *Guided configuration tools:* SAP guided configuration is a content lifecycle management tool that provides the configuration, development, testing, and support needed to deploy SAP products based on an organization's specific selected best practices.

– *Methodology approach:* SAP Activate's methodology is a much more iterative—almost agile—approach than the traditional SAP waterfall approach (project preparation, business blueprint, realization, go-live, and support). The difference between previous SAP implementation methodologies and SAP Activate is that SAP Activate stresses fit-to-standard first instead of morphing SAP to an organization's business processes or custom desires. SAP Activate focuses on minimizing modifications and customizations to an organization, leveraging standard SAP solutions via rapid deployment and minimal business disruption. Figure 2.3 illustrates the SAP Activate methodology approach.

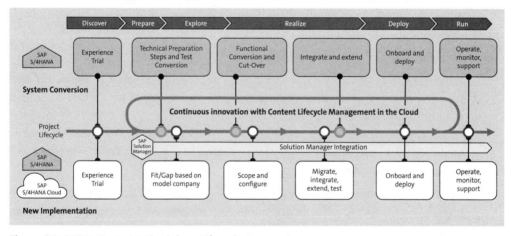

Figure 2.3 SAP Activate Methodology Lifecycle Approach

– *Integration support:* SAP Activate provides a framework for integration between SAP S/4HANA Cloud and complementary applications. Whether those applications are other SAP cloud products rounding out an organization's complementary business processes, such as human resources (via SAP Success Factors), procurement (via SAP Ariba), or e-commerce (via SAP Hybris), or custom cloud development via SAP Cloud Platform, SAP Activate provides support and structure.

For organizations looking to implement cloud ERP effectively and efficiently focused on standard business practices, SAP S/4HANA Cloud exists as a viable option. This focus on standard business processes and commitment to best practices can and should limit both the near-term implementation costs and the ongoing TCO.

2.2.3   The Fit-to-Standard Approach

Organizations' motivations to move to ERP vary widely. On one end of the scale, ERP is a necessary evil for scaling effectively from infrastructure and systems perspectives. On the other end, ERP exists as an innovative differentiating factor for an organization to separate itself from its competition. (Hopefully, most companies approach ERP via the latter viewpoint, not the former.)

Regardless of which end of the spectrum a business finds itself at, all organizations should approach ERP deployment through a common lens and aim to implement ERP with no (or limited) customization. For obvious reasons, including greater support costs, increased complexity, and speed to market, any ERP customization creates more work to maintain for any organization than standard out-of-the-box deployment.

This is where *fit-to-standard* comes in.

SAP S/4HANA's fit-to-standard methodology approaches the critical step of business requirements gathering differently. In the past, organizations would first document their business processes via a series of workshops and then look at how SAP products could map to these business processes. This method of deployment essentially created customer-specific SAP installations, making SAP evolution and upgrades more complicated and expensive.

Understanding the need to modify how SAP recommends deploying its own software, SAP began to drive standard implementation mantras. With SAP S/4HANA's release for both on-premise and cloud versions, SAP further fine-tuned the message by creating the fit-to-standard approach (see Figure 2.4). At each point in this approach, the following occurs:

1. The customer team members gain essential knowledge on the product and best practice processes and the overall solution scope they have signed up for.
2. The consultant explains the process using the best practice process flow.
3. The consultant leverages the pre-configured starter system and delivered data content to demonstrate the system best practices. They highlight areas that likely require configuration decisions.

4. Here, you map the model company best practice content to the customer situation for scope item business processes.

5. The team determines and documents configuration values required for the organization. The customer is responsible for providing value lists; e.g., product group definition.

6. The consultant provides the process flows, test scripts, and users so that the customer can perform the scenarios execution on their own. If necessary, they can create sample customer data to enhance their learning/knowledge.

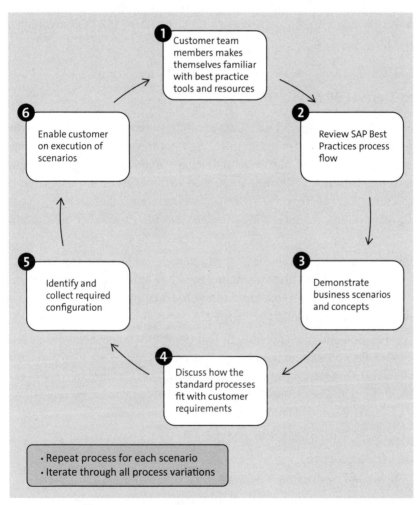

Figure 2.4 SAP's Fit-to-Standard Approach

The primary function of the fit-to-standard approach is to drive requirements gathering from an SAP-first perspective instead of a customer-specific perspective. The underlying approach is to look at how SAP defines a given functional flow (i.e., business process) based on the SAP Best Practices design. Specifically for SAP S/4HANA Cloud, the choice is essentially binary: Either SAP S/4HANA Cloud works as a solution or it doesn't. This is essentially because SAP S/4HANA Cloud provides few configuration options due to its intentional design as a SaaS multitenant platform.

Again, the benefit of implementing SAP S/4HANA Cloud via the fit-to-standard approach is deploying a standard SAP ERP solution with little if any customer-specific customization. No customization equates to a stable platform, low TCO, and higher ROI.

2.3   Two-Tiered ERP Model

Within complex SAP landscapes, the thought of rolling out another location for core SAP products (such as SAP ERP or on-premise SAP S/4HANA) can be both intimidating and discouraging. For years, businesses didn't have much of an option for deployment of SAP products if they wanted or needed to provide a comprehensive IT systems solution. Their choices were manual integration, stitched heterogeneous systems, or massive SAP rollouts. With SAP S/4HANA Cloud, another option now exists.

In large multinationals, companies now can implement on-premise SAP S/4HANA for key foundational business units (including their headquarters) and then implement SAP S/4HANA Cloud at remote locations with less complexity. This solution is known as the *two-tiered ERP model* (see Figure 2.5).

The value proposition and concept behind a two-tiered SAP model lies within a few key premises. These non-SAP marketing and concrete selling points help make the argument for why to potentially implement this model. The following are a few of the best arguments for why an organization would potentially gain value by deploying a two-tiered SAP S/4HANA Cloud landscape:

- Common data model and analytical model
- Common user experience
- Global support and localization
- Central finance at headquarters fed by subsidiaries

- Land and expand (implement a single instance and then implement in more instances once proven)
- Easier adoption of global rollout and digital transformation

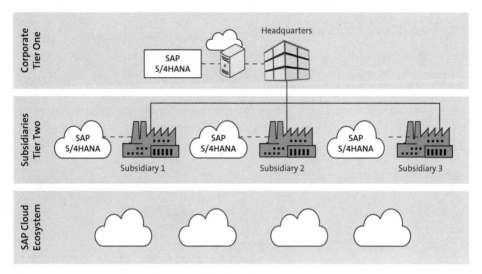

Figure 2.5 Two-Tiered SAP S/4HANA Cloud Landscape

Behind the Curtain: Making the Two-Tiered Model Argument to Executives

Although each of these arguments provides a different value proposition and focuses on a different benefit, the "land and expand" capability speaks most directly to cost, which speaks loudest to executives. It goes without saying that other factors, such as common user experience and a common data model, also support lower overall costs for SAP deployment and TCO; however, the land and expand concept speaks directly to implementation expenses. One of the fundamental basic premises behind land and expand is rapid rollout of subsidiary business units via a templatized approach. This conceptual and actual rollout strategy resonates with the powers that be, because it speaks directly to budget. Templatized rollouts have been around forever with traditional ERP (such as with SAP R/3 and SAP ERP), but SAP S/4HANA Cloud provides a more salient proof of concept, based on the product's design and application.

In the following sections, we'll look at the maturity level of the two-tiered approach. We'll then break down the various use cases for the two-tiered model and why companies are looking at this potential SAP model. This deployment strategy will continue to emerge across the SAP landscape, not only for existing SAP customers looking to extend SAP to smaller business units but for new SAP customers exploring how to leverage world-class SAP ERP in a cost-effective way.

2.3.1   Two-Tiered Approach: Maturity Level

One very important data point to discuss is SAP S/4HANA Cloud's rapidly changing set of innovations. To determine whether SAP S/4HANA Cloud is the right software for your business specifically within a two-tiered SAP landscape platform, you need to understand the functionality roadmap and the innovation being delivered per the SAP S/4HANA Cloud roadmap. Figure 2.6 documents the maturity model lifecycle, beginning with Level 1 and ending with maturity Level 5.

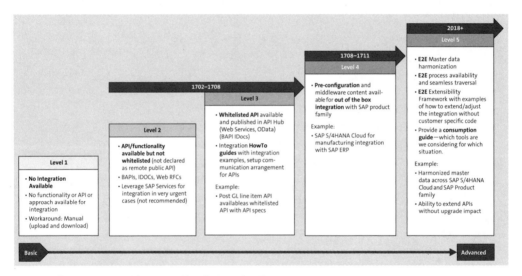

Figure 2.6 SAP S/4HANA Cloud Maturity Flow

In SAP's maturity scale specific to two-tiered SAP landscapes, as described in Figure 2.6, the following levels are defined:

- *Level 1:* No true integration available. Functionality and integration between SAP platforms is simply via old-school upload and download.

- *Level 2:* Automation via an API in the cloud using common interfaces for the on-premise tier 1 system, such as RFC or BAPI.

> **Note**
>
> The cloud API is delivered in the customer project only.

- *Level 3:* Integration becomes more available via whitelisted APIs, which are available via SAP's public cloud and published within the SAP Business API Hub.

- *Level 4:* Integration for SAP S/4HANA Cloud hits a new level with preconfiguration, out-of-the-box middleware available beyond just whitelisted APIs. Provides packaging for out-of-the-box configuration in SAP Best Practices.

- *Level 5:* Additional integration to be developed, planned for 2018 future releases, including end-to-end (E2E) data harmonization. Will provide governance of the entire ecosystem for the two-tiered process.

As you can see, the majority of this maturity in functionality begins to blossom in early 2017 (at the time of writing) and continues to drive innovation with subsequent releases, beginning at Level 3 (SAP S/4HANA Cloud release 1708) and continuing in subsequent innovation cycles.

> **Behind the Curtain: Two-Tiered SAP ERP in Action**
>
> One of the world's leading geospatial component manufacturing companies wanted to deploy an ERP system quickly for their 10-plus European retail locations. The client's headquarters were based in Asia, and the client had been an SAP customer for over a decade. During the client's exploratory study into which ERP system to implement—including NetSuite—SAP S/4HANA Cloud came to market. Unfamiliar with SAP S/4HANA Cloud, the organization viewed this newer SAP solution with hesitation. After learning more about SAP S/4HANA Cloud functionality, the next question centered on corporate integration. The company ultimately selected SAP S/4HANA Cloud as its European lightweight ERP system and is currently rolling it out at the time of writing. This two-tiered SAP model fits perfectly into the company's IT strategy: core SAP ERP at its foundation and ERP SaaS/SAP S/4HANA Cloud at small sites across the globe.

2.3.2   Federated Manufacturing Model

The SAP S/4HANA Cloud federated manufacturing model is one of the prime use cases for deploying SAP S/4HANA Cloud within a two-tiered SAP landscape. With SAP S/4HANA Cloud 1705, SAP's investment in expanding manufacturing capabilities within the product has grown dramatically. SAP S/4HANA Cloud has included core manufacturing capabilities since its start, but for organizations looking for greater business functionality within the manufacturing and production arenas, SAP has expanded its functionality to include more robust manufacturing capabilities.

Manufacturing-focused businesses typically produce goods in a limited number of locations rather than at every location. For businesses looking to deploy SAP products across multiple sites, the two-tiered federated model most likely is a more cost-effective deployment construct than attempting to implement on-premise SAP S/4HANA in every location.

The following decision-making factors typically come into play when deciding how to deploy SAP within a two-tiered manufacturing landscape:

- **Functionality requirements**
  On-premise SAP S/4HANA currently possesses a great deal more functionality than its cloud-based sibling. However, with greater functionality comes greater complexity, implementation cost, and support. For manufacturers that produce more complex goods at a limited number of core manufacturing locations and less complex products at other locations, a core on-premise SAP S/4HANA central instance integrated with SAP S/4HANA Cloud might be the right solution.

- **Cost of deployment**
  Simply put, implementing SAP S/4HANA Cloud is cheaper than implementing on-premise SAP S/4HANA. Assuming feature and function needs are met, a two-tiered federated manufacturing SAP S/4HANA Cloud landscape could be the right solution.

- **Connectivity**
  As SaaS-based technology, SAP S/4HANA Cloud needs the ability to connect to the cloud. Therefore, if a given business wants to deploy SAP S/4HANA Cloud within a two-tiered federated environment in areas with poor connectivity, it presents a challenge. Although there are technical solutions that could provide data staging (i.e., when cloud connectivity goes down, data to be transferred to the cloud is temporarily stored locally), this additional complexity essentially negates the purpose of "simple" SaaS-based solutions. Therefore, poor connectivity should be a show-stopper for implementing SAP S/4HANA Cloud within a two-tiered federated manufacturing landscape.

- **Shop floor requirements**
  SAP S/4HANA Cloud provides the ability to extend functionality, an ability called *extensibility* within the SAP S/4HANA Cloud world. For external integration,

SAP S/4HANA Cloud calls this additional functionality *side-by-side extensibility*. Specific to manufacturing functionality, if an organization requires shop floor business processes, they can only be handled via side-by-side extensibility. If a business requires this functionality, it will need to decide if it's willing to invest in extending its investment into additional software and/or development or opt to use point-to-point integration via open APIs, which do not necessarily involve the SAP Cloud Platform.

- **Manufactured product speed to market**
  If an SAP S/4HANA Cloud prospective customer is looking to more efficiently and rapidly deploy SAP to bring a manufactured product to market quickly, SAP S/4HANA Cloud could provide a competitive advantage from an IT systems perspective. The functionality fit must make sense, but assuming SAP S/4HANA Cloud's business functions meet business requirements, SAP S/4HANA Cloud can be deployed for comprehensive ERP functionality in a fraction of the time as on-premise SAP S/4HANA.

- **Subsidiary acting as subcontractor to headquarters**
  This perhaps is one of the most compelling reasons for deploying SAP S/4HANA Cloud within subsidiaries as part of a two-tiered manufacturing SAP landscape. In this model, the parent headquarters conceptually acts as the customer for the child subsidiary, and the typical business process flows of material requirements planning (MRP), purchase orders, sales orders, production activities, and financial transactions are performed. Figure 2.7 illustrates the two-tiered manufacturing headquarters and subsidiary process flow. The headquarters and the subsidiary each control the following parts of the process:

  - Headquarters:
    - Create production orders and reservations for material including resource capacity
    - Release production order to ensure sufficient stock
    - Create purchase order and issue to subsidiary
    - Good receipts for material
    - Confirmation sent to subsidiary for billing document
  - Subsidiary
    - Create the sales order
    - MRP
    - Planned orders creation of PR or PO

- Release production order
- Create delivery and billing
- Post goods issue to HQ
- Account receivable settlement

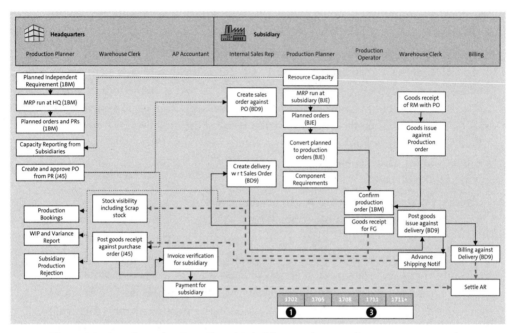

Figure 2.7 Manufacturing Two-Tiered Subsidiary Acting as Subcontractor to Headquarters: Business Process Flow

2.3.3   Holding Company Model

Another effective use case for SAP S/4HANA Cloud applies to holding companies. Organizations focused on managing a portfolio of various businesses can benefit tremendously from leveraging SAP S/4HANA Cloud as their business system of record.

Behind the Curtain: Multinational Holding Company

A multinational holding company with US headquarters had two subsidiaries that were businesses with international footprints: one in Germany and another in the United States. From a systems perspective, they currently possess both SAP (SAP ERP 5.0) and Microsoft (Dynamics) ERP systems implemented for each business or separate legal entity. With two separate ERP backends, the organization is forced to support two separate and distinct ERP systems and their corresponding skillsets. This model is inefficient and overly expensive for the smaller holding company. As of the writing of this book, the holding company is exploring the option to consolidate both ERP systems into a single SAP S/4HANA Cloud platform.

One of the challenges encountered with holding companies is their consolidated financial pictures across all portfolio entities. With SAP S/4HANA Cloud, this challenge can be eliminated. Like some of the value proposition data points described generically for standard two-tiered SAP S/4HANA Cloud landscapes, holding companies can benefit for the following reasons:

- **Ease of deployment**
  As described earlier, SAP S/4HANA Cloud provides a templatized, business-driven deployment approach, which makes rollout much more streamlined. Furthermore, SAP S/4HANA Cloud is built through a business lens, not a technical lens. This means that not only will non-tech-minded folks understand the deployment process much better, because it's business-process-oriented by design, but more importantly its adoption will be that much greater.

- **Minimized implementation cost**
  Ease of deployment equates to minimized implementation cost. Lower cost and less expensive implementations of SAP S/4HANA Cloud will resonate deeply with both a holding company and its management, as well as with the related portfolio company. Holding company management will be pleased to learn that SAP S/4HANA Cloud implementation costs won't eat into the greater holding company portfolio cost structure, and portfolio company management likewise will be delighted by the high potential to have one major component of the portfolio company's compensation tied to profitability.

- **Common business framework**
  A common business framework comprised of a multitude of factors, including common business processes (how an organization handles accounts payable), common data models (how a portfolio company defines its chart of accounts), portfolio company reporting requirements to headquarters (how often the portfolio company is required to provide financial data—quarterly, monthly, etc.), and others, provides a structure for holding company efficiencies.

- **Consolidated financial picture**
  Logically, the more commonality the different business units share within the

greater organization, the easier the holding company can accurately view its consolidated financial picture. SAP S/4HANA Cloud can provide that "common language" for easier consolidated financial reporting.

- **Maturity/sophistication perception of asset**
  Different holding companies are driven by different economic objectives. Many holding companies look to build their portfolio companies strictly to sell for financial gain, whereas others hold businesses for long-term investment purposes. For those looking to sell portfolio businesses, SAP S/4HANA Cloud as an ERP business system framework provides both the optics and the reality of a mature, more sophisticated, well-run business. For this reason alone, implementing SAP S/4HANA Cloud provides a mature system backend, potentially even enhancing an asset's value. (This point will be discussed in greater detail in Section 2.3.4.)

Figure 2.8 shows how a holding company model can be structured from a systems perspective by leveraging SAP S/4HANA Cloud within a two-tiered SAP ERP model.

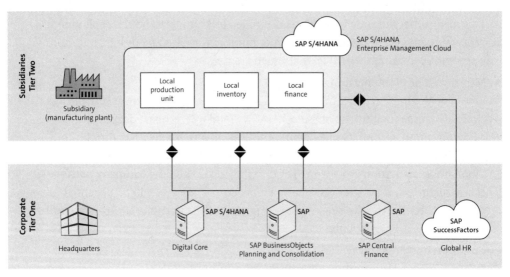

Figure 2.8 Holding Company Two-Tiered SAP S/4HANA Cloud Model

2.3.4   Start-ups and Mergers and Acquisitions

Every day—almost every hour—business ideas are blossoming into real businesses. The start-up has evolved into so much more than simply two people with an idea working out of a garage. Many success factors exist in the creation and, more importantly, the scaling of a start-up. Beyond the fundamentals of business strategy, solving a real problem, financing and investment, and other key growth components, a solid systems infrastructure—both IT and other—is crucial for the success of a start-up's growth and long-term viability. SAP S/4HANA Cloud now exists as a solution for a start-up's ERP platform.

Using the proper systems from a start-up's inception is a crucial foundational success factor. With the flurry of action items facing a startup, IT systems often are overlooked. (This oversight occurs easily when many start-ups face existential issues such as payroll and simply keeping the lights on!) Nonetheless, this important component of IT systems needs to be examined and set underway early on to ensure that scaling isn't impeded by having to retrofit a business (start-up) with IT systems after that ship has sailed.

Behind the Curtain: Leveraging SAP S/4HANA Cloud as a Systems Blueprint for Start-ups

Most start-ups think about ERP long after the business has taken flight. This is understandable; far more pressing issues exist in the genesis and success of a start-up than the ERP setup. However, one potential advantage could exist for start-ups if ERP is considered early on: business process maturity. Most start-ups look towards solving external-facing business problems (e.g., how to provide greater convenience for a consumer by filling some gaps with a service or product) rather than how to run their business internally, but both components are equally important for a business's survival.

This means that regardless of how successful a start-up is in solving a business problem, if the startup fails to effectively build internal functions (i.e., producing proper financials, maintaining solid cash flow, forecasting supply and demand, etc.) to remain afloat, then the start-up will fail. SAP S/4HANA Cloud provides SAP Best Practices as part of its baseline functionality, and these can be used as internal start-up business practices or business function blueprints. These accelerators can provide a much-needed systems (both IT and business) foundation, enabling start-ups to continue to focus externally, on their customers, as opposed to worrying about internal table stakes and very important system functions.

Venture Capital

Start-ups supported and fueled by venture capital receive the advantage of any start-up expertise the venture capitalists bring to the table. This institutional knowledge and expertise provided by experienced scaling and growth experts can be invaluable. Along with the start-up acumen should come experience and foresight related to systems and the investment required to effectively lay a solid foundation for short-term start-up viability and long-term business success. Many venture capitalists already appreciate the value of IT systems, including the suite of SAP platforms; thus, SAP ERP's value shouldn't be foreign to a start-up. However, because many venture capitalists' experience with ERP software might be from older, on-premise versions, such as SAP R/3 or SAP ERP, a bit of education in SAP S/4HANA Cloud might be required. Nonetheless, with a bit of discussion, venture capitalists easily should understand the differences between SAP S/4HANA Cloud as an ERP SaaS platform and its on-premise sibling. Once the value of SAP S/4HANA Cloud is understood, its positioning and purchase should be justified easily; that's one major advantage of being backed by a venture capitalist with deep pockets as opposed to running a self-funded start-up.

Mergers and Acquisitions

According to Deloitte's 2017 M&A index, titled "Fueling Growth through Innovation," the 2017 outlook continues to appear "frothy" (or active), with businesses looking to expand market share and capabilities through strategic acquisition. As the report notes: "Deloitte analysis shows companies using M&A as strategic expedient to capture disruptive innovation growth opportunities. There has been a sharp and continuing increase in M&A deals done with the primary purpose of acquiring capabilities or technologies across key disruptive categories such as Fintech, AI, Robotics, and others" (see *https://bit.ly/2gHYNxO*).

As part of the continued and solid momentum within the M&A space, the need for lightweight and easily deployable ERP solutions continues to rise. SAP S/4HANA Cloud has positioned itself as a front and center option for M&A activity.

Several key advantages exist for SAP S/4HANA Cloud as a go-to solution for the greater M&A market, including the following:

- **The ubiquity of SAP**
  Mature businesses typically choose "red" (Oracle) or "blue" (SAP) when selecting world-class ERP. With blue possessing the world's largest market share within the ERP space, SAP is a clear favorite of M&A organizations based on many factors, including a wealth of SAP talent globally, greater market acceptance, and M&A familiarity. SAP S/4HANA Cloud is one of SAP's newer and more heavily touted products, and it exists as a viable and trusted M&A-driven ERP option.

- **Easy to peel**

  By definition, M&A represents business transactions and activities. The method by which M&A companies build wealth and in turn produce profits for investors is to turn a profit for their shareholders. SAP S/4HANA Cloud not only allows but enables such a premise. SAP S/4HANA Cloud's ability to easily change hands of ownership is a fundamental feature for organizations looking to trade businesses. Via its core features and functions, such as the technical cloud infrastructure with no on-premise footprint, core and common business best practices functions translatable across ownership, few to virtually no IT support staff required for operations, and so on, SAP S/4HANA Cloud provides an easily deployable and agile ERP option for M&A activity. Essentially, the IT system headache is removed.

- **Rapid deployment**

  As discussed, SAP S/4HANA Cloud is easily deployable for many reasons. This feature is very attractive for the M&A market. When M&A organizations look toward acquiring assets (i.e., businesses), building structured systems for repeatable processes is crucial for building value. With SAP S/4HANA Cloud's ease of implementation and inexpensive long-term cost, M&A companies will continue to fall in love with the product's ability to rapidly increase the value of an acquired or held asset. Furthermore, with the ability to quickly deploy SAP S/4HANA Cloud, M&A organizations no longer should be concerned with expensive IT system implementations, assuming SAP S/4HANA Cloud's business functions fit the held asset.

- **Corporate venturing**

  An exciting new business model has begun to emerge: Large Fortune 100 organizations are no longer waiting for smaller, more nimble companies to provide innovation on a start-up scale. With the recent advent of corporate venturing, large multinationals are now creating start-ups *within* their organizations. For example, global consumer packaged goods giant Nestlé has created HENRi@Nestlé, an intrapreneurial program within Nestlé to identify, cultivate, and support innovative entrepreneurial ideas presented by non-Nestlé startups. This corporate venturing innovative approach provides an excellent example of M&A activity in which the pitching companies could potentially implement SAP S/4HANA Cloud as an ERP scalable platform within a two-tiered SAP S/4HANA landscape. (*Note:* Nestlé runs SAP as an innovation ERP platform globally.)

With acquisitions and divestures on the rise, flexible ERP product options such as SAP S/4HANA Cloud provide much-needed flexibility for parent organizations. Figure 2.9 charts responses from large organizations actively involved in M&A activity over the last several years. As you can see, the level of interest and M&A pursuit shows that the market is positioning itself for kinetic business transformation via M&A.

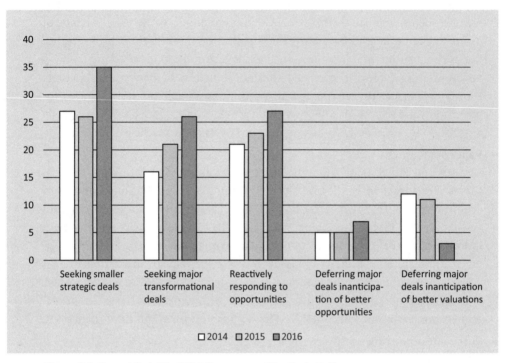

Figure 2.9 Recent Deloitte M&A Responses: Kinetic Activity

As reflected in the industry questionnaire, there are essentially three options for how to most effectively manage and control an acquired entity, as follows:

1. **Integration**

   As part of the business acquisition, the M&A and/or holding company integrates the existing acquiring company's business processes and systems into the existing parent company's corporate processes without any modifications.

   – *Advantage:* Rapid time to value.

   – *Challenge:* Integration is ripe with potential challenges related to a disconnect between the parent and child companies due to using different processes and systems, which potentially equate to different ERP systems requiring higher

TCO, including higher costs for systems maintenance and consistent innovation (i.e., upgrades).

2. **Migration**

As part of an acquired subsidiary, the M&A and/or holding company migrates the acquired company into corporate common processes and systems.

– *Advantage:* The acquired company can benefit from the synergies driving efficiencies.

– *Challenge:* The parent company, as part of the acquisition, requires potentially deep investments from both organizations within IT for project and release schedules.

3. **Innovation**

With this approach, the parent company deploys structure, processes, and systems at the child subsidiaries that align with the headquarters' (i.e., corporate) processes while simultaneously empowering the acquired company to remain independent.

– *Advantages:* This approach leverages SAP Best Practices from the mothership yet maintains flexibility at the subsidiary level, SAP S/4HANA Cloud can be deployed during the acquisition and connect easily to HQ, and the implementation and spin-up for the acquired company is weeks or months instead of years.

– *Challenge:* The acquired subsidiary may be reluctant to adopt the parent company's recommended ERP (SAP S/4HANA Cloud).

2.4 Localization

One of the most frequently asked questions about SAP S/4HANA Cloud relates to localization. Positioned as SAP's ERP SaaS global platform, SAP S/4HANA Cloud's ability to support country-specific needs such as language, currency, tax, and legal requirements is fundamental for product credibility and adoption.

Therefore, SAP is working feverishly to roll out country-specific needs and thus check that essential checkbox. At the time of writing (as of SAP S/4HANA Cloud 1705), SAP S/4HANA Cloud currently supports 23 countries and 10 languages.

Per the upcoming roadmap milestones and corresponding planned SAP S/4HANA Cloud releases through 1802, SAP plans to increase the number of countries supported to 29 and the languages to 17. The following is the list of proposed localization innovations planned through the fourth quarter of 2017 for SAP S/4HANA Cloud:

- *Languages:* English, German, French, Spanish, Japanese, Russian, Portuguese, Chinese (simplified), Dutch, Hungarian, Arabic, Italian, Korean, Swedish, Traditional Chinese, Danish, and Bahasa (Malaysia)

- *Countries:* United States, Germany, Australia, Belgium, Canada, China, France, Netherlands, Japan, Hungary, Philippines, Singapore, Switzerland, United Kingdom, Malaysia, United Arab Emirates, Hong Kong, Luxembourg, Italy, Spain, Taiwan, New Zealand, South Africa, Sweden, Ireland, Denmark, India, Indonesia, and Austria

2.5   Summary

The use cases for SAP S/4HANA Cloud are diverse and sound. If an organization wants to implement a well-designed and best practices-constructed ERP SaaS platform focused on constant innovation and minimal cost rapidly, then SAP S/4HANA Cloud is a viable solution. With any ERP platform (or any software platform, for that matter), business fit is imperative; it's vital that SAP S/4HANA Cloud's business functions are at least an 80 percent match for your specific ERP needs.

Whether your organization is driven by cloud solutions, preconfigured ERP options founded on SAP Best Practices, or a two-tiered ERP model capable of handling parent and child innovation, M&A, and start-up requirements, SAP S/4HANA Cloud has been designed with your prospects in mind.

In this chapter, we discussed the strategic question of *who*; that is, who are the potential candidates for best leveraging SAP S/4HANA Cloud. In the next set of chapters, we'll begin to delve into the tactical question of *how*: How can an organization most effectively implement SAP S/4HANA Cloud?

Chapter 3

Implementation: How Do You Set Up SAP S/4HANA Cloud?

SAP provides critical tools to support the implementation of SAP S/4HANA Cloud, including SAP Best Practices, which provides preconfigured processes, and SAP Activate, a comprehensive methodology that takes full advantage of the preconfigured software to drive an expedited but complete solution delivery.

This chapter will address the methodology and the SAP tools available for successfully and expeditiously implementing SAP S/4HANA Cloud. Because the application is preconfigured with SAP Best Practices, implementing SAP S/4HANA Cloud is different from the laborious efforts required for most previous enterprise-class ERP implementations. With SAP S/4HANA Cloud, implementation project durations can be measured in weeks and months, as opposed to months and years.

In addition, SAP has developed SAP Activate, a rapid, iterative methodology that goes beyond a simple project approach, providing everything from deliverable templates to a prepopulated database that allows users to interact with the system on day one. At the end of the day, the combination of SAP Best Practices and SAP Activate makes the overall implementation a smooth process that not only gets the software up and running for a company quickly, but also engages the user community so that it is ready, willing, and able to accept the new application and new way of doing business.

3.1 SAP S/4HANA Cloud Best Practices

SAP's interactions with businesses over the last 40-plus years have provided tremendous insight into what works well and what doesn't, across multiple industries and companies of every size. This knowledge has been systematized and codified for further application in a multitude of areas, including the configuration of SAP S/4HANA Cloud.

Companies differentiate themselves in several ways, from product design to pricing to customer service, but operational excellence is a must to play the game. The procure-to-pay process for a company won't differentiate it from its competition, but if handled poorly it could affect everything from production cycles to product quality to company profitability, which could prevent a company from being successful no matter how cool its product is or how low its product is priced or how well it interacts with customers. The same holds true for managing the order-to-cash, plan-to-produce, and project services processes, as well as the back-office finance and HR processes. SAP, with its business process knowledgebase, took this premise and created SAP Best Practices. The following two sections will address navigating the SAP Best Practices database and the content within it.

3.1.1   Navigating

One of the intrinsic values of SAP Best Practices is the taxonomy used to provide a structure for all the main processes for an average manufacturing/distribution and/or professional services business. This taxonomy, as well as the SAP Best Practices content, is accessed via the SAP Best Practices Explorer website (*https:// rapid.sap.com/bp*; see Figure 3.1). The website allows even visitors without an SAP user (S-user) ID to browse through SAP Best Practices process flows.

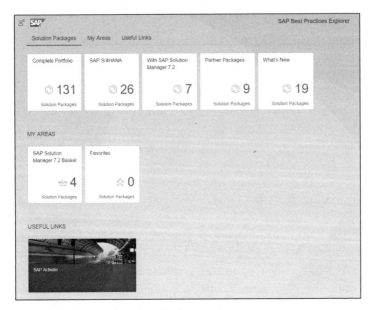

Figure 3.1 SAP Best Practices Explorer

As shown in Figure 3.1, the first step in navigating SAP Best Practices is to select a scope. For SAP Best Practices used to configure SAP S/4HANA Cloud, start by clicking the **SAP S/4HANA** tile. After clicking the tile, you are given the option of selecting a specific solution package (see Figure 3.2).

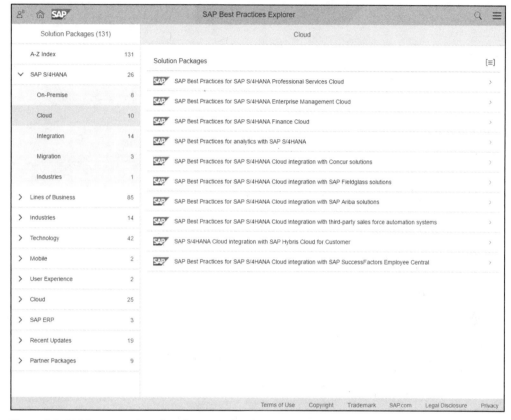

Figure 3.2 SAP Best Practices for S/4HANA Cloud

Click **Cloud** on the left side of the screen to view the list of SAP Best Practices for various SAP S/4HANA Cloud solution packages. After selecting a specific package—for example, **SAP Best Practices for SAP S/4HANA Enterprise Management Cloud**—it's a good idea to select a specific country localization (see Figure 3.3). Localizations will limit functionality to what's applicable for that country. For example, Intrastat processing is unique to EU countries and won't show for others, such as Japan or the United States.

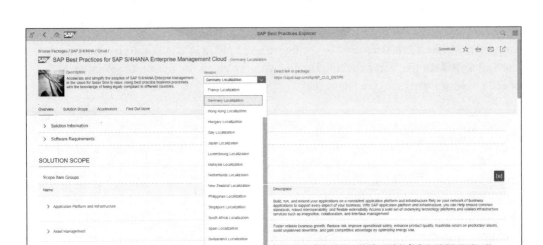

Figure 3.3 Selecting Country for Localization

Once the localization is set, it's possible to view specific functionality or a scope item of interest. *Scope items* are grouped logically, by function. *Scope item groups* can be split into business and technical categories, as noted in Table 3.1.

Business Groups	Technical Groups
▪ Asset management ▪ Finance ▪ Human resources ▪ Manufacturing ▪ Project services ▪ Sales ▪ Sourcing and procurement ▪ Supply chain ▪ R&D/engineering	▪ Application platform and infrastructure ▪ Data management

Table 3.1 Scope Item Groups

The business group scope items include everyday business processes, such as sell from stock (see Figure 3.4) or consumable purchasing, but they also contain integration processes, such as SAP Ariba sourcing integration and SAP Fieldglass contingent labor and invoice integration for finance. The technical group scope items cover processes that would likely be handled by IT support personnel, such as output management (for setting up printing or email and for customizing forms), key user extensibility (for in-app extensions), data aging, master data consolidation, and more.

Figure 3.4 SAP Best Practices: Sell from Stock

Each scope item has multiple drilldown levels for specific content as well as references to the specific edition of SAP S/4HANA Cloud the scope item is in. In the **Sell from Stock** example shown in Figure 3.4, the **Used In** tab would show that the scope item is used in both the Enterprise and Finance Cloud editions.

> **Note**
>
> The edition concept may become obsolete with the current licensing plans only applying to the complete enterprise functionality. Editions, however, are still a part of the SAP Best Practice and SAP Activate documentation and are, thus, referred to here.

3.1.2   Content

As shown in Figure 3.4, each scope item page contains **Description** and **Overview** tabs, which include information about the business benefits of the scope item and the key process flows it covers. In addition, a **Details** section includes the following links:

■ **Test Script**

The test script is a Microsoft Word document that provides the procedures and data requirements for testing the business processes in the scope item. These scripts serve a dual purpose: First, they can be used to guide functionality demonstrations during the fit-to-standard process (discussed in Section 3.2.3). Second, these test scripts are built into the automated test scripts within the Manage Your Application app and can be used for automated regression testing.

The test script is broken into the following sections:

– *Purpose:* A brief overview of the scope item and its business purpose

– *Prerequisites:* Master data, organization data, other test data, and business conditions required to complete the test

– *Overview table:* A high-level overview of the test procedure (see the example for the emergency maintenance scope item in Table 3.2)

Process Step	Business Role	Transaction/App	Expected Results
Report malfunction	Maintenance technician	Report malfunction	Unplanned job is created.
Repair malfunction	Maintenance technician	Repair malfunction	Unplanned job is confirmed, including time recording, con-firming material used.

Table 3.2 Sample Test Script Overview Table

– *Test procedures:* Detailed procedures and expected results for each process step listed in the overview table (see the example for the report malfunction process step in Table 3.3)

– *Appendix:* Overview of related processes

Test Step #	Test Step Name	Instruction	Expected Results
1.	Log onto SAP Fiori launchpad.	Log onto the SAP Fiori launchpad as a maintenance technician.	The SAP Fiori launchpad displays.

Table 3.3 Sample Test Procedures Table

Test Step #	Test Step Name	Instruction	Expected Results
2.	Access the app.	Open **Report Malfunction**.	The **Confirmation** screen displays.
3.	Report malfunction.	On the **Create Malfunction Report** screen, make the following entries: ■ **Tech. Object**: 217100091. Note: You can also search for an object via plain text. Use the value help button and provide a keyword, such as "water pump". In the result list, select the equipment with number **217100091**, a description of **Cooling Water Circulation Pump**, and **Maintenance Planning Plant 1710**. ■ **Description**: Describe the unforeseen event. ■ **Effect**: For example, 2 Production restricted. If default report time needs to be adjusted, make the following entry: ■ **Reported on**: <Date> <Time> Click **Save**. Note the order number and the notification number for the next test.	Order 4XXXXXX is saved with notification 1XXXXXXX.

Table 3.3 Sample Test Procedures Table (Cont.)

■ **Process Flow**

The process flow is a vertical swim lane diagram depicting the main steps in the business process, the order and dependencies of the steps, and the business role responsible for completing each step. Note that these process flows are provided in both a view-only format and in a Business Process Model and Notation (BPMN) 2.0 format for editing or including in other business process documentation using a BPMN 2.0 modeler. Figure 3.5 shows an example process flow.

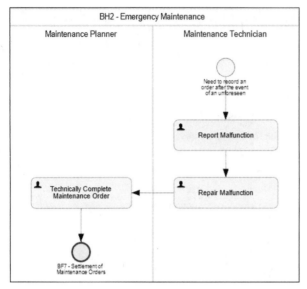

Figure 3.5 Example Process Flow from Emergency Maintenance
Scope Item in SAP Best Practices

- **Set-up Instructions**
  For some scope items for which more technical configuration is required, a technical configuration guide is provided.

All in all, the SAP Best Practices provide an immensely helpful encyclopedia of SAP S/4HANA Cloud scope items, how they should function, and how they should support a business. This valuable information source vastly accelerates an implementation with preexisting documentation and test scripts that serve both to train and to confirm system functionality.

3.2   SAP Activate

Although the SAP Best Practices provide accelerators for understanding and implementing SAP S/4HANA Cloud, they must be paired with a comprehensive methodology to guide and further accelerate an implementation. Designed with SAP S/4HANA and SAP Best Practices in mind, SAP Activate is that methodology. SAP Activate took lessons learned from SAP's previous methodology, ASAP, and combined them with newer, iterative techniques developed for agile methodologies, then leveraged the

SAP Best Practices along with the preconfiguration of SAP S/4HANA Cloud to create this new, lightweight, fast-moving approach to implementation.

Figure 3.6 illustrates SAP Activate's overall implementation and operation lifecycle.

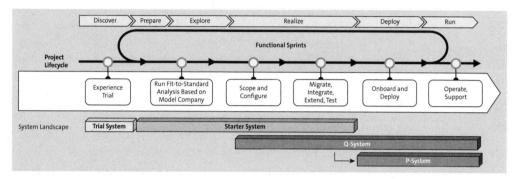

Figure 3.6 SAP Activate Project Lifecycle

Figure 3.6 highlights several important features of the methodology, including the following:

- At the top of the figure, the major phases of an implementation are provided in chevrons from left to right. These phases provide a necessary taxonomy for implementation projects, though they harken back to traditional waterfall methodologies; however, the similarity stops there.

- At the bottom of the figure, the various system landscapes that will be used throughout the project lifecycle are listed, aligned underneath the phases they'll be used in. These system landscapes are as follows:

  - *Trial system:* This system isn't a traditionally delivered landscape, but a free, limited trial version of SAP S/4HANA Cloud. It's populated with sample company data and includes guided tours to help inexperienced users navigate the system and begin to see the system capabilities and adjust to the user experience. This system is only used for the *discover* phase, a preproject phase that prepares business users for the implementation to come and begins the change enablement process.

  - *Starter system:* This system is delivered at commencement of the contract. It contains prepopulated data that's extremely handy for driving the explore phase. Although specific company data can be entered into this system, it won't be carried forward into subsequent landscapes; this landscape is only used to assist in identifying any crucial gaps between SAP S/4HANA Cloud and company business requirements. The starter system can be kept until shortly after the production system goes live.

- *Q system:* The Q or *quality system* is where system configuration takes place. This landscape will survive the implementation, giving customers an environment in which to test new configurations and functions.

- *P system:* The P or *production system* is the ongoing landscape that the business will operate in. While changes must be tested in the Q system, any that remain will necessarily be transported to the P system, keeping the two systems in sync.

- The middle of the figure shows the key steps of the project lifecycle. For example, there are several steps in the explore phase, but the key step in this phase (discussed ahead) is the fit-to-standard exercise. There isn't much new to the world of software implementation methodology here, but note the inference of iterations or *sprints* made by the circular arrows. The SAP Activate methodology, combined with the capabilities of SAP S/4HANA Cloud, allows an implementation to be iterative in nature, with scope-limited sprints rather than a big bang. In addition, this same methodology will apply as new functionality is released.

A single picture can't really tell the whole story of SAP Activate. Figure 3.7 can't tell the whole story, either, but it provides additional noteworthy detail.

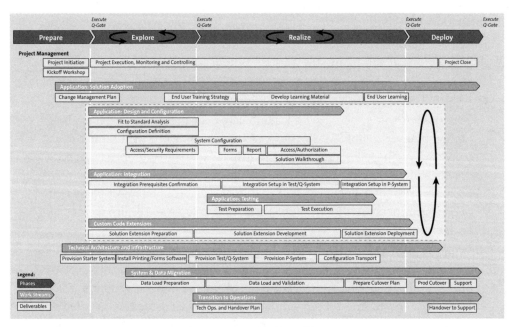

Figure 3.7 SAP Activate Work Streams and Deliverables

Figure 3.7 shows the logical work streams and deliverables created throughout an implementation project. Note the second work stream: solution adoption. Because SAP S/4HANA Cloud is preconfigured, it's imperative that change enablement or user adoption be an integral part of the implementation and not an afterthought. By positioning the work to start early in the project and be active throughout, the methodology assists in ensuring users are not only ready to use the new application, but also eager and supportive of the change in business processes (moving to best practices) that will come with it.

Also note the iterative nature of the design and configuration, integration, extensions, and testing work streams, which provide additional insight into the agile methodology. The integration and extensions work streams also acknowledge that there may be a need to address functional needs outside of what SAP S/4HANA Cloud can provide. The devil will be in the details for these work streams in terms of specific extensions and integrations required, but acknowledging them up front demonstrates the flexibility of the SAP Activate methodology.

The remainder of this section will discuss the various phases in more detail.

3.2.1   Discover

The initial discover phase doesn't directly contribute to the implementation, but it sets up later stages of the project for success. This phase introduces business users and affected stakeholders to SAP S/4HANA Cloud. By providing hands-on experience via the guided tours within the SAP S/4HANA Cloud trial system (see Figure 3.8), the discover phase allows users to become familiar with the *user experience*—that is, the look and feel of the system. They can learn by experience how to navigate the solution, gain insight into the depth and breadth of it, and see what's to come in future project phases.

The SAP S/4HANA Cloud trial system is free only on a limited, 14-day basis, but it's renewable. Note that it does require signing up for an SAP user ID. The trial system provides business roles and predefined scenarios in finance, project management, and purchasing, sales, and production. The trial system can be accessed at *http://sap.com/s4hana-trial*.

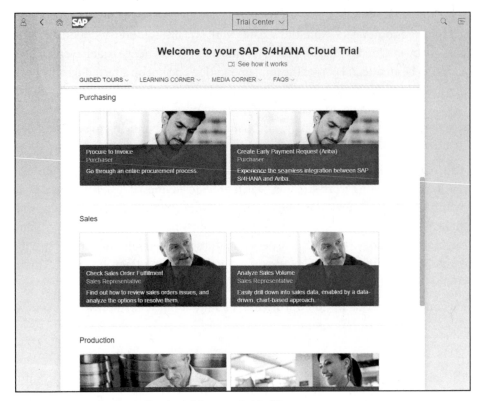

Figure 3.8 SAP S/4HANA Cloud Trial System Guided Tours

In addition, the discover phase allows time for the business and implementation team to review overall company business drivers and priorities that will guide any extension needs identified later, during the explore phase (see Section 3.2.3). In addition, the solution scope can be confirmed, and overall project success factors can be established. Finally, the rest of the implementation approach can be reviewed with all project stakeholders to help establish a common vision for the overall success of the project.

3.2.2   Prepare

The discover phase makes stakeholders familiar with SAP S/4HANA Cloud, but the implementation hasn't really started, because there isn't a defined project yet. Work in the prepare phase formalizes the project, from charter to schedule to team assignments and ultimately to the project kickoff.

Some of the key prepare phase deliverables include the following:

- **Project initiation and governance**

  No project, not even an SAP S/4HANA Cloud implementation, is without issues. As such, a project governance structure is required to address and resolve issues (be they functional decisions or scope changes or budget variances) and address risks. Work in this phase should include setting a governance structure that places decision making as close to the issues as possible while allowing for escalation for cross-functional or more significant issues. The governance structure is usually documented as a project organization (org) chart.

  Along with the org chart, any strategic project (and the implementation of a new ERP system definitely is a strategic project) must have a formal charter that lays out project goals, the business case justification for the project, critical assumptions that will enable success, and constraints (e.g., resources required by ongoing business or other projects). This critical deliverable is the cornerstone for the project and will set the terms for determining success or failure in financial and intrinsic terms. An effective charter also serves to align key stakeholders around the strategic intent of the project.

  Within or attached to the charter is a scope statement that specifically calls out what work is and isn't included in the scope of the project. Many projects run off track due to taking on tasks that were never included in the scope but crept in because there was no scope control mechanism. The scope statement is approved by the project sponsor and/or steering committee and is communicated to the project team along with the process for managing change control. Like the charter aligns stakeholders with the project strategy, the scope statement aligns stakeholders with the tactical project details.

  One final, critical piece of governance to address is communication. Ensure that proper meetings and status report schedules are set up to keep all stakeholders appropriately informed throughout the project (noting that different levels of stakeholders require different levels of detail and communication frequency).

  SAP Activate provides templates for the project charter, business case, and scope statement. All can be readily tailored to specific projects.

- **Project plans, schedule and budget**

  With the scope and overall strategic success factors of the project defined, the tactical plan for implementation can be defined. SAP Activate helps fast-forward this work with two helpful accelerators. The first is an Excel spreadsheet prepopulated with the SAP Activate phases, steps, and tasks (see Figure 3.9).

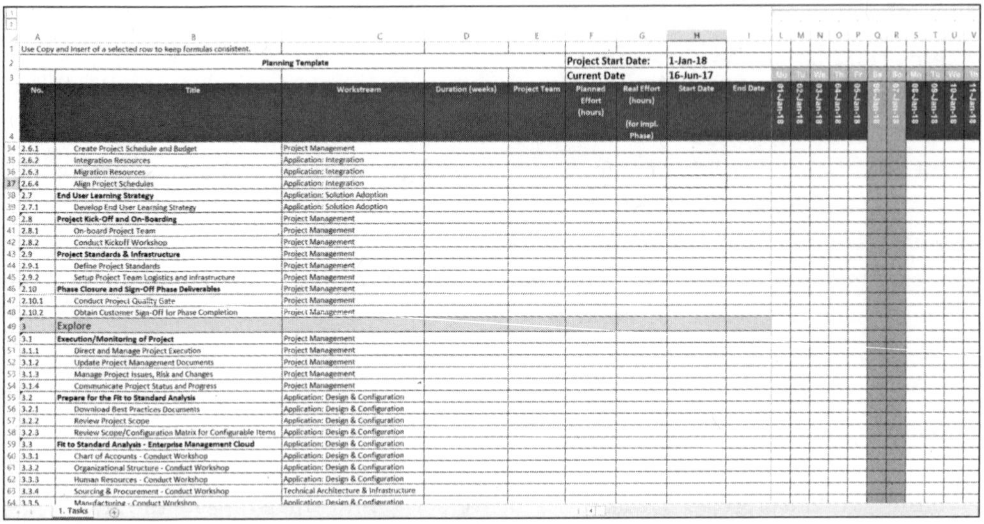

Use Copy and Insert of a selected row to keep formulas consistent.

Planning Template

Project Start Date: 1-Jan-18

Current Date 16-Jun-17

No.	Title	Workstream	Duration (weeks)	Project Team	Planned Effort (hours)	Real Effort (hours) (for Impl. Phase)	Start Date	End Date	Mo 01-Jan-18	Tu 02-Jan-18	We 03-Jan-18	Th 04-Jan-18	Fr 05-Jan-18	Sa 06-Jan-18	So 07-Jan-18	Mo 08-Jan-18	Tu 09-Jan-18	We 10-Jan-18	Th 11-Jan-18
2.6.1	Create Project Schedule and Budget	Project Management																	
2.6.2	Integration Resources	Application: Integration																	
2.6.3	Migration Resources	Application: Integration																	
2.6.4	Align Project Schedules	Application: Integration																	
2.7	**End User Learning Strategy**	Application: Solution Adoption																	
2.7.1	Develop End User Learning Strategy	Application: Solution Adoption																	
2.8	**Project Kick-Off and On-Boarding**	Project Management																	
2.8.1	On-board Project Team	Project Management																	
2.8.2	Conduct Kickoff Workshop	Project Management																	
2.9	**Project Standards & Infrastructure**	Project Management																	
2.9.1	Define Project Standards	Project Management																	
2.9.2	Setup Project Team Logistics and Infrastructure	Project Management																	
2.10	**Phase Closure and Sign-Off Phase Deliverables**	Project Management																	
2.10.1	Conduct Project Quality Gate	Project Management																	
2.10.2	Obtain Customer Sign-Off for Phase Completion	Project Management																	
3	Explore																		
3.1	**Execution/Monitoring of Project**	Project Management																	
3.1.1	Direct and Manage Project Execution	Project Management																	
3.1.2	Update Project Management Documents	Project Management																	
3.1.3	Manage Project Issues, Risk and Changes	Project Management																	
3.1.4	Communicate Project Status and Progress	Project Management																	
3.2	**Prepare for the Fit to Standard Analysis**	Application: Design & Configuration																	
3.2.1	Download Best Practices Documents	Application: Design & Configuration																	
3.2.2	Review Project Scope	Application: Design & Configuration																	
3.2.3	Review Scope/Configuration Matrix for Configurable Items	Application: Design & Configuration																	
3.3	**Fit to Standard Analysis - Enterprise Management Cloud**	Application: Design & Configuration																	
3.3.1	Chart of Accounts - Conduct Workshop	Application: Design & Configuration																	
3.3.2	Organizational Structure - Conduct Workshop	Application: Design & Configuration																	
3.3.3	Human Resources - Conduct Workshop	Application: Design & Configuration																	
3.3.4	Sourcing & Procurement - Conduct Workshop	Technical Architecture & Infrastructure																	
3.3.5	Manufacturing - Conduct Workshop	Application: Design & Configuration																	

1. Tasks

Figure 3.9 SAP Activate Template Project Plan in Excel

This template doesn't include all details for an implementation, but it provides the project structure and, with over 250 task lines, an excellent starting point.

The second useful accelerator is a PowerPoint presentation on running an agile project. The concept of iterative development, though not new per se, may be new to business users and other project stakeholders. This presentation will help ensure everyone is on board with the agile approach of SAP Activate.

- **Starter system provisioning**

  While the project plan is being created, the request to provision the starter system can be made. As discussed earlier, the starter system will be used later in the explore phase (see Section 3.2.3). Requesting it up front can eliminate any unnecessary downtime while the system is being provisioned (which can take a couple of days).

  After the request, three emails will be sent to the contact identified in the SAP S/4HANA Cloud contract: one regarding SAP Cloud Identity activation, one email containing the admin user and starter system URL, and one email with the admin password. The first email specifies two system URLs: the starter system URL and the URL for the administration console for SAP Cloud Platform Identity Authentication. The administration console (see Figure 3.10) is required for user setup and authentication. Some directions are provided in the email, and detailed steps are provided in the SAP Activate methodology. A full user onboarding guide is available on the SAP Help Portal (*https://help.sap.com/viewer/*). The second email contains the technical user password required to initialize the starter system and add business users.

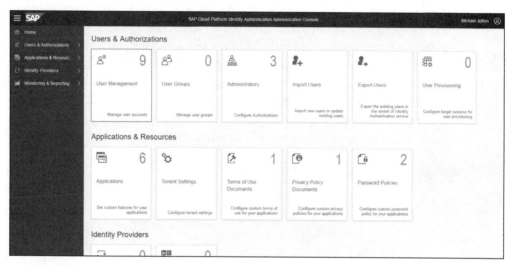

Figure 3.10 SAP Cloud Platform Identity Authentication Administration Console

Another key aspect of this step is confirming the technical infrastructure for the implementation. Although the solution is cloud-based, it's still important to confirm that the end user operating systems and Internet browsers (e.g., Chrome, Internet Explorer, etc.) are compliant. In addition, it's helpful to size the expected Internet usage of this new cloud application. The additional network traffic should be estimated to ensure that the company's current bandwidth and wireless networks (if in use) are properly sized to support expected usage (and avoid network delays that could create unnecessary latency issues, which would ultimately lead to user dissatisfaction). Finally, there are a couple of network server applications (for printing and customizing forms) that need to be downloaded, so it's necessary to confirm server availability and capacity.

- **End user learning strategy and customer team self-enablement**
  There is no guidance and are no templates in SAP Activate for an end user learning strategy deliverable (as of the time of writing), but it's still a critical success factor for implementation and shouldn't be taken lightly. A great deal of user change enablement is built into the methodology, with the discovery and explore phases and the iterative nature of the implementation. Still, a strategy for ensuring users are ready to adapt to and adopt the new system and new way of doing business is

critical to success. Steps should include evaluating the user base to identify training needs and appropriate training methods for the various users.

Once the strategy is built to leverage individual user strengths and balance weaknesses, self-paced training can be enabled as one of the key training resources. SAP provides several self-paced and collaborative training tools. Within the SAP S/4HANA Cloud application is the My Learning app. This app, enabled for users with the *employee* business role (in addition to any other roles they may have), provides a library of role-based, self-paced training. As shown in Figure 3.11, the user first selects the functional role that she/he is interested in and then can choose training topics from four categories, from getting started to role-specific processes to implementation topics and other topics.

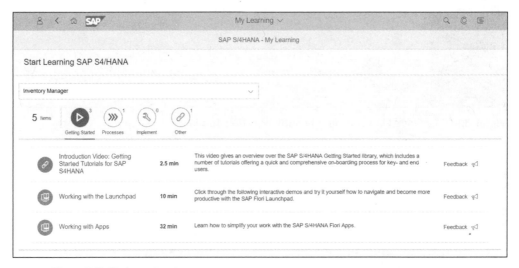

Figure 3.11 My Learning App

Additional SAP training can be accessed from the SAP Learning Hub and from social/collaborative training tools such as the SAP Jam methodologies hub. Ensuring that users have proper access rights and know how to access this valuable learning during the prepare phase will add to their ability to learn about the system before it is released to them.

- **Phase closure and sign-off phase deliverables**
  After the project is officially kicked off (generally the penultimate deliverable of the prepare phase), the phase can be officially closed and all deliverables officially

approved. This final deliverable marks the completion of the phase and confirms, via the sign-off, that all project stakeholders are aligned with the progress of the project and are ready to move to the next phase. This deliverable, along with project management deliverables, is included in every phase of the SAP Activate methodology and is a critical governance gate.

3.2.3   Explore

Many traditional methodologies would move from the prepare phase to some type of design phase. Because SAP S/4HANA Cloud is preconfigured with SAP Best Practices, a great deal of traditional design work has already been done. As a result, SAP Activate doesn't include a design phase; instead, the methodology has termed the next phase *explore* to indicate that this isn't an ordinary methodology. Rather than design screen layouts, data elements, and process work flows, business users are guided through the system by functional experts, exploring how the system already operates. This exploration also turns inward to the business as users seek to learn how the business can adapt to the SAP Best Practices underlying the software, rather than the other way around. Exploration also includes looking outside of the SAP S/4HANA Cloud system to understand what integrations must be addressed, what extensions must be built, and how data from the legacy system will migrate to SAP S/4HANA Cloud.

Some key explore phase deliverables include the following:

- **Fit-to-standard analysis**
  This deliverable is one of the crown jewels of the SAP Activate methodology. The goal of the analysis is to identify, catalog, and assign importance to gaps between SAP Best Practices delivered in SAP S/4HANA Cloud and company processes and data. Most important in this analysis is the perspective taken: business users must start with the assumption that the preconfigured SAP Best Practices are the starting point, *not* the current business processes.

  This starting point requires business users to understand how SAP S/4HANA Cloud works: Enter the starter system, provisioned in the prepare phase. Because this system contains a sample company and sample data, all transactions can be demonstrated to business users, who can then determine what business functions either will need to change or will require some level of extension to the application. When an extension is required, the "gap" is noted in the backlog and gap working document for evaluation and prioritization. The solution allows for iterative development and releases, so not all gaps have to be addressed prior to the initial release. The demonstration sessions, more appropriately named *fit-to-standard workshops*, follow the structure shown in Figure 3.12.

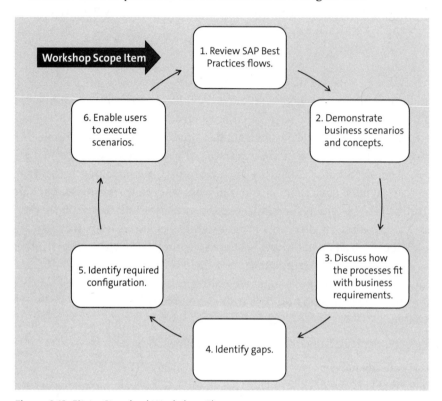

Figure 3.12 Fit-to-Standard Workshop Flow

Workshops are most effectively grouped by functional area and are often broken into multiple smaller sessions. One example of a workshop layout is provided in Table 3.4. Note that this is only a sample; the actual number of workshops will depend on the scope and complexity of business processes relative to a specific company. Also note that SAP Activate lists all potential workshops based on SAP Best Practices scope items and provides additional direction for designing the workshop scope based on configuration applications (see the discussion of the realize phase in Section 3.2.4).

Functional Area	Workshop
Financial workshops	■ Chart of accounts and org structure ■ Accounts payable ■ Credit management and accounts receivable ■ Bank accounts and cash management ■ Accounting and financial close
Sales workshops	■ Sales order processing ■ Sell from stock ■ Customer returns ■ Intercompany sales ■ Contract management ■ Quality management in sales
Procurement workshops	■ Procurement of direct materials ■ Purchase contract management ■ Quality management in procurement ■ Supplier management ■ Consumable purchasing
Supply chain workshops	■ Physical inventory ■ Quality management in stock handling ■ Return to supplier ■ Subcontracting
Manufacturing workshops	■ Production (e.g., make to order or make to stock) ■ Material requirements planning (MRP) ■ Quality management in manufacturing ■ Serial number management

Table 3.4 Sample Fit-to-Standard Workshops

In these sessions, it's important to take the time to review preconfigured system codes, such as return reasons, order types, and so on. These codes are configured in the realize phase, so any potential additions or changes should be identified in the explore phase. Some of the workshops, such as the org structure and chart of accounts workshops, spend much less time on system demonstrations and only focus on data configuration.

- **Output documentation templates definition**
  Even in the digital age, paper forms are required. This deliverable specifies form layouts for master form templates and for specific forms and emails.

- **Prerequisites for SAP S/4HANA integration with other SAP cloud systems**
  Tasks for this deliverable include gathering information on other SAP cloud systems, such as SAP SuccessFactors, Concur, and the like, that will be integrated with SAP S/4HANA Cloud.

- **User access and security**
  Business roles are established to provide access to specific apps and are assigned to users. The system comes with predefined business roles based on the SAP Best Practices process flows. These template roles can be used to create company-specific roles, as shown in Figure 3.13.

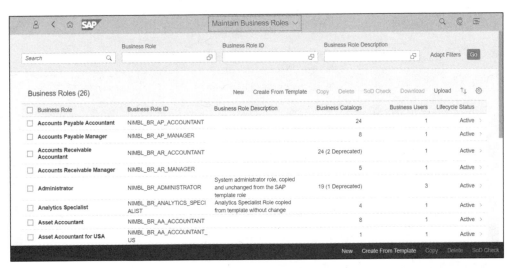

Figure 3.13 Maintain Business Roles

Roles can be combined or split or left as is. The important thing is that the appropriate roles are identified for each business user. As a side note, more sophisticated security management (such as SAP Governance, Risk, and Compliance, available in on-premise SAP S/4HANA) isn't currently available.

- **Solution extension preparation**
  Extensions, covered Chapter 9, must be defined and fully detailed to allow for proper development. Depending on scope and complexity, these efforts can become their own projects within a project and become excellent candidates for iterative releases.

- **Data load preparation**

  Data migration from the legacy system to SAP S/4HANA Cloud can be an extensive effort. This effort is expedited with the SAP S/4HANA Cloud Migration Cockpit, accessible from the Manage Your Solution app. The cockpit provides templates (in the form of Excel spreadsheets; see Figure 3.14) for data loads. Once data is in these templates, the cockpit provides mapping, code variation, and data load tools to automate the entry of data into SAP S/4HANA Cloud. By now, you may have notices that there are a few potential rakes hiding in the grass of this process:

  - First, you need to confirm whether templates exist for all data to be migrated. New templates are being added with each new quarterly release, but it's possible that some data may not fit in a template and will require manual migration.

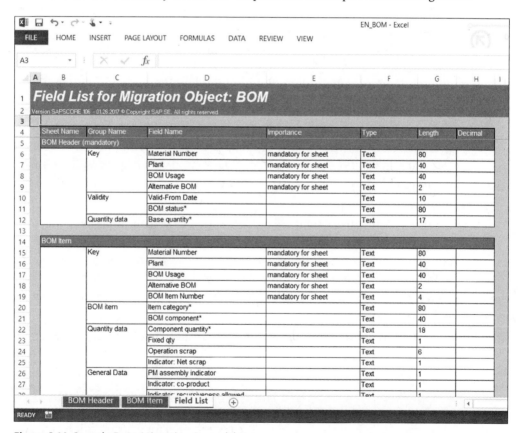

Figure 3.14 Sample Data Migration Spreadsheet

– The next potential hazard is getting data out of the current, legacy system and into the spreadsheets. The analogy of fitting a square peg into a round hole may apply when migrating from 20-plus-year-old systems and from multiple systems. It's a great start to know the form the data has to access, but pulling data out of the legacy system will require significant support from the legacy system maintenance team.

– The final issue to keep an eye out for is bad data. The good news is that the data cleansing tool will find improperly formatted data. More good news is that the cleansing tool allows the user to make corrections within the tool. The challenge is that these corrections can only be made one at a time. For a global issue, handling changes one at a time could be overly laborious. The last piece of news here is good, though: Global issues can be cleansed in Excel and rerun through the Migration Cockpit as often as necessary.

The Migration Cockpit provides an excellent tool to support this effort, but the effort itself must not be underestimated.

- **Test planning**
  Although the SAP S/4HANA Cloud application does not need to be tested per se, the business should define functional tests of critical business processes to confirm they work as expected. SAP Activate provides test plan templates for these test plans. In addition, the test plans available in the Manage Your Solution app can be modified to follow these scenarios, creating an automated testing solution.

- **Provision the Q system**
  Because system provisioning can take a few days, to keep the project moving without unnecessary delay we advise, provided that the fit-to-stand process has been completed and the target configuration chosen, that you request the provisioning of the Q system as soon as possible. This provisioning does require a few key configurations to be completed, however (in the form of spreadsheets sent with the provision request ticket):

  – *Chart of accounts:* A spreadsheet with the SAP Best Practice chart of accounts is provided to allow the accounts to be slightly modified to fit the business. This modification is very limited, so proper time with the chart of accounts must be spent to ensure it's right the first time. Because the SAP Best Practice chart of accounts is preconfigured with accounts for a wide variety of businesses, there may be some accounts that are not required for your specific business. A useful tip here is that for accounts that aren't required, the required eight-digit number can be preceded by "99", making a 10-digit number. When combined with a note that the number isn't required, it will be deactivated. Another limitation is that new accounts can't be added here, but current numbers and definitions can be changed. The number of accounts in the template must match the number of accounts sent to SAP for the Q system provisioning. Should additional accounts be required, they can be added after the system is provisioned. Doing so will require the GL accountant business role and is handled via the GL Account Master Data app (not one of the self-service configuration apps under Manage Your Solution).

- *Organizational structure change:* SAP S/4HANA Cloud can handle multiple organizational configurations, provided they do not overlap with reserved numbers (e.g., 17XX for a US organization, 10XX for a German organization, etc.). As with the chart of accounts, if new organizational structures are required, they need to be entered after provisioning. In this case, the org changes are handled via a self-service configuration app within the Manage Your Solution app. Still, this form must be completed and submitted.

- *Bank-lockbox-Vertex:* This form specifies initial bank information (additional banks can be added after the Q system is provisioned), as well as lockbox information, if appropriate. With the 1705 release, Vertex is no longer mandatory for US customers, but is still available for those who need it. If it's being used, however, the specifics for integration are provided in this spreadsheet.

- *Request questionnaire:* The contains crucial information on single vs parallel ledger, currency, etc., which must be properly completed and should be looked at early in preparation for Q system, supporting the Q provisioning request.

Once these forms are completed (and you have identified the preapproved expert configurations you will ask SAP to execute), they must be attached to a ticket submitted to SAP for provisioning the Q system. Two emails will be sent, because the URL for the Q system is different than that for the starter system. Note that users will need to be added in the same way as for the starter system; no data carries over, but can be uploaded or downloaded from one SAP S/4HANA system to another. With the Q system provisioned and the rest of the explore phase complete, the phase can be closed and signed off, indicating the team is ready for the realize phase. Before moving on, it is essential that you ensure all codes have been confirmed, all data elements defined, and all key processes reviewed; the more time spent in the workshops and in the overall explore phase, the easier the realize phase will be.

3.2.4   Realize

The realize phase is where the rubber hits the road—and then hits it again and again; more appropriately, a series of iterations are performed to incrementally configure and test an integrated solution as defined in the business requirements identified in the explore phase. As these iterations take place, business data is loaded/migrated, user adoption activities continue, and ongoing operating plans are set in place. The hub for a majority of the realize phase is the Manage Your Solution app (see Figure 3.15).

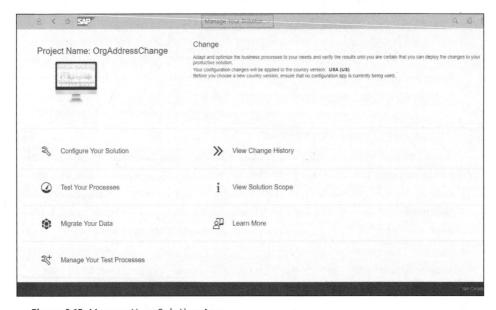

Figure 3.15 Manage Your Solution App

Once a change project is created, the apps to configure and test the solution are enabled for use. In the example shown in Figure 3.15, the change **Project Name** is **OrgAddressChange**, because it was created to make a change in an organization's address. One of the exciting parts of this app is that it's part of the SAP S/4HANA Cloud solution; it is *not* a separate toolset. Although it's not used for all of the realize steps, the Manage Your Solution app will be visited throughout the phase.

Some key realize phase deliverables include the following:

- **Production system provisioning**
  Although this deliverable is part of the realize phase, it's necessary to provision the P system immediately after the Q system is provisioned. Doing so will ensure that both the base release and hot fix levels of the Q and P systems are the same.

Note

Hot fixes, or bug fixes can be applied by SAP intermittently in between the quarterly releases.

The only time these can differ is when a new release comes out and Q is updated and tested two weeks prior to P. Requesting P system provisioning is a little different than the process for Q. First, an administrator for the system must use the Manage Your Solution app to set all self-service configuration user interfaces to **Completed** (see Figure 3.16). No configuration needs to happen; these self-service configuration UIs need to carry over exactly as in the Q system for this initial provisioning. The blue button in the bottom-right corner will say **Proceed to Preset Phase** (as shown in Figure 3.16) for this initial transport only. Once the button is clicked, an incident must be created for SAP to complete the provisioning.

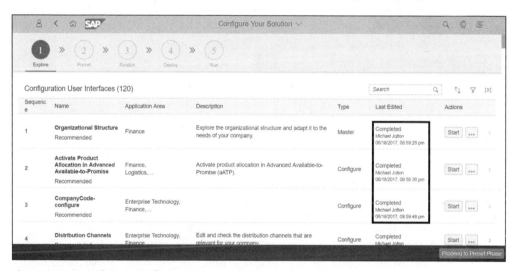

Figure 3.16 Completing Configuration User Interfaces

Another reason to complete the P system provisioning right after Q is that the provisioning may take a day or two; having it provisioned early will prevent any unnecessary team downtime.

- **Solution configuration**
  The solution configuration for SAP S/4HANA Cloud is mostly an exercise in setting master data, such as the chart of accounts and org structure, codes to support

business processes, and so on. Much of the configuration takes place in the self-service configuration UIs (see Figure 3.17); SAP Fiori apps the provide the data to be reviewed and, if necessary, updated.

Figure 3.17 Sample Self-Service Configuration User Interface

The example in Figure 3.17 shows the **Order Reason** codes delivered as SAP Best Practices within the system. If these are acceptable and more are needed, click the **Add** button to create more. If one of the reasons—for example, **Newspaper Advertisement**—is useful but maybe not completely applicable, it can be selected and edited (e.g., renamed **Magazine Advertisement**).

Some configuration (e.g., adding G/L accounts) will take place in the system itself with master data apps. For these apps, the configurator will require the appropriate business role to access and use the app (in the example of adding a G/L account, the configurator will require the GL accountant business role).

If the explore phase was comprehensive, addressing processes and codes, this configuration can be completed relatively quickly just by following the specific requirements. If the explore phase was less complete, the configuration team may spend multiple cycles reviewing codes, accounts, and so on with business users. Although not an ideal situation and not valid rationale for iterative releases, additional change projects can be conducted until the codes and the like meet requirements.

- **Forms adaptation preparation and output management adoption**
  Although SAP S/4HANA Cloud is a SaaS solution requiring no hardware, modifying and printing forms does require separate on-premise applications hosted on a network server. The application for modifying forms is Adobe Lifecycle Designer, and the application for managing printing is SAP Cloud Print Manager. Both applications can be found through the Install Additional Software app within SAP S/4HANA Cloud.

  With Adobe Lifecycle Designer installed, the forms changes identified in the explore phase can be implemented and paper forms and email templates finalized.

- **Test plan creation and execution**
  Test plans are created and executed from within the Manage Your Solution app. The testing suite (see Figure 3.18) provides the ability to define end-to-end tests that, once defined, can be automated for quick regression testing when new releases launch.

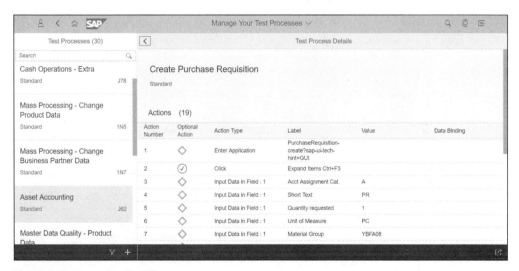

Figure 3.18 Managing Test Processes

All the test scripts from SAP Best Practices are preloaded into the testing tool, making test development much faster than it would be if starting from scratch. The SAP Best Practices test script, or process flow, provides the starting point; specific company data can be provided as needed. Test steps are tracked and monitored to ensure successful execution.

- **Legacy data migration**

  Data migration activities—specifically, loading data into the Migration Cockpit and cleansing the data—should have been started in the explore phase. At this point, in the realize phase, the data should be cleansed and ready to load (see Figure 3.19).

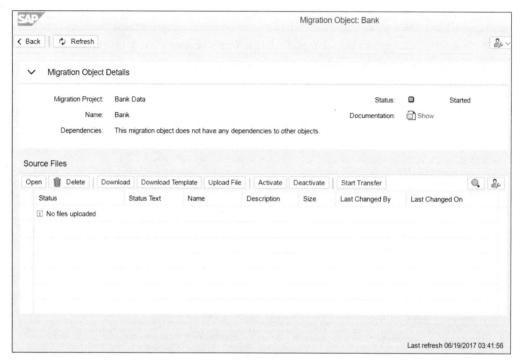

Figure 3.19 Example Migration of Bank Data

Even with the data converted and configuration complete and tested, there's much more work to take place, including the user solution walkthrough, completion of any tailored user learning content, cutover and technical operations planning, and development of any extensions. At this point, the phase is ready for sign-off, confirming that the business and IT stakeholders, as well as the project team, are ready to deploy the system.

3.2.5   Deploy

The deploy phase represents the end of one journey and the start of the next. The new P system will be enabled with the migrated company data and configured processes.

Integrated systems will be connected and extensions fully enabled. Users will be trained and ready to adopt the new system, and the company will officially cutover to the new system.

Some key deploy phase deliverables include the following:

- **Receiving the production system**
  In the same way as the starter and Q systems are received, with two emails and setting up users, the P system must also be received and users set up. By this point, setting up users will be a familiar process, but it must still be done and accounted for in the project plan.

- **Integration and extension deployment**
  Now that the P environment is live and configured, integrations with other SAP cloud solutions, such as SAP SuccessFactors Employee Central and Concur, can be finalized and fully deployed. In addition, other integrations with third-party systems and side-by-side extensions can be fully deployed.

- **End user learning**
  As discussed throughout this chapter, end user learning takes place throughout the implementation. Still, for larger organizations, there may be comprehensive user training programs required for users who weren't involved in the implementation project. This deliverable provides for such training, applying a pilot approach to confirm whether the developed training is effective, along with a general rollout of the training and the ability to evaluate and improve the training as it's delivered.

- **Production cutover**
  Critical to the final P system cutover is the application of nontransportable data. This data doesn't migrate to P as part of the Q to P transport and thus must be recreated manually. Data creation is somewhat administrative in nature, because it's already been handled in Q, so all settings are known. Nontransportable data includes the following:
  - Chart of accounts (beyond standard-delivered)
  - Cost centers
  - Bank accounts (beyond initial)
  - Forms (download/upload)
  - Business roles (download/upload)
  - Profit centers

With this data in place, the final cutover steps can be completed, support officially handed over, and the project officially signed off on, closed, and celebrated.

3.2.6   Run

Deployment, however, is not the end, but a new beginning. The run phase provides ongoing steps for handling each quarter's new releases. Much more on this topic is discussed in Chapter 5. The key point to note here is that SAP and the SAP Activate methodology highlight that though the initial implementation is complete, innovation is a continual process that must be managed throughout the system's lifecycle.

What's Missing? Tips for SAP Activate

As you can see, SAP Activate is a comprehensive methodology, and this chapter only scratches its surface. That said, for the first-time user, the methodology won't capture every nuance of an implementation project. Many such nuances have been discussed in this chapter, including the following:

- Determining how to group scope items for the fit-to-standard workshops
- Limitations for the initial chart of accounts and org structure setups (followed by eventual additions via master data and self-service configuration UI apps)
- Lag time for Q and P system provisioning (which must be built into the work plan to prevent project delays)
- Placeholders for non-SAP-centric activities such as training, for which deliverables and tasks are identified, but templates are yet to be developed

As the SAP S/4HANA Cloud product continues to be enhanced, so does the SAP Activate methodology. Over time, many of these nuances will be addressed, but new ones will emerge. What's important is that this methodology be used as a necessary guide for implementation, supplemented by expert support to catch many of the details that a methodology, no matter how comprehensive, can't address.

3.3   Team Requirements and Timing

Project staffing consists of two categories: the direct project team and the supporting business users and technical team.

When staffing a project team, consider the following:

- *Project scope (e.g., finance only, enterprise management, etc.):* In general, estimate one project team member (also called a *full-time equivalent* or *FTE*) per major functional area (e.g., finance, supply chain, sales and distribution).
- *Potential/likely integration requirements:* Nonstandard integrations will require development support familiar with writing integrations using APIs and SAP Cloud Platform. A general rule of thumb is to estimate roughly two FTE weeks per integration for development and testing. Additional time may be required for more extensive integrations and for deployment.
- *Potential/likely extensions:* The staffing and effort for extensions is highly dependent on specific extension requirements and may not be fully known until the extensions are designed. It's important to note that developers knowledgeable in SAP Cloud Platform and SAP Fiori will be required.
- *Data migration:* The extent of data being converted, in terms of both functional scope (breadth) and volume (depth), will greatly impact the amount of time and number of project team members required for data migration. At a minimum, the project team will need to include project team members familiar with the data structure in the legacy application to assist with the data extraction and transformation, appropriate functional project team members to assist with the data cleansing, and a project team member on the SAP S/4HANA Cloud side to assist with data transformation and loading using the Migration Cockpit.

This core project team will be supplemented throughout the project by key business users and internal IT staff. The roles for these extended members will include providing functional expertise for the fit-to-standard process, as well as assisting in developing test scripts, piloting training material, and more. Figure 3.20 provides a sample project organization chart.

A note about timelines: Project duration and work effort is highly dependent on too many factors to provide an estimate here. Simple finance-only implementations could take as little as eight to 10 weeks, and more sophisticated enterprise implementations with complex organizations and extensive scope could take four to five months on average. As with project team staffing, the project effort and duration will depend on scope, integrations, extensions, and data migration.

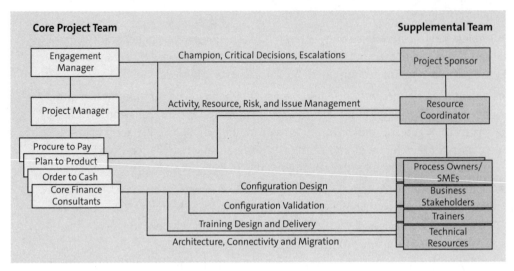

Figure 3.20 Sample Project Organization Chart

3.4   Summary

This chapter provided an overview of SAP Best Practices, the SAP Activate methodology for SAP S/4HANA Cloud, and parameters to consider for project staffing and timelines. SAP Best Practices, along with the SAP S/4HANA Cloud landscapes, preconfigurations, and configuration tools, combine with agile project management concepts to create an implementation approach that's accelerated yet comprehensive and that promotes user change enablement throughout the effort. The net result of applying the SAP Activate methodology should be a quick, less costly implementation with an increased likelihood of successful adoption and system use.

The implementation costs are only one component of overall solution cost, a topic addressed in the next chapter.

Chapter 4

Costs: How Much Will SAP S/4HANA Cloud Cost?

SAP S/4HANA Cloud is focused on driving maximum value to the market via a cost-competitive SaaS product. With quarterly innovations constantly improving the product, SAP S/4HANA Cloud is designed to drive one's business towards a brighter future.
—Melissa Di Donato, chief revenue officer, SAP S/4HANA Cloud

In the previous chapter, we broke down the fundamental components and steps involved in how to set up SAP S/4HANA Cloud at a high level. Understanding the key factors involved in how to implement SAP S/4HANA Cloud provides a foundation for understanding what implementation costs.

In this chapter, we will explore key factors that impact the important questions of cost when implementing SAP S/4HANA Cloud. Key components such as service subscription, functionality, fit-to-standard mapping, and long-term support all drive price. There are methods to trim and even eliminate cost components within an SAP S/4HANA Cloud implementation, but it's important to understand how cost saving decisions impact an SAP S/4HANA Cloud deployment. These factors and corresponding issues will be explored in this chapter.

While weighing direct costs, decision makers would also be advised to look at the financial and operational benefits of the SAP S/4HANA Cloud deployment. If the system can be deployed faster (in a matter of weeks instead of months/quarters), does not require own servers to run on, gets adopted faster due to the user-friendly interface, and upgraded on a quarterly cycle with no disruption to business, all these are advantages that should be considered along with calculations of the up-front deployment cost.

Behind the Curtain: "It Depends"

Questions related to cost are common. As with many consultant responses, the answer to how much SAP S/4HANA Cloud will cost is "it depends." Various differentiating factors impact the best-guess cost. The purpose of this chapter is not to specifically dial in the exact cost for implementing SAP S/4HANA Cloud, but to provide a high-level estimate of the following:

- What factors drive pricing?
- What would a reasonable estimated cost be, based on those factors?
- What are the long-term factors that define an organization's SAP S/4HANA Cloud TCO?

4.1   Subscription Price Structure

Traditional SAP ERP licensing costs were based on metrics primarily driven by the number of users or other major business metrics, such as revenue throughput. With a foundation or starter base cost dependent upon many factors, customers would sometimes find themselves in a morass of SAP SKUs, deciphering foreign bills of materials associated with SAP products they might not even have understood. Also, SAP presents its SAP software pricing via a published list (similar to MSRP [Manufacturer's Suggested Retail Pricing]). Often, the actual price that a customer purchases SAP software is discounted from the published list. This SAP pricing construct has created confusion and sometimes bred distrust.

Section Disclaimer

SAP controls all SAP software pricing and timing and the specifics of its revenue model. SAP can change licensing pricing and its model at any time. This section is meant to provide a clear picture of how SAP has constructed its SAP S/4HANA Cloud pricing model as of the time of writing, but any details herein are subject to change.

The following sections highlight several of the primary decision-making factors involved in the cost of implementing and supporting SAP S/4HANA Cloud. Although implementation and software costs are primary factors, post-go-live cost impact is equally important to consider.

4.1.1 Simplifying the SAP S/4HANA Cloud Licensing Model

To simplify the licensing costs specifically for SAP S/4HANA Cloud, SAP employed the industry-standard SaaS model of cost per user, per month. This cloud pricing strategy reduces the customer's pricing confusion and provides a clear pricing definition.

However, several nuances of SAP S/4HANA Cloud subscription remain. The following are several key factors involved in SAP S/4HANA Cloud pricing:

- **Individual user cost**
  SAP S/4HANA Cloud has adopted the industry standard pricing metric of a defined cost per user per month.

- **Subscription timeframes**
  As a cloud product with a subscription-based model, SAP S/4HANA Cloud's pricing timeframes typically are measured in 12-month increments. SAP typically sells SAP S/4HANA Cloud for multiyear periods, with three years (36 months) being the most common subscription length.

- **Annual maintenance cost**
  Unlike classic SAP on-premise solutions, SAP S/4HANA Cloud doesn't include a charge for any annual maintenance costs. The cost for constant product innovation and support is included in the subscription pricing per user.

- **Tiered pricing**
  Within the SAP S/4HANA Cloud licensing world, SAP incentivizes the customer community with a tiered pricing structure. Specifically, as the number of users increases, the cost per unit (or user) decreases at predefined milestones.

- **Add-ons**
  There are add-ons available that work seamlessly with SAP S/4HANA Cloud and serve specialized/premium functions. These are priced separately.

4.1.2 Current Pricing

If a company wants to implement SAP S/4HANA Cloud, the annual cost would be calculated using the number of users, giving the cost of a license per user, per month. The license cost for SAP S/4HANA Cloud per month or per year would then be calculated using that number along with the cost of any additional add-ons.

The cost might be more than that for QuickBooks, but this it pays for a robust wall-to-wall ERP solution, enabling organizations to drive business value from core finance to sales and logistics to manufacturing. Independent of two-tiered models (i.e., SAP

S/4HANA *and* SAP S/4HANA Cloud) or single ERP instances (i.e., *only* SAP S/4HANA), the SAP S/4HANA licensing pricing shouldn't be an issue.

4.2   SAP's Cloud Extension Model

For those in the know within the SAP world, the timeless idiom of "knowledge is power" rings loud and clear. With an overwhelming amount of SAP knowledge out in the marketplace coupled with constantly evolving products and opportunity positioning, it's difficult for even the most SAP-savvy individual to remain truly up to speed.

Luckily, SAP's cloud extension model helps you keep up. This program enables customers to trade in their on-premise software for cloud solutions. Thus, if an organization possesses SAP "shelfware" that's collecting dust, they can now repurpose that unused software via cloud products, including SAP S/4HANA Cloud. This program provides several benefits, both financial and in terms of business value.

Per SAP's intention with this software-swapping program, customers can reallocate SAP software—whether used or not—from their on-premise solutions to access SAP cloud software. Swapping this on-premise software replaces on-premise licenses and the corresponding maintenance with public cloud or private managed cloud subscriptions. As part of this SAP opportunity, often a customer must expand its SAP investment with the reallocated SAP cloud solutions.

> **Note**
>
> SAP's cloud extension model is part of SAP's strategic offerings and programs. The details of the program can be found on SAP's website, at *https://support.sap.com/ en/offerings-programs/strategy.html*.

The following are several of the key advantages of SAP's cloud extension model:

- **Move to cloud**
  Moving to the cloud provides all the inherent value described in previous chapters. Simply moving to the cloud can reduce a company's internal IT footprint, both from an infrastructure and a personnel perspective.

- **Repurpose the cost of unused software**
  Unused software is a waste of money. Repurposing unused, paid-for software is a tremendous opportunity.

- **Gain business value**

  By repurposing either used or unused SAP software, an organization can immediately recognize business value. For many customers currently on older SAP releases, the daunting task of upgrading to a newer version is intimidating on many levels: effort, business disruption, cost, and more. Trading in outdated or unused software enables organizations to jump immediately to SAP S/4HANA Cloud's constantly innovating ERP platform.

- **Reduce annual maintenance costs**

  By moving to the cloud, organizations immediately lower their SAVs. Most customers would leverage SAP Standard Support or SAP Enterprise Support annual maintenance, and their annual maintenance costs will immediately be reduced by repurposing on-premise software in the cloud.

> **Behind the Curtain: When SAP's Cloud Extension Model Applies**
>
> SAP's cloud extension model is only available for organizations that possess SAP software, not for organizations new to SAP looking to implement SAP S/4HANA Cloud.

4.3   Implementation Cost Components

Beyond the subscription costs for SAP S/4HANA Cloud, the next most expensive component in deploying the product is implementation services. SAP S/4HANA Cloud integrators (i.e., SAP consultants) vary in implementation services and costs, but there does appear to be a recognized implementation cost multiple benchmark related to the corresponding software cost. This multiple for services seems to be more externally driven (i.e., from outside the SAP world) than internally driven (i.e., profit margin-based on an SAP S/4HANA Cloud implementation partner's internal delivery cost).

> **SAPanese: The Definition of Multiple**
>
> The term *multiple* in the context of this discussion refers to the multiplying factor associated between the cost of SAP S/4HANA Cloud software to the cost of consulting services required to implemented SAP S/4HANA Cloud.

Due to the sheer competitiveness within the greater SaaS ERP space, any implementation costs too out of line with the competition (NetSuite, Infor, Workday, etc.) make SAP's ERP SaaS solution—SAP S/4HANA Cloud—noncompetitive. Therefore, the multiple between SAP S/4HANA Cloud licenses and SAP S/4HANA Cloud implementation services reflects the competition's corresponding multiple for greater ERP bake-off alignment.

> **Note**
>
> The term *ERP bake-off* denotes a competitive ERP system selection process between multiple similar ERP systems. This often occurs during an ERP system request for proposal (RFP).

Within an SAP S/4HANA Cloud implementation, there are various components with an impact on the overall services cost. The following are the primary SAP S/4HANA Cloud implementation cost factors:

- **Fit-to-standard process**
  The biggest factor driving implementation cost is how well a customer's business needs fit with SAP S/4HANA Cloud functionality. The objective of SAP S/4HANA Cloud is to meet a customer's business processes as much as possible. The goal is to implement SAP S/4HANA Cloud out of the box and in turn provide SAP Best Practices functionality with little additional customization (i.e., extensibility) or development. If a given organization's business requirements are not mostly met (around 80 percent) with existing or roadmapped SAP S/4HANA Cloud functionality, the cost to implement SAP S/4HANA Cloud could increase dramatically. When additional nonstandard SAP S/4HANA Cloud business requirements are needed, the value proposition for rapid and inexpensive SAP SaaS deployment diminishes.

- **Extensibility**
  SAP S/4HANA Cloud allows for extending its core functionality via *bolt-ons*. These bolt-ons could be SAP S/4HANA Cloud whitelisted APIs or customer-specific extensions designed in and integrated via SAP Cloud Platform. Depending upon the number and complexity of any additional extensions, the additional costs associated with deploying SAP S/4HANA Cloud could be extensive. In some cases, these extensions are rapid and inexpensive, such as simple uploads and downloads or other SAP product integrations (such as SAP S/4HANA Cloud integrating with SAP Analytics Cloud). For new SAP Cloud Platform app development, this

extensibility will be greater. The bottom line is that extensions to SAP S/4HANA Cloud increase implementation costs—especially complex, customer-specific extensions. Table 4.1 highlights the extensibility options provided by SAP, including in-app and side-by-side options. Note the cloud icons, which mark extensibility options available for SAP S/4HANA Cloud.

Key User In-App Extensibility	Side-by-Side Extensibility Based on SAP Cloud Platform
<ul><li>Cloud-enabled development objects</li><li>Custom fields</li><li>Custom analytics and forms</li><li>Custom business objects</li><li>Custom business logic (cloud ABAP web editor)</li><li>No modifications allowed</li><li>Only whitelisted SAP APIs</li><li>Software lifecycle of extensions de-coupled from SAP software updates</li></ul>	<ul><li>Enable an SAP Fiori and mobile user experience</li><li>Integrate with other cloud solutions (for example, from SAP SuccessFactors, SAP Ariba, and third-party solutions)</li><li>Take advantage of SAP Cloud Platform application services (cloud portal, mobile documents, output management, etc.)</li><li>Use a full-fledged development platform to build extension applications (Java, SAP HANA native development)</li></ul>

Table 4.1 SAP S/4HANA Extensibility Options

- **Data conversion**

  Another implementation cost factor is the effort associated with data conversion. Whether migrating from an SAP ERP on-premise platform or another IT backend system, data conversion and migration act as a factor in overall SAP S/4HANA Cloud deployment costs. SAP S/4HANA Cloud implementation costs could be impacted greatly, depending upon the data quality and amount of data to convert. The only scenario in which data conversion doesn't exist as a potential SAP S/4HANA Cloud implementation impact factor is for a net-new implementation with no previous data. If there's no data to convert, no effort is required. One way in which to save implementation services costs is to internalize any data conversion activities if required.

- **Training**

  Like data conversion, training is another area in which customers implementing SAP S/4HANA Cloud can save on implementation costs. Some training should always be included in any implementation partner's scope of SAP S/4HANA Cloud deployment services, but extensive training is normally nice to have rather than a must-have. Training is fundamental to both the short-term and long-term success and sustainability of an SAP S/4HANA Cloud deployment, so while a business can engage an external consulting organization for training services, that company's overall training preparation, rollout, and superuser "train the trainer" should not be outsourced.

- **Custom code**

  If your organization is among the companies that have implemented one of SAP's previous ERP offers, such as SAP R/3, SAP ERP, or even on-premise SAP S/4HANA, and is looking to fully migrate over to SAP S/4HANA Cloud, custom code migration might impact your overall SAP S/4HANA Cloud migration. Often, one of the primary reasons to migrate to SAP S/4HANA Cloud is to simplify your SAP landscape. In that case, removing or eliminating your custom code is not only a good thing but could be a motivating factor for SAP S/4HANA Cloud migration. However, if there's some mandatory business rationale mandating that you must maintain custom code and/or functionality, SAP provides some tools to help you determine the effort of and impact associated with doing so.

- **Analytics**

  A final SAP S/4HANA Cloud implementation cost factor relates to a customer's need for analytics and the extent to which a customer expects SAP S/4HANA Cloud to provide a given level of meaningful reporting. SAP S/4HANA Cloud provides real-time analytics as part of the platform. However, the depth of analytics isn't as robust as that of dedicated SAP analytics products such as SAP Analytics Cloud. As part of the SAP S/4HANA Cloud product analysis researching phase, you must assess what your business reporting needs are and how SAP S/4HANA Cloud fits your specific reporting requirements. Depending upon your requirements, your SAP S/4HANA Cloud implementation costs may increase.

Behind the Curtain: The SAP S/4HANA Cloud Lighthouse Program

At the beginning of the SAP S/4HANA Cloud product launch, a select group of SAP integrators had the opportunity to participate in a dedicated SAP S/4HANA Cloud program called the SAP S/4HANA Cloud lighthouse partner program. As part of this program, these SAP integrators were given training alongside SAP to learn the product functionality, features, implementation methods, extensibility, and deployment methodology. Based on this training, lighthouse partners are uniquely positioned to provide a higher level of SAP S/4HANA Cloud implementation service. We highly recommend leveraging one of these select partners for your deployment. Furthermore, in many cases, SAP won't allow non-lighthouse partners to implement SAP S/4HANA Cloud.

4.4 Estimating Implementation Costs

In the previous section, we deconstructed the various implementation cost components crucial to determining how much an SAP S/4HANA Cloud implementation will cost. However, beyond these data points, how does an organization dial in exactly what implementation will cost for its specific SAP S/4HANA Cloud situation? That's a difficult question to answer fully, but we'll provide some pointers in the following sections.

4.4.1 Fit-to-Standard Process

When engaged with a prospective SAP S/4HANA Cloud customer, the best method to estimate the actual implementation cost is to identify how closely standard SAP S/4HANA Cloud functionality fits a customer's business needs. This process is known as the *fit-to-standard* process.

The fit-to-standard process changes how organizations look at SAP ERP. In the past, business blueprinting workshops were conducted, with business requirements gathered collectively by all required stakeholders. Then, the SAP product was designed around the agreed upon and defined business blueprint outcomes. In the fit-to-standard model, as defined by SAP's newest implementation strategy (SAP Activate), business requirements definition has SAP Best Practices as its foundation. Table 4.2 highlights the paradigm shift in SAP business process requirements gathering.

ASAP, Blueprinting Process	SAP Activate, Fit-to-Standard Process
<ul><li>Consultative approach</li><li>Highly customized solution</li><li>Development, not configuration</li><li>Time-consuming</li><li>Costly</li></ul>	<ul><li>Lead with SAP Best Practices</li><li>Rapid, prescriptive, repeatable delivery steps</li><li>Accelerated by tools, templates, and predefined content</li><li>Agile approach</li><li>Enabled for the cloud</li></ul>

Table 4.2 Evolution of SAP Requirements Gathering Approach, from ASAP and Blueprinting to SAP Activate and Fit-to-Standard

4.4.2 Cost Estimation Process

Prior to the full engagement with an SAP S/4HANA Cloud implementation partner, a customer should engage an SAP S/4HANA Cloud services integrator to assist with a dialed-in SAP S/4HANA Cloud implementation estimate. Hopefully, the SAP S/4HANA Cloud services integrator is an existing trusted advisor. If not, SAP can recommend a lighthouse partner or equally competent services integrator knowledgeable in SAP S/4HANA Cloud. The effort to provide a reliable SAP S/4HANA Cloud implementation cost should be neither extensive nor exhaustive. Although dependent upon many factors, such as number of users and locations, extensibility requirements, and other important data points described previously, the estimate shouldn't take more than a week of discovery from the SAP S/4HANA Cloud implementer and can be as little as several days depending upon the SAP S/4HANA Cloud customer scenario. (*Discovery* is an SAP term defined as the process of learning more about an organization's specific business requirements and how they translate into the effort needed to implement the SAP software functionality.) This week of discovery could include—but doesn't necessarily require—a series of tactical, quick-hit, fit-to-standard workshops onsite at the customer location, in which customers and SAP S/4HANA Cloud partners discuss and define the level of completeness with which SAP S/4HANA Cloud fits the given customer's business requirements.

Example

During a recent SAP S/4HANA Cloud implementation, a customer was looking to deploy SAP S/4HANA Cloud within the United States for one of its business units within the retail space. As part of the process, the consulting partner was asked how long it would take to come up with a dialed-in scope and corresponding services cost. The consulting partner took a two-day on-site visit with the customer to clearly define what's in the SAP S/4HANA Cloud scope. For an implementation of this size (12 locations throughout the United States and Canada for SAP S/4HANA Cloud, with approximately 100 users and no extensibility requirements), a two-day, on-site, quick-hit fit-to-standard workshop was sufficient. Larger, more complex implementations could require more analysis.

The goal of these quick-hit, fit-to-standard exercises is to provide as accurate an SAP S/4HANA Cloud implementation estimate as possible. One of the methods frequently leveraged in estimating delivery cost uses an Excel worksheet to break down the implementation by phase and by resource. After understanding who will be deployed in what implementation phase for what period, resource costs can be allocated, in turn providing a cost structure documenting the resources, rates, and estimated timeline. Figure 4.13 provides an example worksheet recently utilized for an SAP S/4HANA Cloud implementation estimate.

Implementation

Prepare — Hours per Month (add more columns as needed)

	Rate	Total Hrs	Extended	1	2	3	4	Estimated Total Cost
Engagement Manager		40		40				
Project Coordinator		4		4				
Functional Analyst: Core Finance		40		40				
Insert rows above as needed								$ -
Total		84 $	-	84	0	0	0	$ -

Explore — Hours per Month (add more columns as needed)

Role	Rate	Total Hrs	Extended	1	2	3	4	Estimated Total Cost
Engagement Manager		40 $	-	30	10			$ -
Project Coordinator		8 $	-	6	2			
Functional Analyst: Core Finance		160 $	-	120	40			$ -
Functional Analyst: Order to Cash		160 $	-	120	40			$ -
Functional Analyst: Procure to Pay		160 $	-	120	40			$ -
Functional Analyst: Plan to Product		0 $	-	0	0			
Insert rows above as needed								$ -
Total		528 $	-	396	132	0	0	$ -

Realize — Hours per Month (add more columns as needed)

Role	Rate	Total Hrs	Extended	1	2	3	4	Estimated Total Cost
Engagement Manager		90 $	-		30	40	20	$ -
Project Coordinator		8 $	-		2	4	2	$ -
Functional Analyst: Core Finance		360 $	-		120	160	80	$ -
Functional Analyst: Order to Cash		360 $	-		120	160	80	$ -
Functional Analyst: Procure to Pay		360 $	-		120	160	80	$ -
Functional Analyst: Plan to Product		0 $	-		0	0	0	
Insert rows above as needed								$ -
Total		1178 $	-	0	392	524	262	$ -

Figure 4.1 Fit-to-Standard Quick-Hit Implementation Estimate Template

As described in Section 4.3, customers are beginning to expect rough estimates between one and two times the cost of their SAP S/4HANA Cloud licenses. Although this is becoming a more prevalent cost benchmark within the SAP S/4HANA Cloud services world, the cost to implement is still very much aligned with the numerous implementation factors and which partner is performing the work.

4.5 End User Support via SAP Application Management Services

One of the many advantages of implementing SAP S/4HANA Cloud is its very low TCO. As discussed at length in earlier chapters, including Chapter 1, Section 1.5, the beauty of an ERP SaaS is its elimination of many of the traditional constraints associated with on-premise ERP platforms. Still, with many limitations removed via cloud applications and their corresponding infrastructure, SaaS ERP systems in general and SAP S/4HANA Cloud specifically still require some end user support.

Now, let's discuss some factors pertaining to how much end user support you'll need and how you should go about getting it. The amount can vary depending upon several primary factors, including the following:

- **Extensibility usage**
  If an organization has deployed an extensive set of extensions—whether side-by-side or in-app—this extensibility configuration will require an understanding of that which has been implemented, including configuration and development and how to effectively maintain the extensions. The spectrum of extensibility is wide-ranging, from simple in-app extensibility functionality to user screen configuration and all the way to custom-developed SAP Cloud Platform applications that integrate SAP S/4HANA Cloud with non-SAP applications.

- **Custom functionality**
  Like extensibility usage, the more custom functionality is integrated into an SAP S/4HANA Cloud instance, the more specific customer knowledge is needed. As a rule of thumb, the more standard an SAP S/4HANA Cloud instance can be, the lower the TCO and quicker the implementation.

- **Customer SAP knowledge**
  Some SAP customers want to learn as much as possible about SAP technology, features, and functions, while other SAP customers want to focus on their core business. Thus, depending upon which side of this fence your organization falls on, the amount of SAP support differs greatly. This holds true even if an organization is implementing SAP S/4HANA Cloud out of the box.

SAP S/4HANA Cloud end user support can be handled via three methods:

1. Internalize all SAP S/4HANA Cloud end user support.

2. Outsource support completely.

3. Leverage a hybrid model.

For organizations that select either option 2 or option 3, an SAP S/4HANA Cloud AMS organization is a typical end user support mechanism. In essence, the SAP S/4HANA Cloud AMS partner provides a specific set of services based on an agreed-upon price point for a specific set of service-level agreements (SLAs) and metrics.

The extent to which an SAP S/4HANA Cloud AMS provider gives end user support depends heavily on the customer's SAP S/4HANA Cloud instance and outsourcing desire. However, due to the limited amount of configuration and development available within SAP S/4HANA Cloud, the availability of AMS services is significantly lower than for traditional SAP AMS services delivered for on-premise SAP products.

Therefore, due to the limited opportunities for SAP S/4HANA Cloud AMS support, there are only two main support areas: core SAP S/4HANA Cloud and extensibility.

With a strong commitment from the customer to support SAP S/4HANA Cloud internally, these support areas are very manageable. The resource or resources required for internal core SAP S/4HANA Cloud support needs to be more business-savvy in nature, because their support needs will be for more minimal, business-related configuration. The technical modifications and corresponding technical acumen are minimal. Nonetheless, SAP S/4HANA Cloud AMS support can exist as a viable support solution if a customer simply wishes to outsource this software configuration to a dedicated SAP consultancy.

An area that is much more technical in nature, requiring more of a development-type of resource, is SAP S/4HANA Cloud's extensions. These can be internalized with strong, tech-savvy employees, depending upon who developed the extension and its complexity, but they often form a support area that's outsourced. An SAP S/4HANA Cloud AMS provider will have the skills to support complex SAP Cloud Platform applications with resources skilled in the latest and greatest SAP S/4HANA Cloud development services.

Either way, whether internally supported or externally supported (or a bit of both), SAP S/4HANA Cloud's TCO is a fraction of the cost of the traditional on-premise SAP ERP.

4.6   Summary

In this chapter, we broke down the costs involved in SAP S/4HANA Cloud's deployment. We began with the SAP S/4HANA Cloud subscription structure, continued on to the high-level cost construct for SAP S/4HANA Cloud's implementation, and ended with various options for long-term SAP S/4HANA Cloud support. You should now have a much better idea of the all-in investment for successful SAP S/4HANA Cloud deployment. (Add SAP's cloud extension model, and now you have a potential trump card in your back pocket!)

In the next chapter, you'll learn in greater detail about how SAP has constructed SAP S/4HANA Cloud for continued innovation. With quarterly innovation cycles, SAP S/4HANA Cloud promises to deliver value to its customers more quickly and focuses on driving tangible value to your business.

Chapter 5

Maintenance: How Do You Maintain SAP S/4HANA Cloud?

Cloud applications remove a great deal of the overhead required for maintaining a business software solution. That said, you still need to manage and extend the application and enable users to take advantage of the functionality that comes with new releases.

Because SAP S/4HANA Cloud is a relatively new solution, it's being enhanced with new functionality as quickly as possible so that it ultimately will provide capabilities on par with the on-premise version (and eventually beyond the on-premise version). At the same time, new technology, like machine learning and digital assistance, is driving the need for an ever-increasing pace of innovation. Some innovations will be optional for users to accept, but others will be mandatory.

This innovation, however, cannot go unchecked. First, so that all SAP S/4HANA Cloud instances remain upgradable, any new innovations must be backward compatible with existing SAP Best Practices and configurations. Second, any bug released would affect all SAP S/4HANA Cloud customers at the same time, creating a potential nightmare for SAP. Finally, because the on-premise and cloud versions of SAP S/4HANA are built on the same code line, innovations must be coordinated between the two versions even though they're on different release schedules.

Ongoing maintenance for SAP S/4HANA Cloud requires similar diligence in efforts to address enablement and adoption of new functionality and ongoing management of reporting and integrations. Further, because SAP provides quarterly innovations and releases for SAP S/4HANA Cloud, ongoing maintenance must be structured and repeatable.

This chapter will address the unique nature of application maintenance for SAP S/4HANA Cloud. Quarterly releases bring innovation and improvement, but they can also cause significant disruption for the business and for the IT staff who may be working on extensions, custom reports, and so on. Section 5.1 addresses creating a culture of change that embraces these releases as part of a new way of doing business. The following sections address common ongoing maintenance tasks, beginning with report development in Section 5.2. Report management is fairly commonplace; there are, however, nuances to note when working within the SAP Best Practices framework.

Unlike report management, tile management will be a new concept for application maintenance teams. Section 5.3 addresses how tiles that provide visibility into critical key performance indicators (KPIs) can be updated when KPIs change or are added. Section 5.4 then provides a high-level outline of integration management. Integrations are covered in Chapter 8, but it's worth including the topic at a high level here to ensure it's considered when planning maintenance. Not everyone who implements SAP S/4HANA Cloud will want to take on this maintenance effort, which is why considerations for outsourcing this work to an application services provider are provided in Section 5.5 to round out the chapter.

5.1   Quarterly Release Management

To keep pace with the demand for innovation yet keep the quality controls and governance that make SAP so reliable in place, SAP has implemented software manufacturing best practices with a predictable, quarterly release schedule for SAP S/4HANA Cloud (see Figure 5.1). Note that on-premise SAP S/4HANA will have major releases roughly every 11 months.

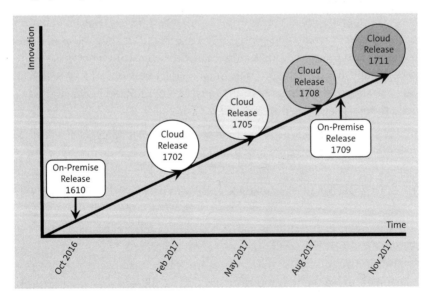

Figure 5.1 SAP S/4HANA Cloud Quarterly Release Schedule

With change at this pace, a concerted communication and change management effort needs to be put in place. This section will address both the need for communication to help enable change and overcome potential barriers that are part of human nature, and the predictable cycle of change. SAP understands the need for this communication effort and properly arms SAP S/4HANA Cloud customers with multiple tools to help. Both internal communications and plans and SAP's communications tools come into play in developing a release plan for the quarterly updates. With this combination of tools working together, quarterly updates will become the new normal for business operations, helping to minimize disruption and promote a culture of embracing change.

5.1.1 Communicating with Users

With SAP S/4HANA Cloud, business users no longer need to wait for overtaxed and understaffed IT departments to deliver needed features and functions at the pace of business. However, with new releases being delivered quarterly, this dream come true for the business has the potential to become a nightmare if communications aren't managed correctly. One reason for this concern is that any given company that uses SAP S/4HANA Cloud may not ask for nor want to make use of specific innovations. Conversely, business users may become frustrated to find that new and desirable capabilities were released, but they weren't made aware of these new features or enabled to use them. Ultimately, the fact is that business users are being exposed to change every three months, and with that change comes a predictable cycle of change adoption that must be accepted and proactively addressed, lest the change be rejected.

Figure 5.2 depicts the typical change acceptance cycle for business users. With little communication, users can quickly turn from viewing an IT change with "uninformed optimism," when little is known about the change but expectations are high, to viewing it with deep pessimism (the "valley of despair"), when unmanaged expectations are met with doubt and concern that the change is bad for the business or not sustainable.

The answer to these concerns is a communication plan that meshes with SAP's release plan in terms of schedule and rigor. Communication and acceptance of business user doubt will help raise confidence and eventual acceptance of the change. To be effective, this communication must be coordinated and enacted in a fashion that becomes predictable to the audience.

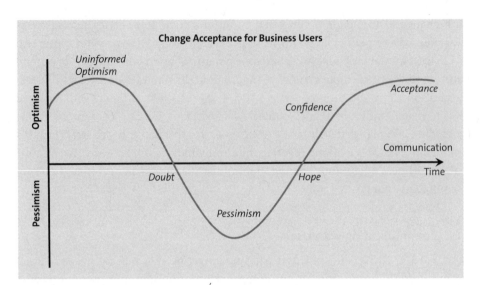

Figure 5.2 Change Acceptance for Business Users

A communication plan will assist greatly in coordinating and controlling messaging around new releases. A successful communication plan will be developed across two dimensions: timing and audience.

From a timing perspective, the communication plan needs to address the following four major phases (as shown in Figure 5.3):

- **New release awareness**
  Even after a year or more of quarterly releases, business people get caught up in the whirlwind of business and need to be reminded about upcoming business disruption. Procedural communications to end users and management should include the following:
  - Highlights of the upcoming release (e.g., business areas affected, including functions that will be enhanced, new functions that will be provided, new technical capabilities)
  - Release timeline (including review/testing and training)
  - Sources (e.g., web links) for relevant release information
  - Expected downtime
  - Scheduled jobs and reports that will be temporarily paused and restarted
  - Reminders to ensure that mission-critical items (e.g., requiring employees to complete a process) aren't due on the same date as the release

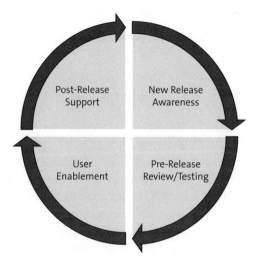

Figure 5.3 Communication Cycles

- **Prerelease review/testing**
  Although each SAP S/4HANA Cloud release will be fully tested by SAP prior to release, review of the new functionality using company-specific data—especially for commonly used applications that receive enhancements or applications that have in-app extensions—will both confirm the enhancements work with company data and assist in developing testing and other prerelease communications. In addition, any integrations that could be affected should be regression-tested to confirm there are no issues. End user communications for this phase should include the following:
  - Specific details about features that will be/were tested (to help build confidence in the new release)
  - Test results, especially noting any concerns that will need to be addressed (note: it's not only okay to be open about concerns, but also highly preferred; users will gain confidence that changes are being managed to allow them to stay productive)

- **User enablement**
  Communications for this phase are provided to fully enable users to make use of enhancements and new innovations. The specific communications depend on the nature of the innovations and the level of end user sophistication. Communications for different levels of end user sophistication should generally include the following:

– Detailed documentation on innovations for sophisticated super users (note that if this information isn't provided, end users will spend valuable time looking for it anyway)

– Web videos or high-level documentation to self-sufficient (but not super-) users

– Classroom training tailored to company specifics, to supplement the high-level documentation for dependent end users

Note that during this phase, user attitude to change must be considered for determining the nature of specific communications and the specific medium and communicator. User attitudes can be classified as follows:

– *Supporters* should be leveraged for communicating change (having business supporters will always help drive overall confidence and acceptance).

– *Neutral* users should be involved and educated with the goal of converting them to supporters.

– *Detractors* are a reality and should be accepted as a good and necessary part of a team to prevent groupthink. When working with detractors, listen to and address concerns as best as possible, with the goal of neutralizing attitudes by providing facts about the change (but not in the hope of converting them to supporters).

User attitude assessment can be captured in a worksheet, such as the one in Figure 5.4.

Release Name:							
Impacted User Name							
Department							
Title							
Reports To							
Assessment What is Changing for this User							
What is Staying the Same							
Perveived Resistance							
Expressed Concerns/Resistance							
Perceived Support							
Expressed Benefits							
Current Level of Commitment							
Influence/Power							
Interest							
User Importance							
Required Level of Commitment							
Approach What this User Should Know to Achieve Required Level of Commitment							
Communication/Change Steps							

Figure 5.4 Business User Assessment Form

- **Postrelease Support**
  Once the new release is live, there should be some follow-up with users to make it clear that they aren't alone and to ensure the application is working as expected (i.e., to confirm that the testing was comprehensive and successful). In general, communications should include the following:
  - One-on-one or group meetings, or a mass email to which recipients can reply, occurring shortly after the release to gather feedback about both the release and the overall communication process
  - Any identified issues that are to be addressed and, if possible, the timeline and/ or approach for addressing them

Regardless of communication phase, the audience for communications should always be considered and calculated as part of the overall communication plan. As previously mentioned, user sophistication will impact the type of user enablement communication. At the same time, employee roles should also be considered. Management and executive levels primarily need to know timelines and business benefits to be expected, whereas users require much more detail. Functional roles also need to be considered. Financial team members, for example, don't need to be informed at a detailed level about manufacturing floor changes (although they may benefit from high-level overviews for functions that could impact financial processes and/or financial data either upstream or downstream).

Figure 5.5 provides an overarching communication plan example.

Release Name:								
Communication Phase	Objective	Audience	Medium	Date	Frequency	Developer	Deliverer	Feedback Mechanism
New Release Awareness								
Steering Committee Release Highlights	Advise application steering committee to enable advocates at management and executive team level	Steering Committee	Meeting	mm/dd/yyyy	Once	tbn	tbn	Discussion in meeting
High-Level Release Highlights	Advise management and executives of expected change impact and business benefits to be gained from new release	Management and Executive Team Members	Email	mm/dd/yyyy	Once	tbn	tbn	Email reply
Release Highlights	Advise users of anticipated business area impacts of new release	S/4HANA Cloud business users	Functional Team Meetings	mm/dd/yyyy	Once per department	tbn	Department Managers	Discussion in meeting
Pre-Release Review/Testing								
User Enablement								
Post-Release Support								

Figure 5.5 Communication Plan Template

5.1.2   SAP Communications

SAP is fully aware of the requirement for frequent and varied communications and has assembled a comprehensive set of tools for SAP S/4HANA Cloud customers. From high-level overviews to videos to detailed release notes, all application-specific information from SAP is made available at *www.sap.com/product/enterprise-management/ s4hana-erp/* (see Figure 5.6). It's important to note that SAP provides information for the current release and the roadmaps for the next three releases (basically, a year of release information) and updates the information with each quarterly release.

Figure 5.6 SAP S/4HANA Cloud Release Information Sources

It's important to review the available SAP documents and videos and then populate the communication plan accordingly.

Along with information about innovations, SAP provides details about release schedules and potential downtime. Releases are made available in a single wave, and the Q environment release precedes the P environment release by two weeks (see sample release schedule in Table 5.1; note that actual dates are subject to change).

SAP S/4HANA Cloud Upgrade Calendar Sample				
Release	1702	1705	1708	1711
Release to customer	Feb. 13, 2017	May 9, 2017	Aug. 7, 2017	Nov. 6, 2017
Wave 1				
Q system upgrade	Feb. 18– Feb. 19	May 13– May14	Aug. 12– Aug. 13	Nov. 11– Nov. 12
P system upgrade	Mar. 4– Mar. 5	May 27– May28	Aug. 26– Aug. 27	Nov. 25– Nov. 26
Wave 2				
Q system upgrade	Feb. 25– Feb. 26	May 20– May 21	Aug. 19– Aug. 20	Nov. 18– Nov. 19
P system upgrade	Mar. 11– Mar. 12	Jun. 3– Jun. 4	Sep. 2– Sep. 3	Dec. 2– Dec. 3

Table 5.1 Sample SAP S/4HANA Cloud Upgrade Calendar

The maintenance windows for regular maintenance and upgrades are available in and subject to the SAP service level agreement for cloud services. To find these windows, go to *https://www.sap.com/about/agreements/cloud-services.html*, then search for "service level agreement". As of the time of writing, the maintenance windows are as follows:

- Regular maintenance: Weekly, from Sunday at 2:00 a.m. to Sunday at 6:00 a.m. local time

- Major upgrades: Up to four times per year, from Friday at 10:00 p.m. to Monday at 3:00 a.m. local time

During a maintenance window, users who try to access SAP S/4HANA Cloud will see a screen like the one shown in Figure 5.7.

Figure 5.7 System Maintenance Announcement

5.1.3   Enabling New Releases

One of the primary steps of ongoing maintenance is the enabling of new releases. Note that during the initial implementation, after the Q system is up and running, the starter system is disabled and no longer available. As a result, there are only two systems to upgrade: the Q system and the P system. As with an on-premise application, the Q system is used for testing the new release; once it's tested, the P system can be upgraded to the new release.

A typical upgrade process might follow the high-level plan in Figure 5.8.

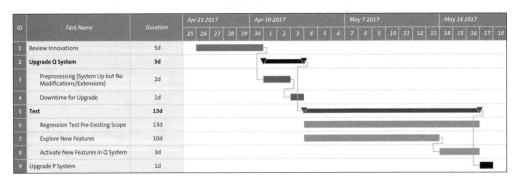

Figure 5.8 Sample Upgrade Process Chart

Before any upgrade begins, it's important to review the new solution scope related to the latest quarterly release. SAP's release notes provide overviews of the new scope in the **What's New** section of the product help documentation. This documentation will list both new functionality and existing functions that have been enhanced. Note that you can focus on new functionality by searching for "scope" and locating scope items with a **New** status.

As in the fit-to-standard process, the new scope items can be reviewed by utilizing the associated SAP Best Practices process models and test scripts. Because the model system data isn't in the Q system, test scripts must be modified to match company data to be tested. Going through the prerequisite steps in the test scripts will help identify any building block master data that needs to be set up to support the new functionality. With prerequisite data loaded and updated test scripts, the tests can be run, allowing key business users to review functionality.

Test scripts should be managed within the Manage Test Processes app (see Figure 5.9).

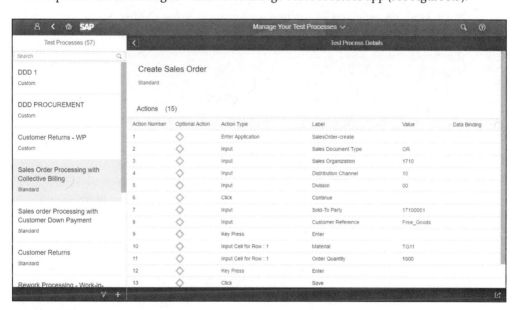

Figure 5.9 Test Process Management

Not all new scope items are required. For optional scope items, the end user review should determine whether the new scope item is something the company wants activated.

> **Tip**
>
> Any scope item cannot be deactivated once activated.

Assuming the scope item is desired—or is mandatory or an already active scope item being enhanced—business users can execute the test plans to identify gaps that will need to be addressed with master data, extensions (or removal of extensions), or process work-arounds. Note that before any extensions are planned, key business users should review the roadmaps for the next three upcoming releases to see if any or all of the identified gaps may be slated to be addressed by SAP.

Activation of scope items isn't automatic; it must be requested via an incident report. Customers can make a single request for activation of all new scope items or can select specific scope items to be activated. Note that any new scope items must be activated in the Q system prior to being activated in the P system, and activation in the P system must occur within two weeks of activation in the Q system (ideally following a plan similar to the one discussed previously). Finally, it's important to note that the Q system and P system configurations (i.e., active scope items) must always match.

5.2   Report Development

Even though businesses are employing more and more digital technology in nearly every aspect of operations, paper reports and forms are still necessary and business users, in general, are continually generating new requirements for paper documents. Some reports are required to support internal analysis or meetings. Some reports or forms are required to conduct business with vendors or customers without digital or integrated data systems. Regardless of the rationale, report and form development is an ongoing maintenance task.

Before developing new reports (or modifying existing reports), it's good to review the list of standard reports and forms. This list is located under the **Accelerators** tab within the SAP Best Practices Explorer, as shown in Figure 5.10.

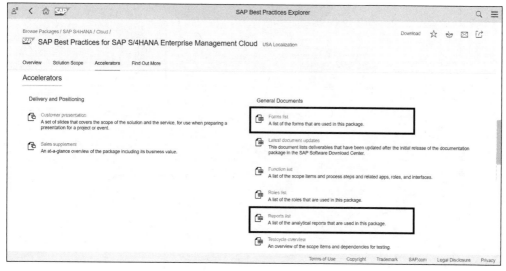

Figure 5.10 SAP Best Practices Accelerators for Reports and Forms

For maintenance activities for reports and forms, because the company has already been through implementation, it's very likely that some of the SAP Activate tasks have already been undertaken, so this work shouldn't be new to the maintenance personnel. Ideally, the external systems required for reporting and forms (i.e., Cloud Print Manager and Adobe Livecycle Designer) will already be downloaded and initialized. From there, the forms adaptation and output management deliverable in the realize phase of SAP Activate contains the necessary tasks for creating and updating reports and forms. The process flow (shown in Figure 5.11) can also be found under the output management (1LQ) scope item in SAP Best Practices.

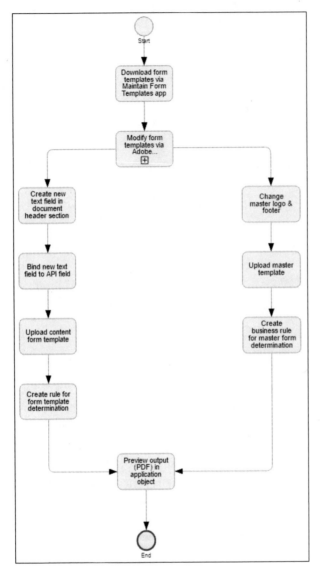

Figure 5.11 Output Management Process Flow

The process begins with downloading form templates from the Maintain Form Templates app (see Figure 5.12). By starting with the templates, customized reports and forms will have a common look and feel, enhancing readability and therefore productivity.

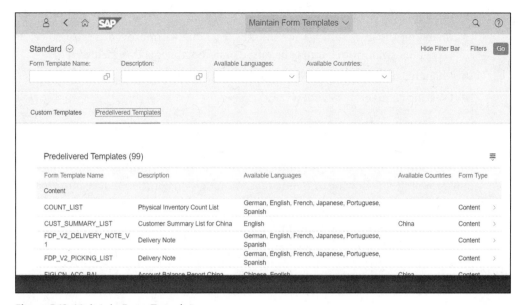

Figure 5.12 Maintain Form Templates

Modifying and developing custom reports and forms should follow a standard and predictable schedule, akin to the quarterly release schedule. A structured process should be in place for making requests, having a steering committee or key user group review the requests to confirm and/or modify the requirements, and development and release of the new or updated reports and forms. Timing for releases can be in conjunction with quarterly upgrades, staggered in between quarterly upgrades, or set up to follow a more aggressive release cycle, such as every two weeks. The critical point is that releases be consistent and be accompanied by proper communications.

5.3 Tile Customization

In addition to providing entry to applications, tiles provide critical KPIs for business users. These KPIs give immediate and critical insight into ongoing operations. Because the needs for different apps change and because KPIs can change, tiles and their use should be maintained actively.

Creating tiles is addressed in Chapter 7. KPI tile maintenance follows a similar process, starting with the KPI Workspace app. Typical tile maintenance will likely include the following:

- Changing the KPI name
- Changing the goal settings for the KPI (e.g., due to improved performance, an acceptable minimum bar may be raised or acceptable maximum lowered)
- Changing other evaluation settings (filters, comparisons, etc.)
- Creating completely new KPIs

Once created and used, KPIs can't be edited; they must be copied and modified, should business needs dictate, by going into the KPI workspace.

In addition to maintaining KPI tiles, business users may want assistance changing tile groupings or showing or hiding tiles. Although this process is very intuitive and user-friendly, business users may still hesitate to undertake it.

Tiles management requires the analytics specialist business role and starts with the Create Tile app (shown in Figure 5.13).

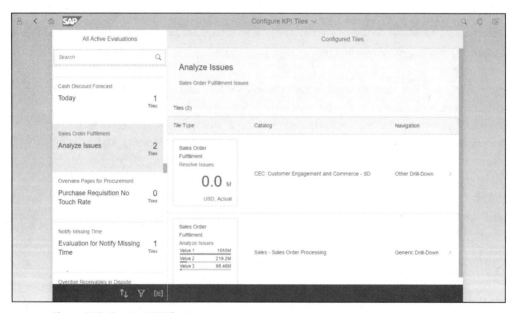

Figure 5.13 Create KPI Tile App

After selecting the appropriate evaluation, the tile in question can be selected and edited in the Edit Tile app (for more information, see Chapter 7). Once developed, custom tiles require little maintenance; however, they should still be tested after an upgrade.

In addition to developing and modifying custom tiles, tile maintenance also includes managing tiles for new and enhanced apps with the quarterly releases. First, it's necessary to ensure new tiles are properly enabled and visible to relevant users. Because new apps are part of an SAP Fiori catalog, that catalog must be associated with the security role assigned to the user; conversely, the user must be assigned to the new security role. The Maintain Business Roles app (see Figure 5.14) lets you view the various business roles, all assigned users to a role, and all related catalogs.

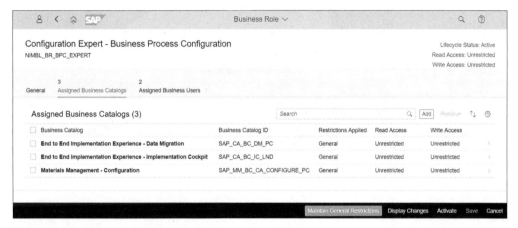

Figure 5.14 Maintain Business Roles App

When a new app is added during an upgrade, it can be added to an existing business catalog or a new business catalog. In the case of a new business catalog, an administrator will need to create the necessary associations and security role changes (see an example of adding business catalogs in Figure 5.15).

Once the security role adjustment is made, the user will need refresh his or her SAP Fiori launchpad to confirm that the tile is visible. If it isn't, the user will need to open his or her user profile from SAP Fiori launchpad, edit his or her home page, open App Finder (see Figure 5.16), locate the new app, and pin it to the appropriate grouping on his or her home page.

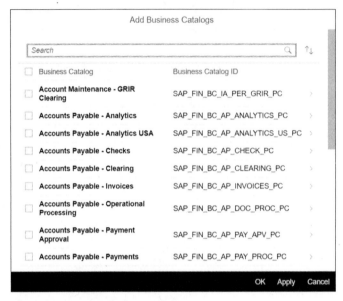

Figure 5.15 Add Business Catalogs

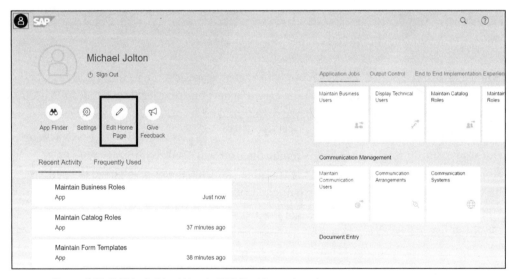

Figure 5.16 Edit Individual User's SAP Fiori Launchpad

The decentralized nature of this maintenance requires significant communication and training to ensure users don't become frustrated. Because users can update their tiles and SAP Fiori launchpad layouts, a healthy maintenance practice would also include periodic spot reviews of specific users to ensure they've optimized their SAP Fiori launchpads.

5.4   Integration Management

Verifying any integrations is critical in the testing phase of a new release. Because SAP requires integrations to use approved APIs, there is a limit to the risk of integrations breaking due to one of the quarterly upgrades. Regardless, it's still important to test integrations.

The very nature of integrations, however, demands that both source and target systems be monitored for changes. As a result, integration testing may need to take place on a different schedule than the quarterly upgrade schedule should the non-SAP system change.

In addition to testing for functionality, integrations should be monitored or spot checked for performance. The Q system environment allows for such testing without disturbing ongoing business.

5.5   End User Support via Application Management Services

As you can see, even though SAP S/4HANA Cloud doesn't require the hardware, networking, systems software/database, and other maintenance associated with on-premise applications, it does still require active ongoing management. Companies looking to eliminate the cost of maintenance need to temper that goal with optimizing the cost of application maintenance. This cost optimization can become tricky when less than a full-time employee or FTE is required for the application maintenance (as is often the case with SAP S/4HANA Cloud). When there isn't additional work available to keep an FTE busy, SAP S/4HANA Cloud customers may want to consider outsourcing maintenance to an AMS provider. AMS providers can capture economies of scale by providing maintenance services to multiple customers.

Outsourcing to an AMS provider must not be taken lightly and offered to the lowest bidder, however. Critical AMS aspects to consider include the following:

- **Strong communications program**
  Much of maintenance is communication. Unlike for customizable on-premise applications, technical skills become commoditized, because sophisticated config-

uration isn't required. Being able to handle communications properly to manage user expectations and acceptance is the real and differentiable skill required, however.

- **Strong business acumen**
  Like communication skills, business acumen is required to assist users in identifying ways to use apps and eliminate reports and poor processes. It's also needed to assist users in defining optimal SAP Fiori launchpad layouts and creating tiles that provide useful information at a glance.

- **Continually updated SAP S/4HANA Cloud knowledge**
  Because updates are released quarterly, AMS providers need to be fully aware of all enhancements and the product roadmap. Specialization in the application becomes a requirement for success.

- **Holistic SAP Cloud Platform skills**
  When integrations and side-by-side extensions are part of an environment, the AMS provider must also be properly skilled in SAP Cloud Platform to be able to maintain those applications. Thus, there are some technology skills that aren't commoditized, but they're limited to this arena.

If these aspects are in balance, AMS providers can be assessed for cultural fit across the companies. AMS providers are day-to-day business partners, not just vendors. They should be selected with due consideration and managed as team members.

5.6   Summary

As you've seen, even though SAP S/4HANA Cloud removes a significant amount of maintenance overhead (with respect to hardware, databases, and much more), a great deal of attention is still required to ensure consistent adoption of innovations and optimized use through tailored reports and tiles. In addition, because this is the digital core of a business, there likely will be integrations that must always be maintained. Although preconfigured and residing in the cloud, SAP S/4HANA Cloud is still an ERP platform woven throughout the daily life of a business and affects many, if not most, of its employees. As a result, ongoing maintenance can't be an afterthought; it must be approached with due attention.

This chapter addressed maintaining the solution. The next chapter will move on to the business functionality provided in the solution.

PART II

Business Processes

Part II dives into the details of SAP S/4HANA Cloud's business capabilities. Because SAP S/4HANA Cloud is a fully functional ERP system, its functional boundaries are too extensive to cover fully. As such, our approach is to present and follow the functional taxonomy provided by SAP and then review critical scope items within that structure. This structure covers all the end-to-end and supporting business processes. From procure-to-pay and plan-to-produce to order-to-cash and core finance and everything in between and around, the complete business map is covered. Not all scope items within these categories can be fully reviewed, and new capabilities and scope items are being added each quarter.

The goal here is to illuminate the depth and breadth of the system while remaining aware that the entire scope is always changing. Beyond the functional scope, understanding the capabilities of SAP S/4HANA Cloud must include a review of the tool's embedded analytics. Business users of this ERP system are dramatically impacted by never having to leave the system to retrieve key performance metrics. Further, the real-time reporting capabilities within SAP S/4HANA Cloud provide the ability to move from insight to action in the click of a mouse. When combined with the full functional scope of the application, SAP S/4HANA Cloud truly becomes the digital core of a business.

Chapter 6

Product Functionality: What Processes Does SAP S/4HANA Cloud Perform?

SAP S/4HANA Cloud is a fully functional ERP application. However, it's capable of supporting manufacturing and service firms with comprehensive tracking and management tools, making it much more than just an ERP platform.

Although SAP S/4HANA Cloud is built on the same code base as on-premise SAP S/4HANA, the product functionality is deliberately limited to the SAP Best Practices preconfigured processes and therefore isn't as broad. Thus, it's tremendously important that customers understand the functionality available.

This chapter starts with a high level overview of the SAP S/4HANA Cloud functionality (expressed as end-to-end workflows like procure-to-pay, plan-to-produce, etc.). From there, the chapter sections explore the functionality within each workflow, starting with streamlined procure-to-pay. The next section, plan-to-product, covers the manufacturing workflows. The sales functionality is next reviewed in the order-to-cash section. Professional services workflows are captured in the next section on project services.

The following sections, starting with core finance, cover supporting functionality that is not, technically, an end-to-end workflow. HR connectivity is the last functional section, but it is extremely brief as human capital management functionality is not included in SAP S/4HANA Cloud. The final section on data management addresses maintaining data integrity. Although most system functionality is covered, because the solution is continually evolving with quarterly releases, this chapter can only provide a point-in-time view. Still, the capabilities of the system and the structure in place for evolution can be seen clearly. This chapter also notes any overlap or integration with some of the peripheral SAP cloud applications. We will end the chapter with a section showing the types of functionality that are added with new releases, using 1708 as an example.

Note

While the content in this chapter focuses on product-based companies, organizations that provide a service rather than a physical product—and this entails a range of professional services companies, government agencies and not-for-profits—can benefit in similar ways from SAP S/4HANA Cloud.

6.1   The Big Picture

Product-based companies follow a somewhat common business model: They procure raw materials and convert those materials into finished goods that they then sell for revenue. Along the way, the company may provide project-based services along with (or apart from) their products. Of course, companies need to account for everything and manage the people that make it all happen. SAP S/4HANA Cloud includes the functionality to make all of this happen, but with the integration, controls, and attention to detail that have come to define SAP.

SAP has organized the SAP S/4HANA Cloud product hierarchically, with business priorities at the top, end-to-end solutions beneath (see Figure 6.1), solution capabilities under that, and finally SAP Best Practices or scope items.

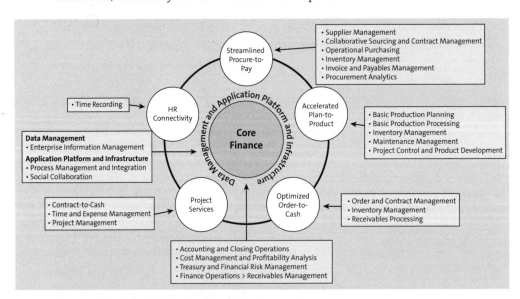

Figure 6.1 SAP S/4HANA Cloud Functional Overview

What's important about this map is the pivot from a transactional view of ERP to an end-to-end process orientation. Business users become fully aware of upstream and downstream processes, expanding the purview beyond individual tasks.

SAP S/4HANA Cloud takes full advantage of this process orientation, building in interactive views of entire work streams, such as the one shown in Figure 6.2. With these tools and the real-time data that accompanies them, managers can view an entire functional lifecycle to identify bottlenecks and potential process breakdowns.

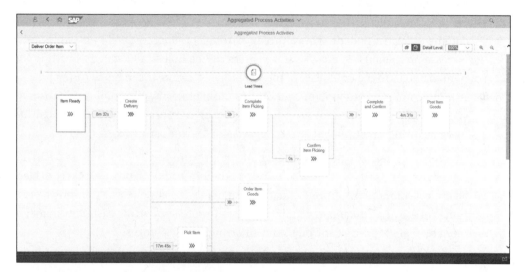

Figure 6.2 End-to-End Workflow Example

End-to-end business process flows can be analyzed by volume of activity and by cycle time. The benefit of this insight is the ability to not only optimize individual business processes, but also create exponential improvements by optimizing how processes work together (i.e., viewing the business as a holistic unit).

In addition to the simple ability to see and manage the business as a set of interrelated processes, SAP has already optimized the business processes with the preconfigured SAP Best Practices. Businesses that adopt SAP S/4HANA Cloud are getting not only a solution that allows them to improve business operations with end-to-end process management, but also the benefit of years of cross-industry experience in the form of preconfigured SAP Best Practices processes built into the system from the start.

6.2   Streamlined Procure-to-Pay

The procure-to-pay process is often seen as the start of the overall business process flow, but nothing is produced nor sold in this critical end-to-end process. Still, manufacturing can be severely impacted by late procurement or procurement of substandard materials, and company profitability can be impacted if material costs are higher than forecasted due to factors such as premiums on rush orders because raw material inventory was depleted and wasn't replaced in time. Viewed more positively, because manufacturing costs are generally fixed but raw materials costs can vary greatly, optimized procurement practices can dramatically reduce overall product cost and thus significantly increase profitability. Success in this process can be holistically stated as getting the right materials to the right place at the right time to ensure the manufacturing process isn't interrupted and to support overall gross profit projections by minimizing costs. As such, though it's perhaps not as exciting as sales or as respected as product design and manufacturing, procurement is a strategic factor for company success.

SAP certainly realizes the importance of the procure-to-pay function and has designed the SAP S/4HANA Cloud solution to promote a smooth process that considers all critical components, from evaluating and managing suppliers to minimizing carrying costs by optimizing raw materials inventory to supporting cash flow management by maintaining a controlled and efficient payables process.

SAP subdivides the procure-to-pay end-to-end business cycle into logical process groupings. This section covers each process while following the business cycle, beginning with a look at procurement master data and supplier management. Operational purchasing covers the actual procurement process for both direct materials (inventoried and consumables) and indirect (MRP) materials. Then, we'll cover optimizing procurement spend with contract management and collaborative sourcing. Following the business cycle, we'll then discuss the next processes of putting materials into inventory and, ultimately, paying for them. The section concludes by reviewing the procurement analytics made available for tracking and managing this entire business cycle.

6.2.1   Procurement Master Data

Before going into further detail on procurement, it's worthwhile to step away from the process flows and discuss the master data concepts that will greatly enhance the overall process. SAP S/4HANA Cloud, thanks to being on the same code base as its on-premise relative, can be as sophisticated as necessary to cover a multitude of situations. At its most basic, the master data is fairly straightforward, requiring the entry of materials and suppliers. By going a little further and paying proper attention to the master data detail at the start, downstream processes can be improved dramatically. For example, when a new material is entered into the system, one or more suppliers also can be identified and entered. Then, through the Manage Sources of Supply app (see Figure 6.3), specific suppliers can be tied to the materials. Downstream, when a purchase requisition is created, the supplier data then doesn't need to be entered.

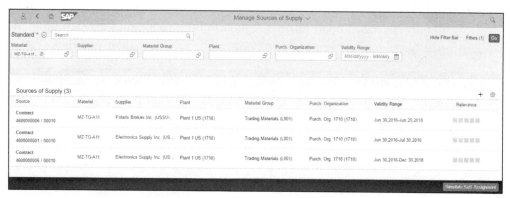

Figure 6.3 Manage Sources of Supply

6.2.2   Supplier Management

The procure-to-pay process begins with finding the right suppliers and then managing those suppliers to maintain a healthy relationship. SAP S/4HANA Cloud supports supplier management with three scope items grouped under two solution capabilities, as follows:

1. *Supplier evaluation*, including the following scope items:
   - 19E: Supplier classification and segmentation
   - SL4: Supplier evaluation and performance monitoring
2. *Classification and segmentation*, including the following scope items:
   - 19C: Supplier activity management

Supplier Evaluation

SAP promotes efficient supplier management by allowing the creation of supplier portfolios with the supplier classification and segmentation scope item. This portfolio approach begins with the creation of purchasing categories. Categories can be established following any taxonomy a company chooses. Typical taxonomies are logical product groupings, such as electrical supplies or computer equipment. Suppliers could also be categorized by geographic location, size, or however else a company might want to manage them. It's important to note that suppliers can exist in more than one category, allowing for highly flexible comparison options.

The strategic buyer business role is required to manage categories. Once the category taxonomy is decided upon, business users with this role can create categories and then assign suppliers, company employees, and materials to them (see Figure 6.4).

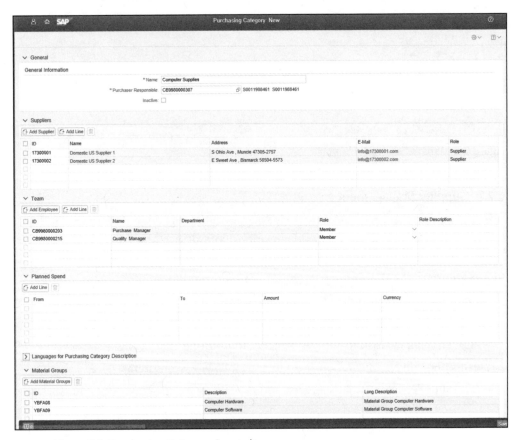

Figure 6.4 Purchasing Category Example

Once established, categories allow for improved supplier comparisons, which will support the optimization of the procurement process and cost reduction. Comparisons can be built from performance data and from internal or external questionnaires and qualification templates completed for a specific category. With side-by-side comparisons, the procurement manager is granted an increased ability to continuously balance the supplier mix and coach suppliers to improve performance.

New in version 1702 is the supplier evaluation and performance monitoring scope item. This function supports the process of developing, administering, scoring, and evaluating questionnaires on supplier performance (see Figure 6.5).

Figure 6.5 Supplier Evaluation

The process flow is straightforward. Someone with the business role of strategic buyer will use the Manage Questionnaire: Evaluation app to create the questionnaire. Different types of questions can be created, such as those with multiple choice or free-text answers. In addition, questions can be assigned weights to emphasize importance. Finally, questions can be identified as mandatory or optional. Figure 6.6 shows an example of adding a questionnaire.

Once questionnaires are established, employees with the employee-procurement business role can appraise various suppliers by filling out the questionnaire. Responses can be monitored to ensure the completeness of the survey exercise, and results are available via a dashboard.

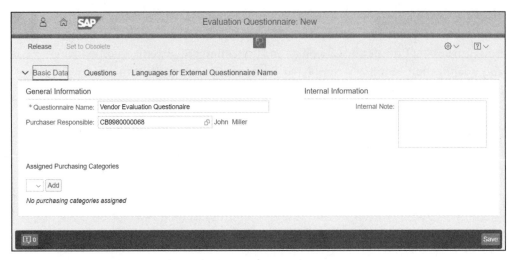

Figure 6.6 Adding Vendor Evaluation Questionnaire

Making this process repeatable with a baseline rating brings the best practice of continuous improvement to supplier management. It also allows for subjective input from employees who work with the vendors daily, providing a full 360-degree view. The result is an optimal set of vendors that are continually assessed and motivated to provide the best pricing and services possible.

Supplier Classification and Segmentation

Classification and segmentation solution capabilities are primarily covered under the *supplier classification and segmentation (19E)* scope item, which falls under the *supplier evaluation* solution capability in the SAP scope taxonomy. Still, SAP, in the current scope documentation, has a *supplier classification and segmentation* solution capability that is separate from the 19E scope item. As such, naming the solution capability supplier classification and segmentation would appear to be a misnomer and is potentially subject to change. What isn't readily subject to change is the highly valuable *supplier activity management* collaboration scope item. This scope item allows internal company personnel to collaborate on an effort and for everyone involved to track that effort and the tasks associated with it. The process starts with creating an activity via the Create Activity app (see Figure 6.7).

Users can provide information about the activity and tie it to one or more suppliers and then one or more participants. Once the activity is created, tasks can be created by selecting first a participant (see Figure 6.8) and then, if desired, one or more suppliers.

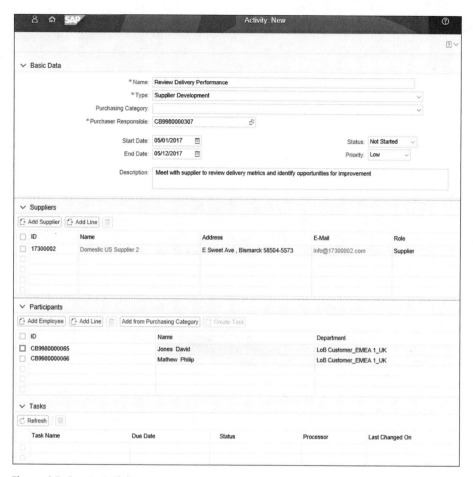

Figure 6.7 Create Activity

From there, the activity and tasks can be tracked and updated as progress is made. In essence, the procurement department now can track and manage all of the one-off activities that were previously subject to falling between the cracks as other priorities arose.

The strategic buyer business role is required to create and monitor/update procurement activities and tasks. The strategic buyer can make use of the app to notify participants about tasks or updates to tasks. Status can be maintained as well. Note that this scope item can be enhanced further with a custom tile that identifies assigned tasks for a specific participant—a constant reminder to that person that there is important work that still needs to be done (potentially eliminating the need for an email and further improving the overall process).

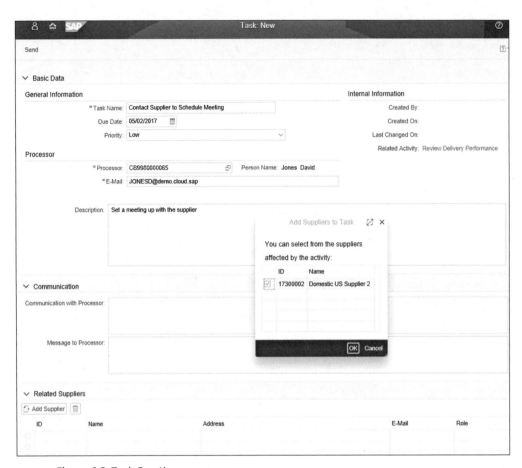

Figure 6.8 Task Creation

6.2.3   Operational Purchasing

The core of procurement entails identifying requirements and processing purchase orders to meet these requirements. Collaboration with suppliers, leveraging SAP Ariba, can significantly enhance the overall experience. As such, certain solution capabilities are grouped together under the operational purchasing end-to-end solution, as follows:

- *Requirements processing*, including the following scope items:
  - 18J: Requisitioning
  - 1L2: SAP Ariba—quote automation for procurement

- *Purchase order processing*, including the following scope items:
  - BMR: Scheduling agreements in procurement
  - J45: Procurement of direct materials
  - BNX: Consumable purchasing
  - BLL: Serial number management
  - 1JR: Analytics for stock management
  - 1JI: Real-time reporting and monitoring for procurement
  - BLF: Batch management
- *Purchase order collaboration*, including the following scope item:
  - J82: SAP Ariba—purchase order to invoice with procurement

Indirect Materials

There is no scope item section for indirect materials (though scope item BNX is relevant), per se, but because the procure-to-pay process is greatly simplified for indirect materials (also known as maintenance, repair, and operations [MRO] support materials), it's worth noting why. The reason the process is simplified is that these materials aren't inventoried, and they don't need to be tracked with the same rigor as direct materials that end up in finished goods.

The business roles for consumables purchasing (scope item BNX) are the same as for direct materials purchasing. Purchase order creation and approvals follow the same process and use the same apps as with direct materials. The specific data in the purchase order will be different, and **Material Number** isn't a required field. When received, the purchased goods are posted in the same way as direct materials (and with the same options).

Requirements Processing

Procuring supplies can be rife with opportunities for waste and control issues (like guarding against kickbacks and other unsavory behaviors). As such, SAP S/4HANA Cloud requisitioning is built to allow proper segregation of duties, yet with variable controls to allow for proper governance without excessive constrictions that restrain performance. The result is a process that uses up to five distinct roles, as shown in the SAP Best Practices process flow in Figure 6.9.

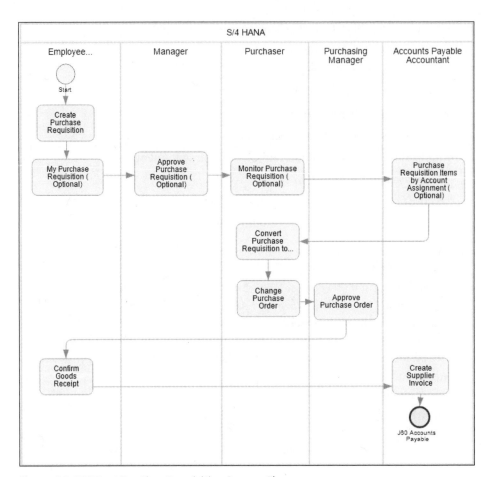

Figure 6.9 SAP Best Practices Requisition Process Flow

Although purchase requisitions likely will be created most often automatically through the material requirements planning (MRP) process, they can also be created manually. Almost like shopping on an Internet website, an employee can search for materials from a catalog and add them to a cart, which becomes the purchase requisition. If an item isn't available in the catalog, free text can be entered for the purchaser.

Once the purchase requisition is made, it's subject to management approval. Approval thresholds, if desired, are set in the purchase order, configure approval guided configuration process available via the Manage Your Solution app (see Figure 6.10).

Figure 6.10 Setting Purchase Order Approval Thresholds and Approvers

The approver (or processor) can be set by rule, such as the requesting employee's supervisor, via the **Processor Type** field. Alternately, a single, specific approver also can be selected.

Additional optional steps are included for a purchaser and/or accounts payable accountant to review the purchase requisition. Once reviewed/approved, the purchaser converts the requisition into a formal purchase order, which will go through a mandatory approval gate from the purchasing manager. Once the supplies are received by the employee, she or he will confirm receipt, and accounting will be notified to create a supplier invoice and start the accounts payable process.

The addition of SAP Ariba for quote automation can further enhance the procurement process for items that can be competitively bid for online (usually commodity items). Quote automation with SAP Ariba integration allows SAP S/4HANA Cloud customers to continually get the best available market price for supplies by digitally requesting price updates from suppliers. Naturally, this scope item requires additional subscriptions for the setup and use of SAP Ariba. The integration setup will also allow quote requests to go either only to approved suppliers that have been set up in SAP S/4HANA Cloud or to all Ariba Network suppliers. The setup allow allows SAP S/4HANA Cloud users to take advantage of the United Nations Standard Products and Services Code (UNSPSC) classification domain for mapping commodities. Alternately, a company may choose to provide company-specific commodity mappings. To set up and maintain the Ariba Network configuration, the Ariba Network integration configuration business role is required.

Purchase Order Processing

The purchase order processing solution capability group contains most scope items under operational purchasing. Once purchase requisitions have been approved, purchases can't simply be executed at will. The purchase order must be executed and coordinated with manufacturing and inventory management, making this solution a critical junction in the supply chain highway.

Although challenging vendors to offer the lowest price on supplies is often a primary goal for the procurement function, it is also important to lower other operational costs, like inventory carrying costs, while still having materials available when manufacturing needs them. The *scheduling agreements in procurement* scope item (with the SAP Best Practices process shown in Figure 6.11) addresses this goal in two ways.

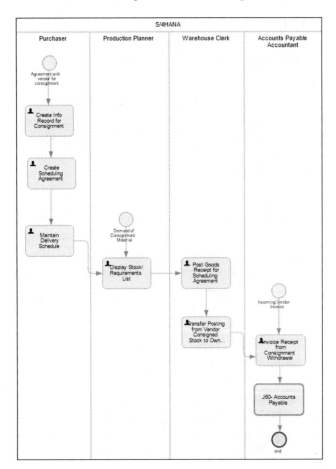

Figure 6.11 Process Flow for Scheduling Purchase Agreements

First, this scope item allows a company to create a large, single purchase order that can have scheduled deliveries over time. As a result, it's possible to receive a volume discount on the large purchase while not loading up the warehouse with supplies that won't be used for months on end. Second, the single order reduces the overhead associated with creating and managing multiple purchase orders. The delivery schedule can be fully itemized to account for different amounts of supplies at different times. The itemized schedule can be used to accommodate seasonality, planned plant downtimes, and other scheduling needs. All in all, this one scope item could save a company significant costs and greatly improve overall productivity by reducing purchasing cycle times.

The current app for delivery scheduling is shown in Figure 6.12. This app presents an opportunity to demonstrate that SAP has been moving SAP S/4HANA Cloud apps to SAP Fiori (for more on SAP Fiori, see Chapter 7, Section 7.1).

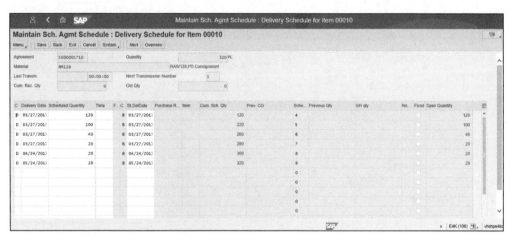

Figure 6.12 Delivery Schedule Example

Scheduling deliveries in advance is one tool for optimizing inventory management and minimizing carrying costs. Another approach is to place the burden of managing the inventory on the vendor with consignment processing. In this arrangement, the vendor owns and maintains the inventory on the customer site. When supplies are needed, they're pulled from stock and ownership transfers to the purchaser, with invoicing taking place periodically.

The purchaser business role is required for setting up and maintaining a consignment or advance purchase schedule. Having the production planner role or working with a production planner who has that role is helpful for reviewing the stock situation, optimizing the delivery schedule, and even executing an MRP run to determine material requirements if desired. Because the process ends with receipt of goods, a warehouse clerk will ultimately complete the process.

Absent a schedule, direct materials are procured through a standard workflow that progresses from purchase requisition to purchase order generation to purchase order issuance to the vendor and ultimately to goods receipt and invoice processing. SAP S/4HANA Cloud provides multiple variations on this standard flow, beginning with the generation of the purchase requisition. As mentioned previously, purchase requisitions can be generated manually via the requisitioning workflow. In addition, an automated process that utilizes MRP functionality (discussed in Section 6.3) will generate the appropriate purchase requisitions for a production run.

The purchase requisition itself allows for significant detail (see Figure 6.13).

Figure 6.13 Create Purchase Requisition

At a minimum, the requisition must include the **Material** being requested, the **Quantity**, and the **Plant** the material is being requested for. Remember that the better the master data, the easier downstream processes like creating a purchase requisition are.

Once a purchase requisition has been created, the SAP Best Practices workflow provides for a gate review for accuracy. A procurement employee with the purchaser business role can review open purchase requisitions via the Manage Purchase Requisitions app (see Figure 6.14). The app starts with a list of open requisitions, along with header data about each requisition and an indication of whether a purchase order has already been created for it. When a user selects a specific requisition, menu items to create a contract, a request for quote, or a purchase order are enabled; then, with just a few clicks, a purchase requisition can be converted to a purchase order.

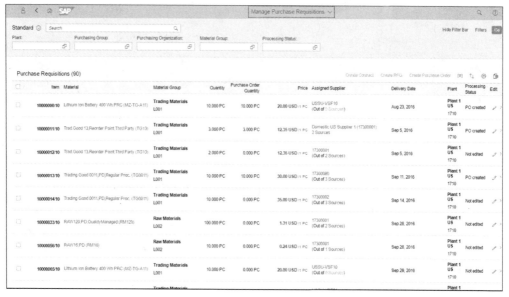

Figure 6.14 Manage Purchase Requisitions

As an additional level of flexibility, SAP S/4HANA Cloud also allows appropriately secured personnel to manually create a purchase order. As with the requisition, the purchase order is subject to approval based on a predetermined amount.

The SAP S/4HANA Cloud output manager handles transmitting the purchase order to the vendor. The purchase order can be printed and sent manually, emailed manually, emailed automatically, or formatted as an XML or PDF file. These options are determined and configured in the Output Parameter Determination app—a sort of configuration process normalization that allows for centralization of output processing setup and maintenance.

From here, the process transitions from ordering to receiving and managing supplies. For posting received goods, the warehouse clerk business role is required and the Post Goods Receipt app, shown in Figure 6.15, is used. This app ties the received goods to the purchase order, allowing closed-loop tracking and three-way matching. Note that SAP S/4HANA Cloud has additional apps that allow for reviewing goods receipt details and reversing goods receipts.

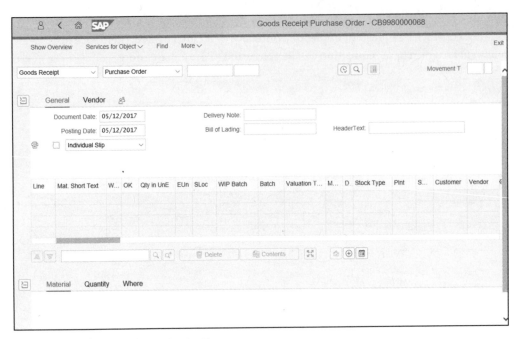

Figure 6.15 Goods Receipt Posting

Once the goods are received, the J45 scope item includes provisions for periodic processes, like analyzing stock overview, analyzing material documents, and a warehouse manager checking valuated stock and managing stock.

For some companies, managing stock must occur on a much more granular level. To that end, SAP has included both *serial number management* and *batch management* functionality within SAP S/4HANA Cloud. Serial number management provides the ability to differentiate individual material items with unique serial numbers. The result is extremely detailed tracking and control across the entire value chain for a product. Batch management provides similar tracking capability, but at an aggregated batch level. This type of tracking might be more prevalent in a process-based manufacturing environment, such as for a chemical manufacturer. In this case, a procured material is tagged with a unique 10-digit alphanumeric code. The batch number promotes uniquely sorting the material inventory and allows a company to maintain the characteristics, chemical composition, or product specifications at the time of a material's procurement. Note that this functionality can also be applied to produced materials.

At this point, the end-to-end process is handed over to the accounting department. Using the accounts payable accountant business role, a supplier invoice can be created for further payment processing. Multiple options exist for getting the supplier invoice into the system. One obvious option is to use the Create Supplier Invoice app (see Figure 6.16). This app gives the accountant the opportunity to start from an existing invoice when working with multiple deliveries from the same vendor.

Figure 6.16 Create Supplier Invoice

Purchase Order Collaboration

Another option for vendor invoice creation is to take advantage of the built-in integration with SAP Ariba and make use of the Ariba Network for automation of sending purchase orders and generating vendor invoices for suppliers in the network. A third option is to make use of the built-in integration with OpenText for automated invoice document recognition and supplier invoice creation. With this solution, an uploaded document is run through the OpenText optical character recognition (OCR) engine and the necessary invoice data is extracted for use in creating a vendor invoice in the SAP S/4HANA Cloud system. The vendor invoice can then be posted automatically or staged as a draft for review and posting by an appropriate accountant. Note one last point about vendor invoice creation: There's an option to create the invoice with a reduction (e.g., for damaged goods) and then create a complaint letter.

6.2.4   Contract Management and Collaborative Sourcing

Sourcing doesn't always require purchasing. Subcontracting is a common practice, so provisions are made for it in SAP S/4HANA Cloud. Subcontracting is also grouped in with general contract management in the SAP functional hierarchy, as follows:

- *Operational contract management*, including the following scope items:
  - BMD: Purchase contract
  - BMY: Subcontracting
  - 1B6: Sales rebate processing
- *Source assignment*, consisting of the following scope item:
  - 1AO: SAP Ariba—sourcing integration

Operational Contract Management

The purchase contract functionality provides the ability to record and maintain contract details for negotiated purchases. Tying contracted purchases to a manufacturing run supports cost tracking and therefore improved profitability and margin control. To this end, the SAP S/4HANA Cloud purchase control functionality allows contracts to replace purchasing information records and to be assigned in the source list as a fixed source for MRP runs. Additional contract functionality ties purchase requisitions and purchase orders to contracts so that someone monitoring a contract can check released purchase orders against it.

While purchase contracts focus on raw materials, subcontracts support the process of sending raw materials to a vendor for additional value-added manufacturing and ultimately return them to inventory (as revised). For repetitive process optimization, subcontracting can be tied to the MRP process for automated subcontract purchase requisition. Alternately, a subcontract purchase order can be requested manually.

Regardless of how the subcontract requisition is generated, the key is that it uses the same apps as the direct material procurement process, promoting improved efficiency and a better learning curve for users. A purchase requisition is assigned and a subcontract order created by a user with the purchaser business role, using the

Manage Purchase Requisitions app. The purchase order is approved by a purchasing manager via the Approve Purchase Order app. At that point, a warehouse clerk posts a goods movement to transfer components from a storage location to stock at vendor. This stock can be viewed via the Display Subcontracting Stocks by Supplier app (see Figure 6.17).

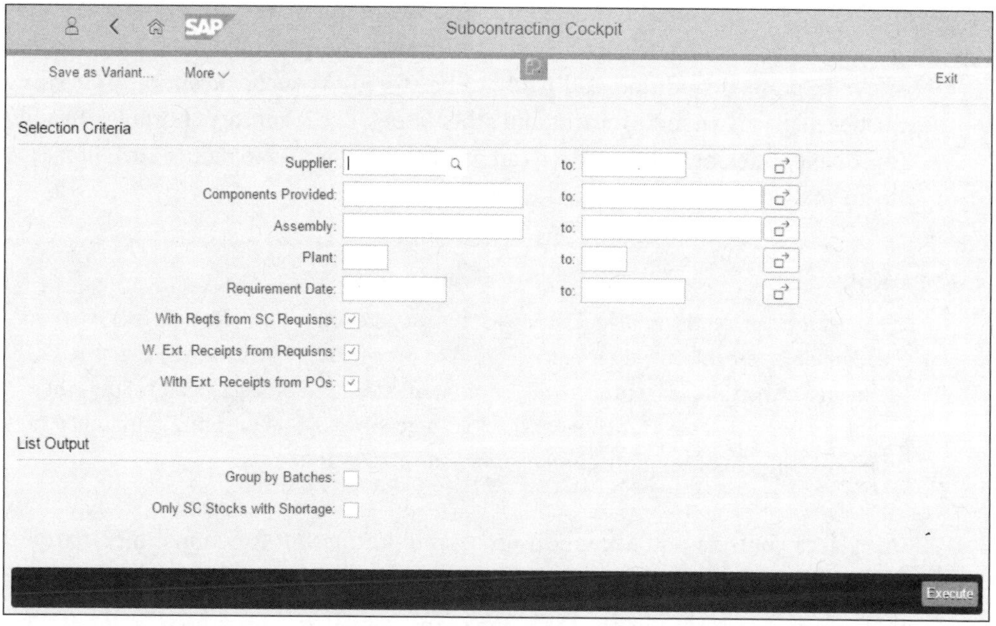

Figure 6.17 Subcontracting Cockpit

Once the subcontracted materials have been received back into stock, the goods movement is posted and the supplier invoice created.

Source Assignment

SAP S/4HANA Cloud supports efficient and flexible contract and subcontract management, but SAP Ariba Sourcing takes procurement to an even higher level with digital bidding for supplies via the Ariba Network. Once the optimal vendor bid is accepted, SAP Ariba automatically converts those bids to contracts or purchase orders in SAP S/4HANA Cloud. The integration between SAP Ariba Sourcing and SAP S/4HANA Cloud is built in, and once a company is subscribed to SAP Ariba Sourcing, the integration can be activated via guided configuration with no development work required. The result is a seamless, optimized procurement process.

6.2.5   Inventory Management

It goes without saying that purchasing is just the beginning of the procure-to-pay end-to-end process. The middle child of this process involves receiving the procured materials and moving them into the proper locations for effective movement to the manufacturing process. SAP has applied the *Pareto principle* in the SAP Best Practices process flow, including the process for putaway of purchased materials in the *purchase of direct materials* scope item. Unfortunately, procured materials are not always in perfect condition and ready to be stored. As such, exception processing must be in place to handle returns and other issues, like inventory shortages. In addition, quality tracking and reporting can help pinpoint issues to reduce such breaks in the normal process.

> **Note**
>
> The Pareto principle is also known as the *80/20 rule*. This principle states that roughly 80 percent of the time, the standard process will be followed; the other 20 percent of the time, exceptions will require non-standard processing. It follows then that it's best to design for the standard 80 percent and deal with the remaining 20 percent through often more cumbersome exception handling.

SAP places controls and exception processing in the SAP functional hierarchy for inventory management, as follows:

- *Goods receipt*, including the following scope items:
  - 1FM: Quality management in procurement
  - J82: SAP Ariba—purchase order to invoice integration with procurement
- *Basic shipping*, including the following scope items:
  - BMC: Stock handling—rework, scrap, blocked stock
  - BMK: Return to supplier
  - BML: Physical inventory—inventory count and adjustment
  - 1MR: Quality management in stock handling

Goods Receipt

Before vendor materials are accepted into inventory, it's a best practice to inspect them for quality. Because it's not practical to inspect every item, a statistically significant inspection lot can be set aside. The quality management in procurement scope item provides for this inspection. After a warehouse clerk posts goods receipt for a purchase order, a quality technician can set up inspection lots and conduct inspections. To preserve segregation of duties, where required, a quality engineer can make decisions about use of the materials. (In a smaller operation that doesn't require such controls, the same person could have both business roles.)

The inspection process is an optional call-out from the fully encompassing direct materials purchase process. After inspection, the material disposition options include the following:

- Accepting the materials and posting them to unrestricted stock
- Accepting the materials other than the sample materials (because they were used for or damaged by the testing)
- Rejecting the materials and posting to blocked stock for further disposition
- Rejecting the materials and posting to return to the supplier without delivery
- Rejecting the materials and posting to a blocked stock location for returns to supplier with delivery

Depending on the disposition, the direct materials procurement process is continued or the rejected materials are returned to the supplier and the procurement process is interrupted.

A particularly interesting function, which has the potential to be enhanced with machine learning in time (though nothing is on the SAP roadmap currently) is a dynamic modification rule that tightens quality inspections based on previous unacceptable test results (or, conversely, loosens them in the case of repeated acceptable tests). Suppliers are ultimately rated based on the quality scores that come out of this testing process.

Along with quality testing, goods receipt functionality includes the SAP Ariba purchase order to invoice integration (discussed in Section 6.2.3) due to the automation of goods receipt processes.

Basic Shipping

The basic shipping functional grouping includes the scope items to handle managing the stock once it's received.

The core inventory management scope item provides for all stock movements, from scrapping stock to blocking and unblocking stock for various reasons. Scrapping requires an inventory manager role, whereas the stock movement activities require a warehouse clerk role.

Scrapping stock can occur for two reasons. One reason is that stock is scrapped as part of a production process (or for another reason), in which case the value of the stock needs to be considered in product profitability calculations. In this case the goods movement posting would be handled as part of the profitability analysis process, and the Post Goods Movement app is used, as shown in Figure 6.18.

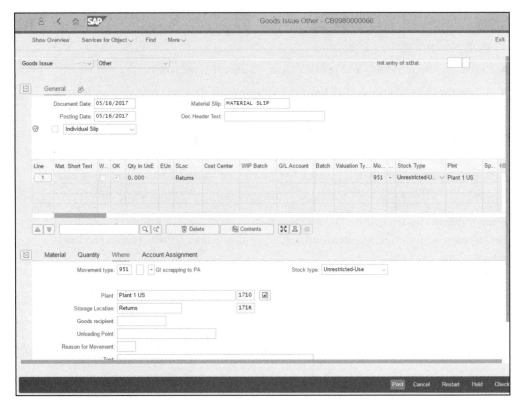

Figure 6.18 Post Goods Movement

When this process is complete, the quantity and value of the goods are removed from stock, and the goods' value is posted to the account and to profitability analysis.

In the other scenario for scrapping stock, materials are consumed by the cost center as part of production or for MRO. In this case, the goods movement financial posting is done via the cost center, and the simple-to-use Manage Stock app can be used for the process, as shown in Figure 6.19.

Manage Stock

Storage Location: Std. storage 1 (171A)
Stock Type: Unrestricted-Use Stock
Current Quantity: 9,677.000 PC

Document Date: 05/15/2017

Posting Date: 05/15/2017

Stock Change: Scrapping

Cost Center: R&D (US)

Quantity: —   10   +

Attachments: 🖇

Post   Cancel

Figure 6.19 Scrapping Stock to Cost Center

The remaining stock movements are handled with the Transfer Stock app (see Figure 6.20). This flexible (and friendly) SAP Fiori app is similar in look and feel to the Manage Stock app and makes recording stock transfers a piece of cake. Transfers using this app include blocking stock (e.g., stock that requires rework and thus can't be used for logistic purposes and must be excluded from MRP calculations) and unblocking stock (e.g., making blocked stock available for returns delivery), moving blocked stock to inspection (for quality control), and changing stock location. Note that the stock movements can be within a plant or across plants; the option chosen will determine which Transfer Stock app (i.e., in-plant or cross-plant) to use.

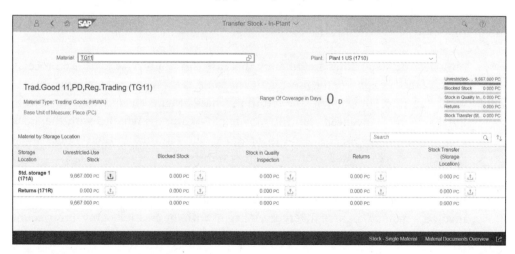

Figure 6.20 Transfer Stock: In-Plant

Stock that must be returned eventually to the supplier follows the return to supplier process (see Figure 6.21).

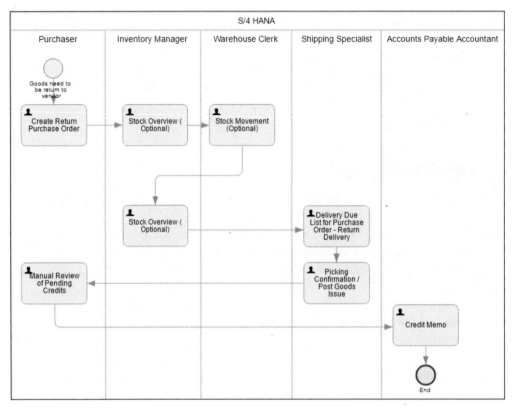

Figure 6.21 SAP Best Practices: Return to Supplier Process

Although the step names are different (because this is a reverse logistical process), many of the key apps for the process are the same as those for the standard procurement direction. For example, the return purchase order is created using the Create Purchase Order Advanced app. The movement of stock is handled with the Stock Transfer: In-Plant app. The result is that goods are returned to the supplier and a credit memo is generated to offset the stock transfer.

The remaining scope items for basic shipping provide control over the process. The first is physical inventory, inventory count and adjustment. Because the process involves a manual count of inventory, it begins with the creation of inventory count sheets. As actual inventory counts are completed, results are entered into the system for comparison and reconciliation. The system allows for recounts and closes with final posting of inventory levels. Note that there currently isn't an API to support automated entry of inventory counts, but there is an outbound API for the count sheets. It would be logical to expect that an inbound API will be delivered in time.

Whereas a physical inventory provides a control on inventory shrinkage, the *quality management in stock handling* scope item provides a check on damage of stock items during the storage and handling of materials. When damage is identified, a warehouse clerk can flag it for investigation. The material will then be posted to inspection stock (with an inspection lot automatically created). The quality engineer must then inspect the stock to see if it's still usable. Like the purchasing quality inspection, the stock can be posted back to unrestricted, blocked, or scrapped based on the inspection.

6.2.6 Invoice and Payables Management

The procure-to-pay end-to-end process logically completes with invoicing and payables management. As a result, many of the complete process scope items in the functional grouping are included in the procurement and even inventory management solution groupings. The scope item hierarchy is as follows:

- *Invoice processing*, including the following scope items:
  - J45: Procurement of direct materials
  - 18J: Requisitioning
  - 1LE: Vendor invoice management by OpenText
- *Accounts payable*, including the following scope items:
  - J60: Accounts payable
  - 19O: SAP Ariba—payment and discount management integration with finance
- *Invoice collaboration*, including the following scope items:
  - J82: SAP Ariba—purchase order to invoice integration with procurement
  - 19W: SAP Fieldglass—contingent labor and invoice integration for finance

> **Note**
> Since the invoice collaboration scope items are handled by SAP Ariba and SAP Fieldglass and not by SAP S/4HANA Cloud itself, they will not be discussed in this book. However, it is good to be aware of the relevant integrations.

Invoice Processing

The invoice processing functionality of the J45 (procurement of direct materials) and 18J (requisitioning) scope items were discussed in Section 6.2.3. Invoice automation is enabled with the 1LE (vendor invoice management by OpenText) scope item. This functionality, also discussed in Section 6.2.3, is enabled with configuration of built-in integration between the two applications.

Accounts Payable

Although accounts payable is listed as a scope item, it's extensive in depth and breadth. The deep functionality within accounts payable covers the management of payable invoices created in the purchasing process, as well as the ability to plan for future payables, analyze payment outcomes, and take advantage of cash discounts. Analytics are provided to help manage payables aging and more. As with the purchasing controls, there are also options to set up two-step approvals for payments. Accounts payable is also provided as a scope item under core finance and will be explored in more detail with the rest of core finance in Section 6.6.

As with the other SAP Ariba integrations, the SAP Ariba payment and discount management integration with finance puts the payables process into a high, digitized gear that allows for the following:

- Enabling electronic payment advices to be sent to suppliers via the Ariba Network
- Establishing dynamic discount terms to optimize cash discounts
- Updating payment terms in supplier invoices in SAP S/4HANA Cloud

This integration works alongside the end-to-end SAP Ariba purchase order to invoice integration as well.

The last scope item in this grouping covers another built-in integration. This integration is provided for the procurement and payment of contingent labor via SAP Fieldglass. Contingent labor has become a mainstay of business, allowing companies to manage fluctuations in human resource requirements for any number of reasons (seasonality, ramp-ups for projects, etc.). With the power of SAP Fieldglass and the integration with SAP S/4HANA Cloud, a company can digitize and automate the transfer of electronic invoices for independent contractors.

6.2.7   Procurement Analytics

Procurement analytics is the final functional grouping for the procure-to-pay end-to-end process, but it's far from an afterthought. The capabilities within SAP S/4HANA Cloud provide much more than reporting; one of the true powers of SAP S/4HANA Cloud is the ability it grants to move from insight to action. The scope item hierarchy is as follows:

- *Spend analytics*, including the following scope items:
  - 1JI: Real-time reporting and monitoring for procurement
  - 1JR: Analytics for stock champion
- *Real-time reporting and monitoring*, including the following scope item:
  - 1JI: Real-time reporting and monitoring for procurement

SAP S/4HANA Cloud provides the following avenues for analytics provision and consumption:

- Interactive SAP Fiori tiles
- Interactive graphics
- Static and dynamic reports

Interactive SAP Fiori tiles provide an immediate activity dashboard for the purchasing manager (see Figure 6.22). From contract-related metrics like off-contract spend and expiring contracts to purchase requisition performance to supplier evaluation metrics, the telltale signs of procure-to-pay performance are available at a glance. With the ability to customize tile parameters, the values can also be color-coded to draw attention when performance falls outside acceptable levels. With a quick glance, the purchaser or purchasing manager can see in real time how a function is performing and where attention must be spent, rather than waiting for an email or an angry phone call or digging through reports of stale data.

The tiles in this case provide much more than just key metrics. They're the first level of insight in a process that can lead to direct action in any critical area. Clicking a tile opens the details behind the metric. As shown in Figure 6.23, the details can be presented graphically to draw attention to outlying issues. The details can also be provided in a tabular format and, if desired, exported to Excel at the click of a button. In addition, by clicking the **Open In...** link at the bottom right of the screen, the user is given intelligent options for drilling in further from the report to a transactional application in which the data can be acted upon. This quick insight to action is a true jewel of this application, enabled by the triad of preconfigured SAP Best Practices, SAP Fiori, and the real-time view of data available from the SAP HANA database.

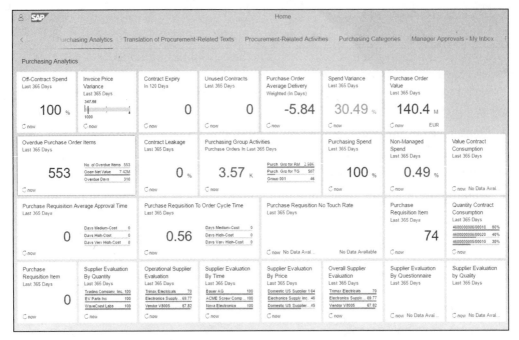

Figure 6.22 SAP Fiori Purchasing Analytics Tiles

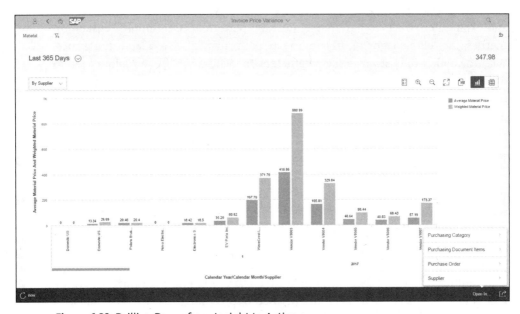

Figure 6.23 Drilling Down from Insight to Action

SAP S/4HANA Cloud also provides a more detailed dashboard in the Procurement Overview app (see Figure 6.24). This more traditional dashboard consists of individual graphics, or *cards*, that can be sorted differently or hidden, as customized for the user. In addition, there are filters at the top of the screen that allow for quick drill down to specific suppliers, plants, materials, and more. These filters also can be customized, prepopulated, and saved for repetitive use. As with the tiles, each card has behind it a more detailed graph, with the ability to view the data in tabular format, export it, and, more importantly, drill down to actionable transactions when necessary.

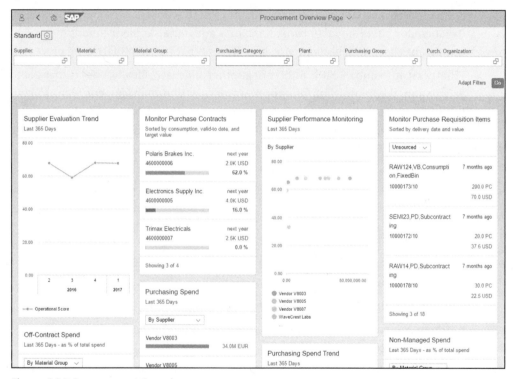

Figure 6.24 Procurement Overview

Additional reports and dynamic queries also can be developed to meet specific company and analysis requirements.

The net result of the SAP S/4HANA Cloud procure-to-pay process is much more than a collection of transactional applications to complete a business function; it's continual business improvement across the entire business cycle.

6.3   Accelerated Plan-to-Product

Effective production planning smooths out the use of production resources, be they materials, machines, or people. Whether materials requirements planning (MRP) or manufacturing resource planning (MRP II), the ultimate goals are as follows:

- Make sure materials are available for production runs while minimizing inventory levels to control inventory carrying costs.
- Make sure products are available for customers when needed.

Along the way, effective management of the process will help remove waste and reduce cycle times. One of the management tools to reduce waste and cost is *kanban* (Japanese for *visual signal* or *card*). Kanban is a materials replenishment methodology that has been widely adopted, especially for repetitive manufacturing processes.

Whether using kanban, MRP, MRP II, or another approach, ideally, once things get to production, the manufacturing process takes over and management turns to control of the run. Of course, things break, materials can be defective, and myriad other issues can arise. As a result, visibility into the manufacturing process is extremely important.

In general, there are two basic manufacturing models: *make-to-stock* and *make-to-order*. In make-to-stock, the company creates a demand plan to fill anticipated product orders. A goal is to reduce costs by gaining economies of scale when producing in volume. The products are generally uniform in nature with customization limited to the nature of the production run. Make-to-order focuses on unique customer requirements (or specific orders), with the ultimate goal of managing production for a single customer.

Whether making to stock or order, the following manufacturing techniques exist:

- *Discrete*: Production of finished goods that are distinct items capable of being easily counted, touched, or seen
- *Process*: Production of goods that are typically produced in batches or bulk quantities, like chemicals
- *Repetitive*: Production of typically homogeneous goods in rapid succession

Although basic in its capabilities, the initial release of SAP S/4HANA Cloud supports all these manufacturing techniques, as well as make-to-stock or make-to-order models. Because new releases come out every three months, the capabilities in the plan-to-product end-to-end business process continue to evolve and mature to the level customers have come to know from SAP.

SAP divides plan-to-product into four categories, discussed in detail in the following subsections. The first, basic production planning, is primarily focused on planning and on securing materials for the production run. The next section, basis production processing, covers the actual production of goods. The manufacture of goods usually requires inventory management for raw materials, work-in-process, and finished goods; this functionality group is covered in the inventory management section (Section 6.2.5). The fourth category of functionality addresses both the financial controls required for manufacturing and what could be termed *product controls* (managing the engineering bill of materials to maintain control of what goes into the product).

6.3.1   Basic Production Planning

The SAP S/4HANA Cloud plan-to-produce scope items are broken down into functional groupings, like the procure-to-pay scope items. As with some of the procure-to-pay scope items, there are several cross-functional grouping boundaries due to their end-to-end nature. The basic production planning grouping is primarily the materials requirements planning process, but it includes several of the end-to-end production scope items as well, because they start with an MRP step. The basic production planning grouping is as follows:

- *Material requirements planning*, including the following scope items:
    - J44: Material requirements planning
    - BJ5: Make-to-stock production—discrete manufacturing
    - BJ8: Make-to-stock production—process manufacturing
    - BJE: Make-to-order production—finished goods sales and final assembly
    - BJH: Make-to-stock production—repetitive manufacturing

Because MRP will tell a company what materials must be procured for a production run, two basic inputs are required: a demand forecast (i.e., the number or amount of products to be produced) and the raw materials required to produce the finished goods. Of course, raw materials inventories are constantly changing, and production run times will impact when materials are required, which is why computing power is required to determine proper production run requirements.

For the demand forecast, SAP S/4HANA Cloud uses the term *planned independent requirements* (PIRs). As of the time of writing, there were two options for generating PIRs: automated and manual. If the process is handled manually, it's assumed that some outside forecasting is involved and that the PIR is being generated via the Create PIR app (see Figure 6.25).

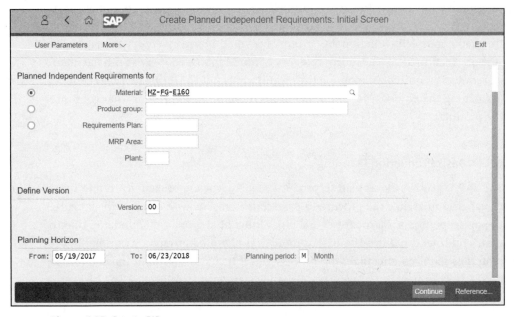

Figure 6.25 Create PIR

Release 1702 provided the ability for the system to look at previous consumption over time (by period) to produce a forecast for a PIR. While new and limited in forecast ability, the functionality is still beneficial to the forecasting process and, we imagine, will continue to mature and evolve with more complicated algorithms over time.

Before initiating an MRP run, a materials planner can view material coverage with existing inventories. Via easy-to-read graphics, shown in Figure 6.26, a planner can easily see whether current inventories can cover requested demand and for how long.

Once a requirement for an MRP run is determined, the execution is as simple as the click of a button (click the **Start MRP Run** hyperlink at the bottom right of the screen). In addition, MRP runs can be scheduled based on several factors (see Figure 6.27).

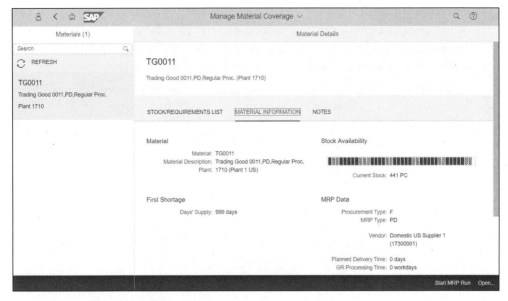

Figure 6.26 Manage Material Coverage

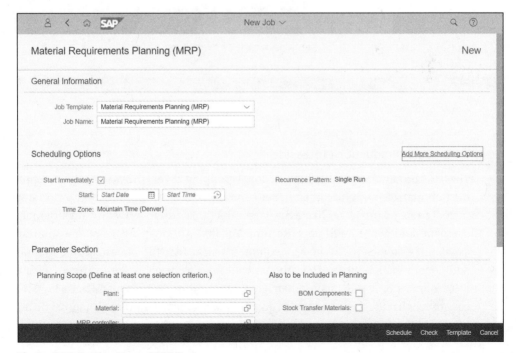

Figure 6.27 Setting Up an MRP Run

Of course, a great deal has been set up behind the scenes to make this simplicity possible. Whether for bills of materials or recipes, the master data for what raw material requirements are necessary drive the details of the MRP run. This master data is set up during system implementation but can be maintained as needed.

The results of the MRP run are shown as purchase requisitions in the Manage Materials Coverage app, as shown in Figure 6.28.

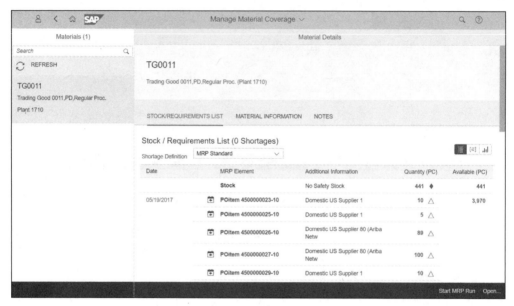

Figure 6.28 MRP Output

6.3.2   Basic Production Processing

The basic production processing functional grouping covers the various types of production management discussed in Section 6.3.1. In addition, production processing includes related processes like external production or subcontracting, quality management, and available-to-promise functionality. Although many of the solution capabilities only contain one scope item, it's clear that the hierarchy will support additional functionality as the product continues to develop. For example, release 1702 contains only one quality management item (for discrete manufacturing); it's easy to see that SAP is poised to add quality management for process manufacturing in a later release. The basic production processing scope hierarchy is as follows:

- *Basic production execution*, including the following scope items:
  - BJ5: Make-to-stock production—discrete manufacturing
  - BJ8: Make-to-stock production—process manufacturing
  - BJE: Make-to-order production—finished goods sales and final assembly
  - BJH: Make-to-stock production—semifinished goods planning and assembly
  - BJN: Rework processing—stock manufactured material
  - BJQ: Rework processing—work in process
- *Inspection planning*, including the following scope item:
  - 1E1: Quality management in discrete manufacturing
- *Basic order processing/ATP*, including the following scope item:
  - 1JW: Advanced available-to-promise processing
- *Basic subcontracting*, including the following scope item:
  - BMY: Subcontracting
- *Basic external processing*, including the following scope item:
  - BJK: Production subcontracting—external processing
- *Kanban*, including the following scope item:
  - 1E3: Kanban supply into production

Make-to-Stock Processes

For the make-to-stock discrete manufacturing process flow, planned orders from the MRP process are converted to production orders to trigger the production process. The process flow then has two production cycles: one for production of subassemblies and another for final assembly. There are several steps in the manufacturing process flow, but the process is straightforward, with few apps required. The first step is to pick and stage subassembly materials for production using the Stage Materials for Production app. The outcome of this step is getting the required materials from inventory to the shop floor for the production run. If adequate supplies are available for the production order, no line items will be generated from this action. With materials staged and ready, the subassembly production order is released. The operations for the production order can be monitored while the production run is in process, using the Monitor Production Orders app. This app contains all the details of the production run, including details of the operational steps (see Figure 6.29). The result is management visibility into the behind the scenes processes of a production run.

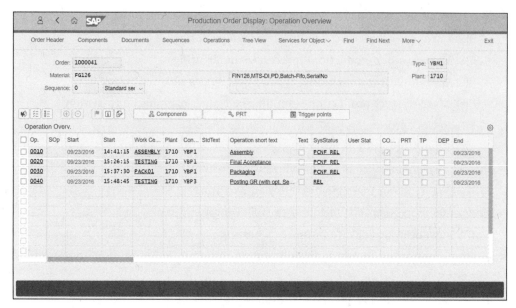

Figure 6.29 Production Order Operation Overview

When the production run is complete, the subassemblies are posted to inventory. The final assembly production cycle operates in a similar manner. The subassemblies are staged, the production order is released and monitored for completion, and the finished goods are ultimately posted to inventory. The addition of serial numbers to finished goods for postproduction tracking for the life of the product is another function available. There is also functionality provided for reviewing scrap after the production run to help drive improvement in production efficiency.

The make-to-stock process manufacturing functionality starts with the same MRP process, but its differentiation can be seen immediately in the SAP Best Practices process flow (see Figure 6.30). First, there's only one production run (with no provision for subassembly because it won't be required). Second, the process allows for the raw materials to be tracked in batches (which is much more common for process manufacturing). Otherwise, the process manufacturing functionality is currently in a basic state, with significant sophistication on the near horizon.

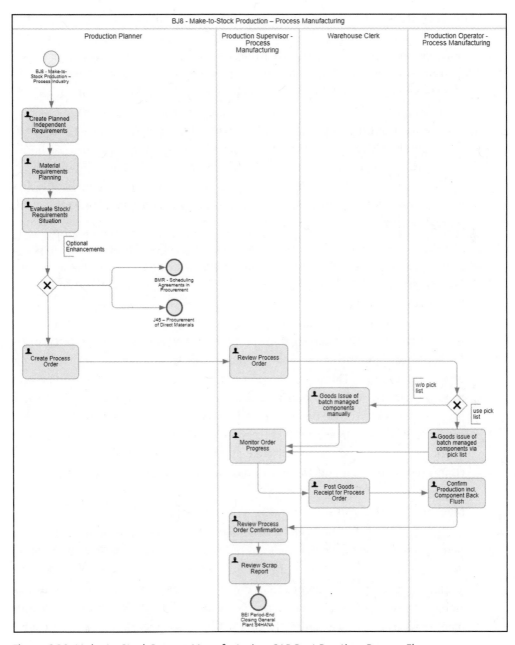

Figure 6.30 Make-to-Stock Process Manufacturing, SAP Best Practices Process Flow

Make-to-stock repetitive manufacturing provides an additional methodology that differs from those for discrete and process manufacturing. Rather than tying the production run to a sales order, it's tied to a run schedule that determines the dates and quantities for the run. Requirements for the run are still created following the PIR and MRP process as for discrete and process manufacturing. Materials are staged, and the manufacturing process is monitored to completion. The products are produced in quantity over time, not to discrete lots. Also unlike discrete manufacturing, products follow an identical sequence on the manufacturing floor; the focus is on homogeneity to drive operational efficiency. Upon completion, the **Confirmation** step sets up the finalization activities, including finished product goods receipt, backflush of component materials, posting of costs to cost collector, and creation of material and journal entries.

Although repetitive manufacturing removes individuality of products, the make-to-order approach is designed for ultimate flexibility, with an ideal aim of tailoring production runs to specific customer orders. To help drive some operational efficiencies, SAP S/4HANA Cloud provides two SAP Best Practices process flows for make-to-order manufacturing: one for semifinished goods planning and assembly and the other for finished goods. The semifinished goods process flow allows for manufacturing of semifinished components, common for make-to-order products, prior to the receipt of a customer order. This preproduction run provides some manufacturing economies of scale and reduces production cycle time for the finished product once customer orders are received. Because no order precedes this process flow, the demand process follows the PIR and MRP processes of discrete manufacturing, and the production process is similar to the discrete process as well, with the exception that the completed goods are inputs to a make-to-order finished goods production run.

Make-to-Order Processes

The make-to-order finished goods manufacturing process varies significantly from make-to-stock, starting at the beginning of the process flow. No PIRs are used for demand planning. Instead, the process begins with a sales process, which begins with a sales quotation and results in a sales order (for more information, see the discussion of the order-to-cash end-to-end process in Section 6.4). When the production planner receives the sales order, the production process starts. Semifinished products, if applicable, are staged along with requisite raw materials. The remainder of the production process is like that for discrete manufacturing. At this point, it's clear that

SAP has normalized processes to create a system in SAP S/4HANA Cloud that promotes SAP's "Run Simple" concept by maintaining consistency across functions.

Rework Processes

Even with simplicity built into production process flows, things go wrong. To accommodate exception processing, SAP S/4HANA Cloud includes two rework processes: one is for defections found during a production run that can be corrected within that same run, and the other is for defects caught after a production run. Although the shop floor will take care of the rework, it's critical that the ERP system capture associated costs and defects for management tracking.

For reworking work-in-progress, the workflow utilizes the Confirm Production Order Operation and Manage Production Operations apps, both of which are part of the standard production run process. By doing so, defects are recorded within the time ticket confirmation, and the additional rework operation is automatically inserted in the parent production order. Once the rework operation is confirmed, costs are settled within the original production order. As you can see, the system is designed to complete the rework within the normal course of the production run, minimizing any overhead and additional costs for handling an issue that is, by its nature, already adding to the cost of production process.

For rework of materials that have made it through a complete production run, the process mimics a normal production run: A rework production order initiates the process, the defective products are pulled from inventory, the rework is completed, and the corrected products are posted back into stock. In this case, however, the material to be reworked is recorded as both input and output. As with work-in-process rework, the goal remains to have the products fixed and back in the finished goods inventory with minimal overhead and minimal variance from normal production processes.

Quality Management

The quality management in discrete manufacturing scope item is provided to help reduce rework and scrap via improved monitoring and continuous improvement. Like the rework scope items, but within one scope item, provisions are made for testing materials while in process and for testing finished goods materials. For finished goods, at goods receipt from production the material is posted to quality inspection stock and an inspection lot is created. This sample lot is determined from a previously developed inspection plan. Inspection results are recorded, and a quality engineer decides to accept or reject the products. Based on that decision, the products can then be posted to unrestricted or blocked stock or to scrap. For quality inspections within the production process, the same apps and processes take place, but a quality assurance or inspection gate can trigger the quality process, and materials can be blocked or scrapped from within the production process.

Advanced Available-to-Promise Functionality

Because production runs aren't always complete due to quality issues or machine or other issues, and because demand planning isn't a perfect science, SAP S/4HANA Cloud provides advanced available-to-promise (AATP) functionality. Although this functionality will mostly likely be used in the sales process (order-to-cash) as opposed to the manufacturing process (plan-to-product), the scope item is included here because the AATP process checks in on product availability from manufacturing and can result in a backorder if stock isn't available. AATP can be used for individual material-plant combinations and for sales orders created in a sell-from-stock scenario. Stock availability is checked from the Monitor Product Availability app (see Figure 6.31), which can be launched independently from a tile or from within a sales order.

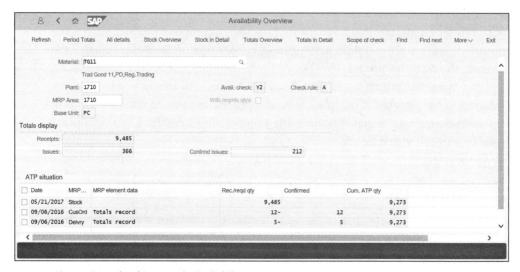

Figure 6.31 Checking Stock Availability

When there isn't a shortage, sales orders won't be changed during the AATP process. If the available quantity of a specific material-plant combination is insufficient to fulfill a sales order, backorder processing can be triggered. Backorder processing also can be scheduled to run automatically via a schedule or timetable.

Subcontracting

To supplement production runs in the case of shortages, or to provide specialized manufacturing capabilities, subcontracting is often a requirement and is therefore provided for in the SAP S/4HANA Cloud plan-to-product functionality. Two scope items provide alternatives for subcontracting a component of a product (from within a production run) or for subcontracting a finished good. The basic subcontracting scope item was addressed earlier in Section 6.2.4. For subcontracting a specific production step during the manufacturing process, when a planned order for production is converted to a production order, the system checks if operations require external processing. In this way, the system supports completion of an external operation but still from within a production order. When the order is processed and the operation to be handled externally is reached, the system creates a purchase requisition, triggering work-in-process material to be transferred to the external subcontractor. The finished material is received back, the goods receipt is posted, and the next operation step is initiated.

Kanban

The last scope item in the basic production processing grouping is kanban supply into production. As discussed earlier, kanban processing creates a pull for materials in the production process, getting them from the previous step "just-in-time" for the next production step. Kanban replenishment is commonly used in repetitive manufacturing environments but can be applied elsewhere when appropriate. For SAP S/4HANA Cloud, replenishment levels are set in master data, and stock levels are monitored during the production process. When the preset replenishment level is reached, the order is triggered automatically by the system. Kanban, along with the other scope items in this grouping, provides for optimized basic product manufacturing and a structure that will eventually support much more sophisticated manufacturing capabilities.

6.3.3   Inventory Management

Inventory management is woven throughout the production process, but broken out into its own functional grouping to allow for future growth and specialization. The functional hierarchy is as follows:

- *Goods issue*, including the following scope item:
  - BMY: Subcontracting
- *Goods receipt*, including the following scope items:
  - J45: Procurement of direct materials
  - 1E1: Quality management in discrete manufacturing
- *Basic shipping*, including the following scope items:
  - BMC: Stock handling—rework, scrap, blocked stock
  - 1MR: Quality management in stock handling
  - BMK: Return to supplier
  - BML: Physical inventory

As of release 1705, each of these scope items is part of another functional grouping, either production processing (Section 6.3.2) or procurement (Section 6.2.5), and therefore they have been addressed already.

6.3.4   Maintenance Management

Maintenance management is another function related to and woven throughout the production process. Maintenance activities, however, are only indirectly related to production, because they're concerned with maintaining the tools and machines necessary to produce products. There are three maintenance scope items currently accounted for in S/4HANA Cloud:

- *Maintenance execution* includes the following scope items:
  - BH1: Corrective maintenance
  - BH2: Emergency maintenance
  - BJ2: Preventative maintenance

Corrective maintenance is the set of activities required to address and remedy tool and/or machine issues after they've occurred. Corrective maintenance is scheduled via a service order and follows a process that allows for ordering parts and costing the repair. Any employee can create a maintenance request (see Figure 6.32), empowering the entire workforce to keep the plant running at an optimal level.

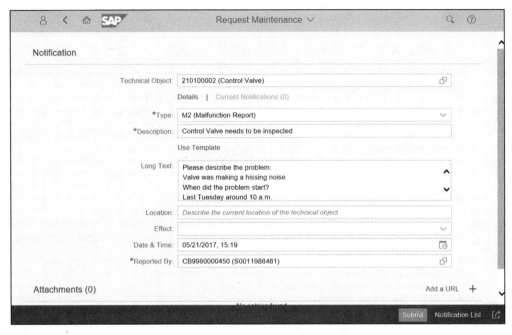

Figure 6.32 Maintenance Request

Emergency maintenance is like corrective maintenance in that an issue needs to be addressed. In the case of emergency maintenance, however, a breakdown has occurred or a system has fallen out of acceptable tolerances, and emergency service must be provided; there isn't time to create a service request. In this case, the maintenance technician is empowered to address the issue first and then, after the fact, fill in the maintenance information for the materials and time required to complete the repair.

Preventative maintenance is scheduled to service working equipment before it can fall out of tolerance or break, preventing costlier scheduled or emergency repair and, worse, system downtime. Processes are provided to plan, in advance, the scope of and time needed for inspection and maintenance work and then to track that work and related costs. At the highest level, preventative maintenance is governed by a *maintenance strategy*, which represents a rule for the sequence of planned maintenance and inspection tasks. The strategy provides parameters and schedules for maintenance—for example, once a month, or every 300 operating hours. Additional scheduling parameters, such as shift factor, preliminary and follow-up buffers, and hierarchy, also can be specified. Different plants can use the same or maintain separate maintenance strategies. At a lower level, specific maintenance tasks can be specified for different types of maintenance to ensure completion of the proper steps (preventing a critical task from being skipped by accident). These tasks are coupled with a maintenance strategy to create a specific maintenance plan to be scheduled and carried out.

Whether for preventative, emergency, or scheduled maintenance, SAP S/4HANA Cloud provides a comprehensive suite of tools to keep plant equipment operating at its most efficient.

6.3.5   Project Control and Product Development

The final functional grouping under plan-to-product, project control and product development, is new to SAP S/4HANA Cloud as of version 1702. As such, it shows potential for future extensibility but is somewhat limited currently. The grouping hierarchy is as follows:

- *Project financials control*, including the following scope item:
  - 1NT: Project financial control
- *Product development foundation*, including the following scope item:
  - 1NR: Engineering bill of materials version management

Development of a new product is often handled as a standalone project requiring project coordination, staffing, and progress and cost tracking. To support this project cost tracking, SAP S/4HANA Cloud lets you create a work breakdown structure (WBS) as an accounting structure to categorize, plan, and track project costs. Once the WBS is set up, the SAP Best Practices scope item lets the project financial controller monitor the project costs, generate settlements when appropriate, and ultimately close the project. The result is the prevention of runaway costs for new product development.

The other scope item in this grouping addresses the new products themselves, as opposed to the financial controls relative to the new products. When developing a new product, engineering will create an engineering bill of materials (EBOM) to define the product as designed. Versioning is used to provide controls in product development and ensure the proper EBOM is handed over to manufacturing. Once the EBOM is complete, a version is assigned, locking the document from further changes and thereby maintaining control of the product design.

As such, this review of plan-to-product ends at the beginning, with planning activities. SAP S/4HANA Cloud has a comprehensive functional structure for manufacturing that's being extended and matured continually, rounding out the product as a comprehensive ERP offering.

6.4   Optimized Order-to-Cash

The saying goes that "cash is king," but an optimized order-to-cash process truly focuses on the customer. As such, SAP S/4HANA Cloud provides a comprehensive order-to-cash suite to handle the myriad ways customers buy and interact. The system also provides flexibility to handle how businesses want to sell—for example, from stock or orders, with or without contracts, with free delivery, and more. Because companies often sell products from a third party, SAP S/4HANA Cloud provides for those models as well.

Having the ability to handle multiple transaction types is only a portion of the battle. SAP S/4HANA Cloud takes the next step by leveraging the real-time analytics capabilities of SAP HANA to provide management with insightful dashboards that use graphics to highlight critical areas in which support is needed. The result is an order-to-cash process that is not only flexible, but also optimized and continually improving. In the following sections, we'll summarize the order-to-cash processes that have been covered in previous sections before moving on to order and contract management.

6.4.1   Order-to-Cash Scope Items Covered in Other Functional Groupings

Like the other end-to-end processes, order-to-cash is divided into subcategories. In this case, however, SAP has grouped most of the functionality under the order and contracts management category. This function and its scope items are covered in Section 6.4.2.

Note that several order-to-cash scope items are part of other functional groupings and aren't covered in this section. These include the following:

- *Goods issue*, including the following scope items:
  - BMY: Subcontracting
  - 1MP: Quality management in sales

- *Basic shipping*, including the following scope items:
  - BMC: Stock handling—rework, scrap, blocked stock
  - BMK: Return to supplier
  - BML: Physical inventory—inventory count and adjustment
- *Receivables processing*, including the following scope item:
  - J59: Accounts receivable

The inventory scope items are covered in the procure-to-pay process (Section 6.1) and accounts receivable is covered in the core finance process (Section 6.6). The one scope item not covered in this or other sections of the book, but worth mentioning, is quality management in sales. Like the other quality management functions, this scope item provides for inspections of materials during the sales process, with the ability to address defects as needed. As with the end-to-end process flows, the quality management functions provide for continuous process improvement across the entire order-to-cash process.

6.4.2   Order and Contracts Management

Sales orders come in many shapes and sizes, from many different sources and for different types of products and services. As such, the majority of functionality for the order-to-cash process rests with sales orders and contracts and the different types of processing required to handle them. The currently available scope items are as follows:

- *Sales order management and processing*, including the following scope items:
  - 1IQ: Sales inquiry
  - BDG: Sales quotation
  - BD9: Sell from stock
  - BDH: Sales order entry with one-time customer
  - 1JQ: Advanced available-to-promise processing
  - BKJ: Sales order processing with customer down payment
  - BKZ: Sales order processing with collective billing
  - BDA: Free-of-charge delivery
  - 1MI: Delivery processing without order reference
  - BDN: Sale of nonstock item with order-specific procurement
  - BD3: Sales processing using third party with shipping notification

- BDK: Sales processing using third party without shipping notification
- BKA: Free goods processing
- BKK: Order fulfillment monitoring
- BDW: Returnables processing
- 1EZ: Credit memo processing
- 1F1: Debit memo processing
- BKL: Invoice correction process with credit memo
- BDQ: Invoice correction process with debit memo
- 1B6: Sales rebate processing
- BDT: Intrastat processing
- 1IU: Customer consignment
- *Claims, returns, and refund management*, including the following scope items:
  - BDD: Customer returns
  - BKP: Accelerated customer returns
- *Sales contract management*, including the following scope item:
  - 19I: Sales contract management
- *Sales monitoring and analytics*, including the following scope items:
  - 1BS: SAP Fiori overview pages for sales and distribution
  - BKN: Order-to-cash performance monitoring
- *Billing and invoicing*, including the following scope items:
  - 1HO: Intercompany sales order processing—domestic
  - 1MX: Intercompany sales order processing—international

Sales Order Management and Processing

Naturally, the largest concentration of scope items is found in sales order management and processing. In general, the sales process begins with a sales inquiry from the customer. Because a sales inquiry is an inbound request from a customer, permissions for creating an inquiry are granted to the internal sales representative role. A sample inquiry is shown in Figure 6.33.

As of version 1702, this app still operates in the older web GUI. Although lacking the benefits of SAP Fiori, the app still provides significant functionality and offers a great deal of intelligence to the internal sales rep while creating the inquiry; for example, the app has one-click icons for the rep to see if the products are available and to learn more about the products and pricing. In addition, a rep can easily search for products to build the inquiry.

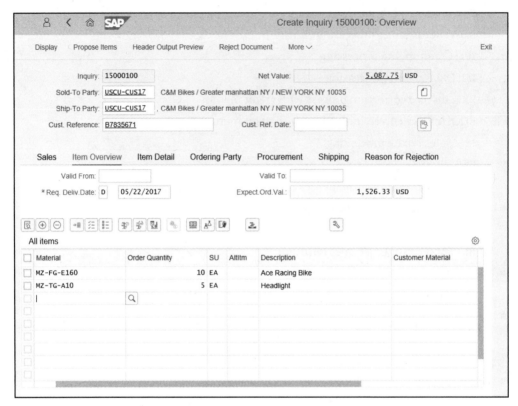

Figure 6.33 Sales Inquiry

With an inquiry created, the information is in the system to help project demand. The customer can still change or cancel the inquiry; ideally, however, the customer will want to move from inquiry to purchase. In that case, the logical next step is for the customer to request an official quotation (for items sold to order) or to buy the items (for items sold from stock).

A quotation represents a formal set of terms provided to a customer. The document itself, accessed from the Manage Sales Quotations app, looks like a sales inquiry, with the same fields and options (e.g., for checking availability, scheduling line items, etc.). The big difference is that a quotation can be referenced in the sales order.

Although a sales quotation isn't required to sell from stock, it can kick off the sell-from-stock scope item. The quotation scope item is more or less a standalone transaction, but the sell-from-stock scope item is a complete process (as shown in Figure 6.34).

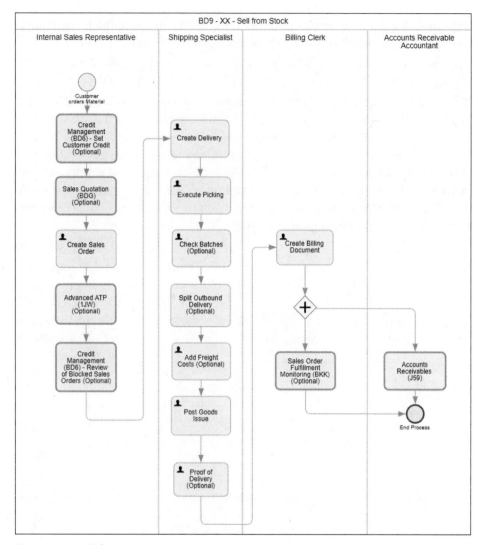

Figure 6.34 Sell-from-Stock, SAP Best Practices Process Flow

This process covers a standard scenario for selling product from stock, with several options that connect to other scope items. The first optional step is to establish a credit limit for a customer. The next scope item is the previously discussed sales quotation. At this point, the actual sales order can be created. The sales order creation will have the same look and feel as the quotation and inquiry, with matching functionality. Before moving forward with the sales order, another external scope item, advanced available-to-promise, can be executed to confirm and prioritize stock availability. Prior to completing the sales rep process steps, the credit management scope item can be reaccessed to check the customer's credit and ensure the sale can be made.

Once everything has been approved, the process moves to the shipping department for creating the delivery and working through the pick, pack, and ship process. The system allows splitting shipments when required. Shipments can be split by item or within items if desired. Another option is to add freight costs to the order. Because the items have been picked at this point, the actual weights and dimensions will be available, and accurate freight costs can be determined and applied. Once shipped, if a customer is set up to require proof of delivery, the quantity delivered, as confirmed by the customer, can be recorded so that billing can commence. The entire process concludes with the creation of a bill and, if required, accounts receivable processing (which is also another standalone scope item).

From this baseline process, there are several variations, as well as standalone scope items. One variation, common for companies that receive inbound sales inquiries, is sales order entry with a one-time customer. In this scenario, a sales order is created, but there's no customer master record to reference. A dummy customer record must be used to create the order. When this dummy customer ID is entered, the system triggers a form to fill out address information for the customer (see Figure 6.35).

Figure 6.35 Address Form for Dummy Customer

At this point, the actual customer information can be entered. The customer master is not updated, but this one-time customer information is captured for use throughout the rest of the sales order process, which follows the standard sell-from-stock process.

Another sales process variation provides for making sales with a customer down payment. Down payments might be necessary for several reasons, such as the following:

- The cost of the item is significant and the customer needs to provide financial goodwill that he or she will complete the purchase.
- The purchase exceeds a customer's credit limit, so a down payment is used to pay down the potential receivable into a range within the approved credit limit.
- Company policy requires down payments to support cash flow management.

The sales order processing with customer down payment scope item (BKJ) makes use of the billing plan functionality within the order-to-cash process (see Figure 6.36). A request for down payment is first established when creating the sales order. This request creates a billing block that prevents further processing until the down payment is requested and received. Once the down payment is received, it's recorded, and the delivery of products is initiated (in accordance with the standard sell-from-stock process).

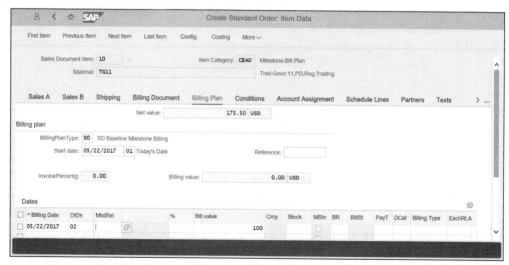

Figure 6.36 Billing Plan

A billing block once again halts processing to ensure the final invoice is adjusted for the deduction of the received down payment. This integrated process both controls the movement of products before a down payment is received and allows the maintenance of proper document flow between the sales and financial transactions.

Another billing option within the sales order process is *collective billing*. This option still follows the standard sell from stock process, but this scope item provides for grouping sales orders for delivery and billing. Shipping costs are minimized by grouping the sales orders to be delivered to the same customer into one delivery document. Similarly, the grouped deliveries are consolidated into a single invoice document and revenue is posted to accounting accordingly.

One more billing option in SAP S/4HANA Cloud is not to bill at all, using the *free of charge delivery* scope item. This process can come in handy when sending customers samples or goodwill items. The process flow follows the familiar pattern of sell from stock but makes use of the Manage Sales without Charge app to create the order. When entering the order, there are two options to handle invoicing via the item category. The default option automatically transfers costs to accounting and creates a proforma invoice (even though the customer won't be paying anything). Alternately, the order can be completed upon delivery with no transfer of costs or invoicing, thus minimizing overhead for a non-revenue-generating order.

SAP S/4HANA Cloud provides additional flexibility beyond billing options. With delivery processing without order reference, goods can be sold without a preceding sales order. Although a sales order isn't required, this abbreviated process requires that customer master data be set up in the system. With customer information in place, a shipping specialist can open the Create Outbound Delivery without Order Reference app and initiate the delivery.

Note that the system can be set up to check stock availability at delivery creation using the available inventory and replenishment lead time. Without sufficient stock, there's nothing to pick or ship, so the process is temporarily halted. Once sufficient stock for delivery is available, the system will create the delivery and the picking process can start. In this way, open deliveries can be prevented by using the app options to check inventory at order creation. Alternately, deliveries that lack confirmed quantities can be prevented by configuring the system to not allow incomplete deliveries to be saved. Other options exist for allowing the delivery to be created even if stock isn't immediately on hand, making use of an extended replenishment lead time during the stock availability check and providing a longer window for the stock to become available. Once the delivery is set, the Analyze Outbound Delivery Logs app can be used to review all created deliveries.

Beyond open orders, in situations in which stock is short for an order, SAP S/4HANA Cloud provides the ability for the sales order to trigger a purchase request to replenish the stock from a third party, specifically for that order. The *sales of nonstock item with order-specific procurement* scope item covers this situation. The purchase request is converted to a purchase order and, when the goods are received, to customer and special stock. Delivery and customer and vendor invoicing follow from there (see Figure 6.37).

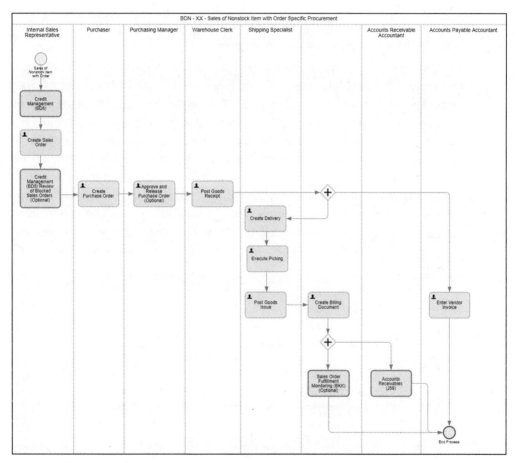

Figure 6.37 SAP Best Practices Process for Sale of Nonstock Item with Order-Specific Procurement

When stock isn't available or when an item is never stocked, some companies will make use of a third party to send product directly to a customer (as opposed to having the items delivered to stock and then shipped to the customer from there). Two options, in separate scope items, support this type of sale. One of the scope items supports the third party sending product directly to the end customer without notification of delivery. In that case, the sales order automatically creates a purchase order for the goods from the third party (to be delivered directly to the end customer). When the third-party invoice is received, the billing quantity is updated and the customer invoice can be created (and the payables process is also initiated). The other third-party option uses shipping notification, as opposed to an invoice, to trigger a statistical goods receipt (as the goods are received by the end customer), which is then used to generate the customer and vendor invoices.

Free goods processing allows a company to provide a volume discount, in the form of a quantity of free products based on the volume of products purchased. In this case, a company is likely offering a promotion like "buy two, get one free." Although it seems like a simple transaction, ensuring the accounting is correct for profitability and cost analysis requires effective tracking throughout the process. As a result, SAP S/4HANA Cloud provides the *free goods processing* scope item to cover this special, but not uncommon situation. The promotional policy can be set up via master data. For example, say that the promotional policy for the TG11 product requires a minimum purchase of 1,000 units. At 1,000 or more units, 10 units are provided for free for every 500 purchased. In Figure 6.38, only 250 units have been ordered, so the app provides a warning that the minimum number of units for the discount hasn't been met.

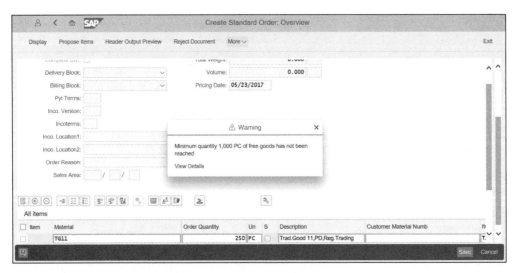

Figure 6.38 Minimum Quantity Warning Example

Even though the minimum hasn't been met, the order can continue; there just won't be any free goods.

In the example shown in Figure 6.39, 1,500 units were entered for the order. Upon entry, the system automatically splits the order into two line items: one for the first 1,470 that will be charged at full price, and one for the 30 items (10 per each 500 items) that will be free of charge. The remainder of the sales process proceeds in accordance with the standard sell from stock process.

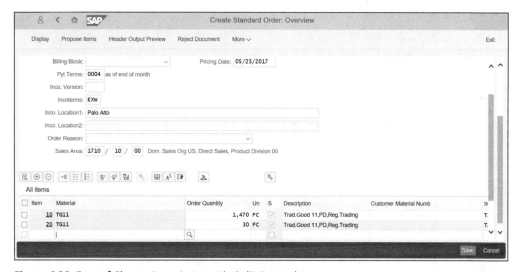

Figure 6.39 Free of Charge Item Automatic Split Example

Another way for companies to incent customers to make volume purchases (or just purchases in general) is to offer rebates. SAP S/4HANA Cloud provides many options for handling rebates. Volume-based condition contracts, generated after the customer invoice is created, drive the rebates.

One additional method for moving product to customers, specifically in wholesale situations in which the customer will be reselling the product to an end customer, is consignment-based sales. In this circumstance, product is shipped to the wholesaler, but not actually sold. The wholesaler is in essence another warehouse to store products until they're sold to the end customer. SAP S/4HANA Cloud allows for stock to be posted via the customer consignment scope item to "consignment stock" until sold. The processes in this scope item also cover return of consignment stock when it's not sold.

Regardless of the type of order, or even when an order doesn't exist, any number of issues can crop up that would interrupt or delay the sale or prevent it from completing. To promote a structured approach to exception management, SAP S/4HANA Cloud provides multiple, targeted processes within the *sales order fulfillment monitoring* scope item. The four process threads include the following:

1. Incomplete items
   - Incomplete sales inquiries
   - Incomplete sales quotations
   - Incomplete sales documents
   - Incomplete sales contracts
2. Sales order issues
   - Fulfillment issues
   - Sales blocked for credit issues
   - Incomplete sales orders
   - Sales with delivery blocks
   - Sales with billing blocks
3. Shipping issues (sales due for delivery)
4. Billing issues
   - Collective invoice creation issues
   - Blocked billing documents
   - Schedule billing issues

The appropriate analyst can search for specific sales orders or filter issues by stage (e.g., order, supply, delivery, invoicing, or accounting). From there, SAP S/4HANA Cloud is designed to drive the analyst to action to resolve issues. This "insight to action" design of SAP S/4HANA Cloud is one of its distinguishing features. The system provides issue data directly from apps like the Sales Order Fulfillment app (see Figure 6.40).

Data can be provided in tabular form or in a more insightful graphical format to help focus attention where it belongs. When reviewing issue logs, menus tailored to the nature of the issues being investigated prompt the analyst to select the correct transaction in the system for addressing and correcting the issue. For example, at the bottom of the screen shown in Figure 6.41, there's a comprehensive, ribbon-style menu of actions to take depending on the issue type. When an issue is selected, the relevant menu items are highlighted and activated.

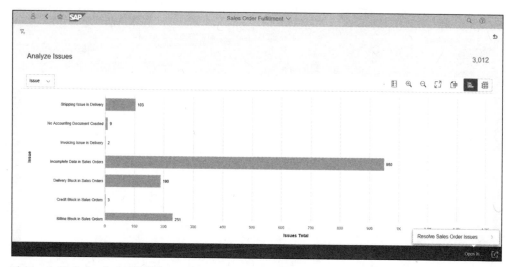

Figure 6.40 Sales Order Fulfillment Issues Summary View

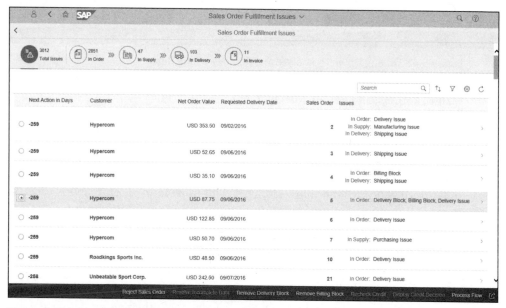

Figure 6.41 Sales Orders Fulfillment Issues Example

From there, the analyst can drill down to a specific issue (as shown in Figure 6.42), and elements like billing blocks can be investigated and removed to keep the process moving.

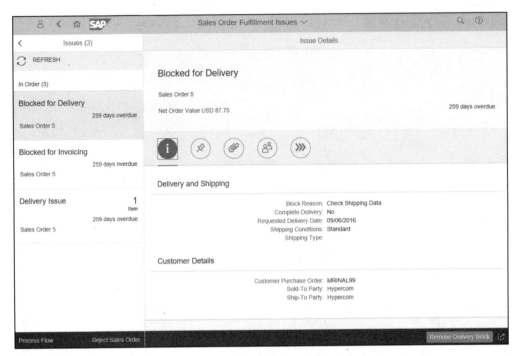

Figure 6.42 Drilling Down to Analyze and Remove Billing Block

Claims, Returns, and Refund Management

Although order fulfillment monitoring keeps outbound processes running smoothly, for companies that deliver goods on pallets, the return of those pallets also needs to be managed. SAP S/4HANA Cloud provides pallet return functionality through the *returnables processing* scope item. In this scenario, when creating a standard sales order, during the pick and ship steps, a pallet (or other form of returnable packaging) is added to the delivery. Customers return pallets using a pallet return order. The process follows with pallet return delivery and goods receipt or a pallet return delivery without reference and goods receipt. If a customer doesn't return pallets, a debit memo request can be issued.

Debit and credit memos are a common practice within the sales order management and processing function and as such are provided for with appropriate scope items that allow for memo creation with or without invoice correction. When a customer has been undercharged (e.g., due to a pricing or sales tax error), but before the invoice has been created, a debit memo is issued. For detailed tracking, the debit memo can be tied to a specific sales document or order. In the same way, credit memos can be generated when a customer has been overcharged. When the invoice has already been generated, the credit or debit memo can be associated with the invoice for proper accounting.

For EU companies, when using the localization for EU countries, an additional scope item—intrastat processing—is available under sales order management and processing for statistical tracking of goods moving between EU countries.

However much as companies don't want to deal with them, sales operations aren't complete without being able to handle returns and refunds. SAP S/4HANA Cloud provides two scope items to handle these reverse processes: *customer returns* and *accelerated customer returns*. Both scope items allow for full processing of a customer return. The standard process uses multiple apps to accomplish the process, whereas the accelerated option provides a single app with automated handling of the various reverse logistics documents. Regardless of how the return is initiated, it can be tracked through the entire process to ensure product is returned and posted to appropriate stock (depending on whether the product is defective) and that the financial portion of the return is completed. Status data is available, but the system also provides a useful graphical representation of the return process and what stages are in process (see Figure 6.43).

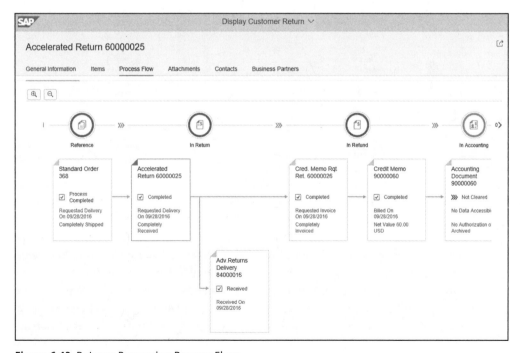

Figure 6.43 Returns Processing Process Flow

This view highlights to the returns clerk where there could be issues that need to be addressed.

Sales Monitoring and Analytics

Intelligent graphics, like that for the returns process, are one of the hallmarks of SAP S/4HANA Cloud. Some of the graphics are within scope items, as shown in Figure 6.43, but additional monitoring and analytics for the entire order-to-cash process are available from the order-to-cash performance monitoring and SAP Fiori overview pages for sales and distribution scope items. The showcase for these graphics is the Order-to-Cash Overview app (see Figure 6.44).

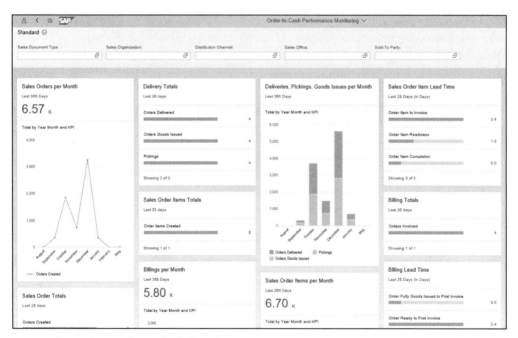

Figure 6.44 Order-to-Cash Overview App

This app contains multiple cards that provide critical success factor metrics for the overall process, providing an end-to-end view of the health for the overall order-to-cash process. The app provides the ability to filter by different criteria, such as **Customer**, **Sales Organization**, **Timeframe** (e.g., **Calendar Year**, **Quarter**), **Material**, and much more. In addition, you can click any card to drill down to a lower level of detail to explore data of concern. Even more powerful is the ability to dynamically create additional graphics (grouped as an *analysis path*) to view data differently and gain additional insights (see Figure 6.45).

Figure 6.45 Analysis Path Example

One additional analysis item of note is the ability to view both counts and lead-time metrics for every major step in the order-to-cash process (see Figure 6.46).

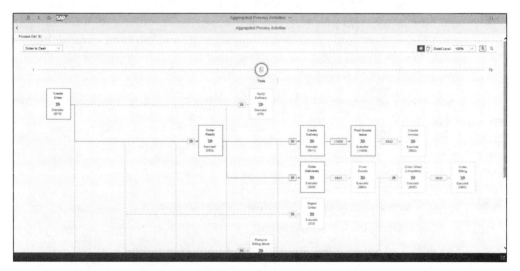

Figure 6.46 Aggregated Order-to-Cash Process View

This view and data gives companies the ability to manage and improve the overall process, not just individual, standalone transactions.

6.5   Project Services

Although the order-to-cash process covers the sales and distribution of material products, SAP S/4HANA Cloud also provides for sales and management for project-based services as well. To handle project-based services, SAP S/4HANA Cloud allows you to contract projects and to plan, deliver, and then bill for these projects. For project management and billing, time-management functionality is also provided. Billing options are provided for fixed price, time and materials, and periodic invoicing contracts. The application also covers both customer projects and internal projects.

In this section, we'll divide the discussion of project services into three sections. Section 6.5.1 covers the processes of planning and controlling project tasks. Section 6.5.2 covers the process of linking a customer project to a contract, which will ultimately lead to revenue for the company. Finally, Section 6.5.3 covers time and expense management, critical for project controls and invoicing.

6.5.1   Project Management

Project management is not an end in itself, but it is required to deliver a project successfully. Effective project management ensures getting the right work done at the right time by the right people. The project management functional hierarchy contains the necessary scope items for managing both customer and internal projects and the human and material resources required for those projects. The project management functional hierarchy is as follows:

- *Customer and internal and project management*, including the following scope items:
  - J11: Customer project management
  - BGI: Customer project analysis
  - BGJ: Utilization analysis
  - 1KC: Resource management—project-based services
  - 1A8: Internal project management
  - 1JB: Social collaboration integration
- *Service and material procurement*, including the following scope item:
  - J13: Service and material procurement—project-based services
- *Project controlling and accounting*, including the following scope item:
  - 1IL: Event-based revenue recognition—project-based services

The primary scope item in this grouping is customer project management. This scope item covers all the major steps involved in planning, resourcing, tracking, and billing a customer project. Creating a customer project is extremely straightforward with the Create Customer Projects app (see Figure 6.47).

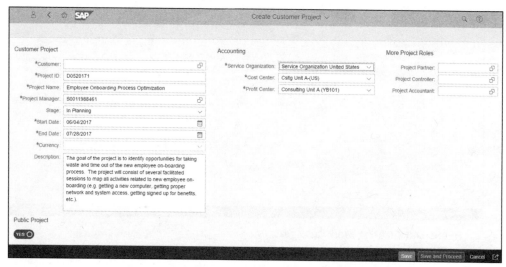

Figure 6.47 Creating Customer Project

Master data for the customer and the company organization must be set up already in the system. From there, the project planning starts at the top down and works down; in other words, start and end dates are provided, then work packages are defined for the project, then roles assigned to the work packages, then resources assigned to the roles. As of release 1702, work packages are a two-tiered structure, with multiple work items underneath work packages (see Figure 6.48). Although additional tiers and links (or *dependencies*) aren't available in this release, the two tiers still can handle effective planning for defining a project from the top down. It's also important to note that SAP has an API for exporting project data. With the ability to export, extensive projects that require more detailed WBSs can be planned and accounted for correctly within SAP S/4HANA Cloud and then exported to a bottom-up-oriented tool for detailed planning.

The work item tier is defined by creating roles to complete the work items (see Figure 6.49). As a role is created, it's associated with a work item and effort. In the example shown in Figure 6.49, a junior consultant is needed for four different work items under the *discover* work package. With master data set up for the definition of a junior consultant in the selected delivery organization, the standard costs and revenue can be determined and are provided. Multiple roles can be set up for any work item. Note also that required skills can be indicated for the roles.

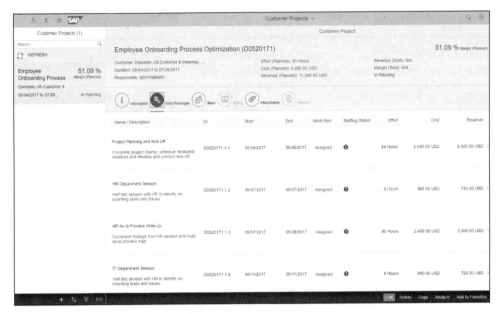

Figure 6.48 Creating Work Packages

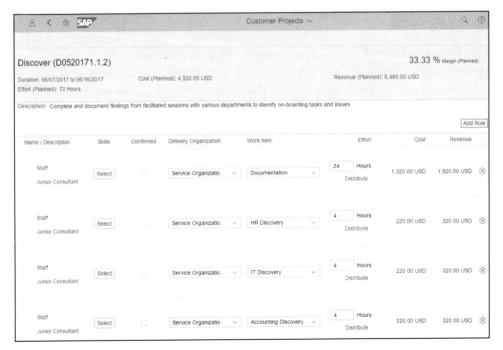

Figure 6.49 Creating Work Items

Resourcing the roles (which is both within the customer project scope item and its own standalone scope item) is extremely simple as well. Clicking the **Staff** hyperlink opens a resource selection screen (see Figure 6.50) showing team members and their availability. The **Search Relevance** stars are determined based on availability and skill match, helping to identify the best resource to staff.

Figure 6.50 Resourcing Project Roles

Once resources have been requested, the resource manager can review and confirm them for the project. At this point, the customer project is planned, estimated, staffed, and ready to roll.

With the project established and running, SAP S/4HANA Cloud provides analytic capabilities with rich and flexible graphics, using the margin and utilization analysis scope items. Both analysis scope items make use of the analysis path capabilities discussed in Section 6.4.2. Figure 6.51 provides an example of a margin analysis path. Project profitability can be viewed by project, by customer, by planned versus billed work for a project, and more. Utilization analysis looks at both billable and nonbillable utilization across similar parameters. Figure 6.51 shows one graph from an analysis path, but on the left of the screen additional graphs are provided. Note that graphs can be added or removed and presented as tables instead of graphs, and the analysis path can be saved for easier access in the future. Because billable utilization and profit margin are the lifeblood of services companies, this rich analysis capability is invaluable.

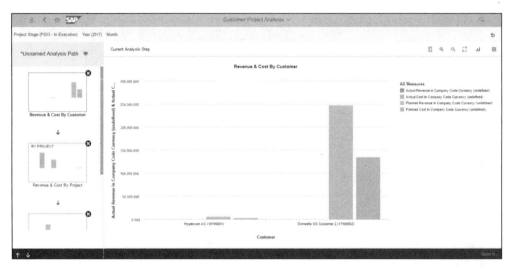

Figure 6.51 Margin Analysis Path

The customer projects scope item continues with steps for entering time, billing, and more. Because these steps are also addressed in distinct scope items, they'll be addressed separately. Before we do so, however, it's important to note that SAP S/4HANA Cloud has a separate scope item for internal projects. The general process is the same, but different applications are used, because the accounting is different and doesn't require billing. One of the common steps across the two is service and material procurement for projects. Projects often require procurement of supporting materials, such as hardware, but the requirements (accounting and tracking for projects) are different than for procurement for products. There are three types of scenarios this scope item covers:

1. **Outsourcing of a service for a project**
   In this scenario, a third party is required to perform a subset of work for a project (like subcontracting the roofing for a new house). SAP S/4HANA Cloud accounts for the service order and the supplier invoice and subsequent payment.

2. **Materials required that will be consumed by the project**
   In this scenario, consumables for the project, such as office supplies or other mate-

rials required to complete a project, are requested, ordered, received, and in-voiced/paid for.

3. **Materials/products from a third party necessary for the project (e.g., hardware to support on-premise system implementation)**
   The materials are purchased and accounted for within the project but shipped directly to the customer.

Additional shared steps/scope items are covered in the next section and Section 6.5.1.

6.5.2   Contract-to-Cash

The contract-to-cash functional grouping contains many sections, but only four scope items (one of which is custom project management, discussed in Section 6.5.1). The grouping hierarchy is as follows:

- *Contract and engagement setup*, including the following scope items:
  - J14: Sales order processing—project-based services
  - 16T: Intercompany processing—project-based services
- *Project controlling and accounting*, including the following scope items:
  - 1IL: Event based revenue recognition—project-based services
- *Usage consumption capture*, including the following scope item:
  - J11: Customer project management
- *Fixed price billing*, including the following scope item:
  - J11: Customer project management
- *WiP management and revenue recognition*, including the following scope item:
  - 1IL: Event based revenue recognition—project-based services
- *Sales order management and processing*, including the following scope item:
  - J14: Sales order processing—project-based services
- *On-account billing*, including the following scope item:
  - J11: Customer project management
- *Time and materials WIP clearance bills*, including the following scope item:
  - J11: Customer project management
- *Periodic billing processes*, including the following scope item:
  - J11: Customer project management

- *Electronic bill presentment and payment and e-invoicing*, including the following scope item:
  - J14: Sales order processing—project-based services
- *Resource-related intercompany billing*, including the following scope item:
  - 16T: Intercompany processes—project-based services

Within this grouping, the sales order processing scope item covers everything from setting up the services contract to billing. Debit memos are used to generate customer invoices. The process then proceeds to accounts receivable.

Event-based revenue recognition often is a necessary practice for project accounting. Revenue, billed or not, may not be recognizable until certain project milestones are met. Event-based revenue recognition is available for fixed price and for time and materials and periodic service projects. An account assignment object is set up and document line items defined for the recognition event. When all assigned document line items are complete, the revenue can be recognized. The system handles reconciliation at period end.

The last scope item in contract-to-cash is *intercompany processing for project services*. This scope item covers the ordering and accounting for project services that are provided between affiliate companies.

6.5.3   Time and Expense Management

Of course, project management and invoicing is stymied without time and expense recording and management. Otherwise, only fixed price or periodic projects could be undertaken, and such projects couldn't be accounted for accurately for costs and profitability. The grouping hierarchy is as follows:

- *Time and expense management*, including the following scope item:
  - J12: Time recording—project-based services
- *Usage consumption capture*, including the following scope item:
  - J11: Customer project management

The key scope item in this grouping is time recording for project-based services. SAP S/4HANA Cloud supports timesheet entry tied to project tasks via a simple, user-friendly SAP Fiori app. The exciting aspect of this functionality is that because the app is built in SAP Fiori, time can be entered from a mobile phone or any other mobile device (see Figure 6.52). Timesheet entry is a necessary evil, adored by management and abhorred by project team members. Making the process simple and mobile greatly enhances the likelihood of accurate and timely time entry.

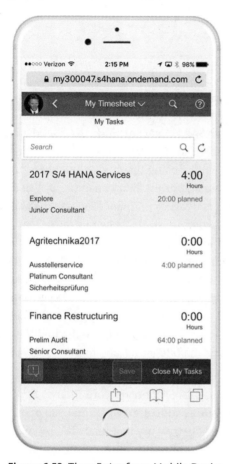

Figure 6.52 Time Entry from Mobile Device

Expense entry is provided through the fully mobile-enabled and cloud-based Concur Expense application. Expenses can be entered along with pictures of related receipts. A comprehensive report can be easily generated as well. This application is integrated natively with SAP S/4HANA Cloud to provide a seamless experience (for both the user and the IT department).

All in all, the project services capabilities of SAP S/4HANA Cloud have strengths in look and feel, resource management, and integration with accounting, but some current weaknesses in detailed project definition. Although these weaknesses can be worked around via integrations with more detailed project planning tools, they'll likely be addressed quickly and continually with the regular SAP S/4HANA Cloud quarterly updates.

6.6   Core Finance

Procure-to-pay, plan-to-product, order-to-cash, and project services all have one thing in common: they all tie back to the heart of SAP S/4HANA Cloud, *core finance*. Backed by the power of real-time analytics from SAP HANA, SAP S/4HANA Cloud provides a comprehensive and mature suite of financial applications with core finance. Most of its functionality lies with accounting and closing operations, but there are also end-to-end solutions for cost management and profitability analysis, as well as treasury and financial risk management. Major advances in finance include the ability to post and report by accounting principle, which is especially helpful as the world becomes more financially integrated. In another major functional leap in the world of finance, SAP S/4HANA Cloud takes advantage of the simplified SAP HANA data structure (i.e., the universal journal), which eliminate aggregates and indexes and makes financial data much more accessible. Also, the SAP Fiori-based user experience provides major benefits from fact sheets and SAP Smart Business apps. Finally, key integrations throughout the core finance function provide extensive flexibility for additional functionality for reporting, planning and budgeting, and more.

Core finance is less an end-to-end process than a collection of processes that take place throughout a company's ongoing operations. SAP breaks core finance down into four areas. Accounting and closing operations addresses most financial operations. Additional areas include statutory reporting, treasury and financial risk management, and receivables management (*credit and collections*).

6.6.1   Accounting and Closing Operations

Behind every accounting system is the *chart of accounts (CoA)*. This all-important structure, along with the company organization structure, guides accounting reporting across the organization. As such, setting up the CoA is part of the initial configuration of the system, and the basic structure isn't changeable thereafter. The following are some key points to note about the CoA setup:

- SAP will provide an SAP Best Practices CoA to start with and a spreadsheet to specify modifications. SAP will take that spreadsheet and set up the CoA in the system;

this set up, called *expert configuration*, is included in the subscription fees and doesn't incur an extra charge.

- Although account numbers can be changed from those provided in the SAP Best Practices CoA, they must be eight digits in length to prevent future issues with subsequent releases.

- When setting up the initial CoA, existing SAP Best Practices accounts can be changed, but new accounts can't be added. New G/L accounts can be added *after* the initial CoA is created, however.

- Accounts that won't be used can be flagged during setup with a 10-digit account number starting with 99 and with a "Do Not Use" note in the new long text. This will let SAP know that these accounts are to be blocked so that they won't show up or affect reporting or accounting.

Once the CoA is set and the rest of the accounting master data (cost and profit centers, etc.) is set, from accounts receivable to payable to fixed assets, the "stuff" of accounting is contained within the accounting and closing operations end-to-end solution grouping, as follows:

- *Accounts payable*, including the following scope items:
  - J60: Accounts payable
  - 19O: SAP Ariba—payment and discount management integration with finance
  - 19W: SAP Fieldglass—contingent labor and invoice integration for finance
- *Accounts receivable*, including the following scope items:
  - BD6: Credit management
  - J59: Accounts receivable
  - 1MV: Machine learning—SAP Cash Application
- *Asset accounting*, including the following scope items:
  - J62: Asset accounting
  - BFH: Asset under construction
  - 1GB: Asset accounting—parallel ledger
  - 1GF: Asset under construction—parallel ledger
- *Revenue and cost accounting*, including the following scope item:
  - J54: Overhead cost accounting
- *Inventory accounting*, including the following scope item:
  - BEJ: Inventory valuation for year-end closing

- *Closing operations*, including the following scope items:
  - J58: Accounting and financial close
  - 1GA: Accounting and financial close—parallel ledger
  - BF7: Period-end closing—maintenance orders
  - BEI: Period-end closing—plant
  - 1IL: Event-based revenue recognition—project-based services
  - 1PO: Event-based revenue recognition—project-based services
  - BNA: Period-end closing—projects
- *General ledger*, including the following scope items:
  - 1J2: Statutory reporting framework reports
  - 1GI: General ledger allocation cycle
  - 1GP: Intercompany processes—cost allocation in general ledger
- *Financial reporting*, including the following scope item:
  - 1J2: Statutory reporting framework reports

Note

The general ledger scope items are fairly self-explanatory without much additional material; as such, they will not be covered in this chapter. The final financial reporting scope item is redundant, but has been listed here for the sake of completeness.

Accounts Payable

Although integration scope items exist for payment and discount management with SAP Ariba and for contingent labor invoice integration with SAP Fieldglass, the accounts payable function is primarily supported via the accounts payable scope item. This comprehensive scope item provides multiple tools for managing open vendor invoices, whether created automatically through the procure-to-pay process or created manually when a purchase order doesn't exist.

The first step in the process is creating and/or maintaining vendor master data. With SAP S/4HANA Cloud and the simplified data model, vendors are maintained much like customers and even employees, as business partners through the Maintain Business Partner app (see Figure 6.53). Having a single application greatly simplifies training and allows bilateral (e.g., vendor/customer) relationships.

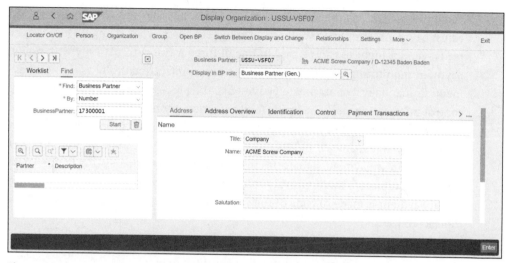

Figure 6.53 Maintain Business Partner

For companies that use checks, online management of checkbooks and check printing are also available (see Figure 6.54).

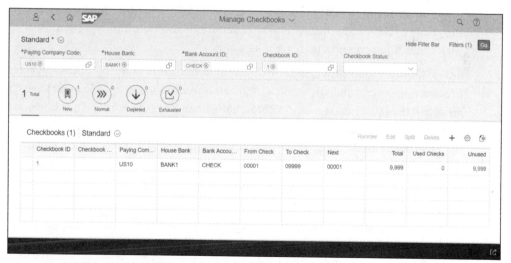

Figure 6.54 Checkbook Management

With vendors and checkbooks set up, open items can be managed. In the first step, invoice payment preparation, an accounts payable accountant can view the open vendor line items (via the Supplier Invoices List app). If desired, the accountant can adjust payment terms or due dates of an invoice to adjust when it's paid. Once they're ready, vendor invoices can be paid in one of three ways: automatically with online payment monitoring, as part of a payment run; semiautomatically as a single payment; or manually. For automated payments, the process starts with setting up the control information and scheduling (and subsequently releasing) the payment proposal. If more rigorous control is desired, a two-step approval process (first from an accounts payable manager and then from a cash manager) can be set up. Approver IDs are set up as payment signatories in the master data setup. Posting manual payments isn't subject to this approval process and doesn't create any type of check; the actual payment is made outside of the system (e.g., directly through an online bank transaction).

Once payments are processed, checks can be printed or, in the case of electronic payments, payment notifications created (to be printed or emailed).

Note that down payments are also processed through the accounts payable scope item. A down payment is requested and posted, an invoice is created, and the payment processed.

As one additional available process improvement, SAP S/4HANA Cloud also supports the ability to connect to the SAP Financial Services Network, simplifying connectivity with banks for payments and bank statements.

SAP S/4HANA Cloud provides for management and control of the entire payables process with several analytics tools. One of the most important tools to mention isn't an app in the traditional sense: SAP Fiori launchpad (see Figure 6.55). The launchpad tiles provide a high-level dashboard for accounts payable activities and metrics. From days payables outstanding to cash discounts available and utilized, multiple metrics are available immediately, without launching an application.

Behind the tiles are graphics and tabular details, which can be viewed in a multitude of ways for evaluation and action (see Figure 6.56). These reports are extensive and should meet most needs, but with the click of a button the data can be exported to a spreadsheet for further analysis. More importantly, the system provides "insight to action" capability by allowing the user to jump to an app to manage supplier line items. For the accounts payable manager, the view can be sent as a link in email to a specific accounts payable accountant or purchasing manager to investigate further.

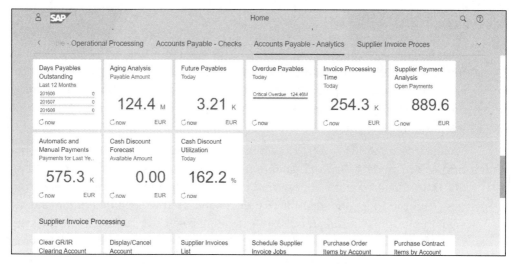

Figure 6.55 Accounts Payable Launchpad Metrics

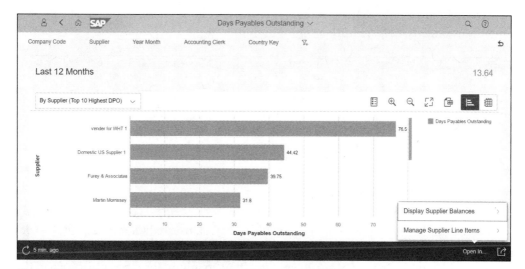

Figure 6.56 Drilldown Report from Days Payable Outstanding Tile

With the ability to plan future payables and analyze the outcome of payments, the accounts payable function can remove process waste and become part of a culture of continuous improvement.

Accounts Receivable

Accounts payable process improvement can reduce cost and waste and improve cash flow, but the accounts receivable process is even more important for getting all important revenue in the door. There are three accounts receivable scope items that cover the entire end-to-end process: credit management, accounts receivable, and—one of the revolutionary innovations available in SAP S/4HANA Cloud—machine learning for cash application.

Having a customer who *won't* pay represents a significant risk to any business, but having a customer who *can't* pay is a much greater concern. For this reason, SAP S/4HANA Cloud provides robust credit management functionality. Creditworthiness data can be maintained for customers and used to help determine and set credit limits, thus limiting the risk of extending credit to customers. When a sales order exceeds a customer's credit limit, a block is placed on the order. The block can be removed, but only by authorized personnel.

Because blocks can be removed and because some customers can exist without a credit limit, SAP S/4HANA Cloud provides ongoing tracking of credit exposure by customer (see Figure 6.57).

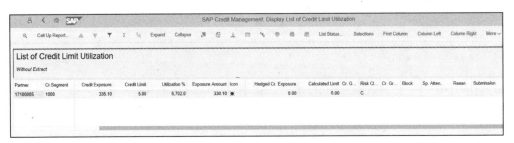

Figure 6.57 Credit Utilization Tracking

The system monitors sales (that aren't blocked) against credit limits to identify exposure risk. Other checks available, which can also be set up as tiles for easy access, include reviewing the oldest open item, the maximum dunning level, or when the last payment was received.

Accounts receivable functionality provides the complete process for monitoring open invoices and processing payments against those invoices. Payments can be processed and posted automatically by importing bank statements (see Section 6.6.3) or manually. Because customers can miss an invoice or might just need a reminder to pay, statements of account can be generated easily (see Figure 6.58), and, when needed, dunning letters can be generated with the appropriate history maintained. The accounts receivable scope item also includes functionality for processing down payments that are required in the sales process.

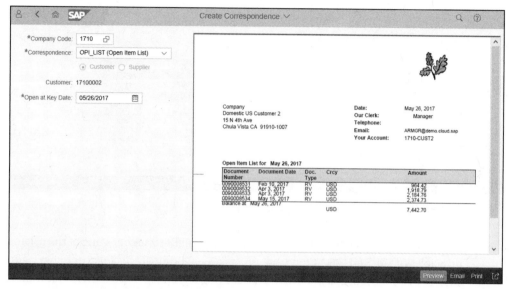

Figure 6.58 Previewing Statement of Account

As with accounts payable, SAP S/4HANA Cloud provides extensive analytics tools for managing accounts receivable, beginning with the SAP Fiori launchpad tiles. Metrics available at a glance include outstanding receivables, overdue receivables, promises to pay, and more. Recall that tiles can be customized to highlight when variables such as total receivables exceed (or fall below) acceptable tolerances. Behind the tiles are details and actionable data, in both graphical and tabular formats. One example is the **Overdue Receivables** tile, behind which is an overdue receivables report that can be displayed graphically by aging category (as shown in Figure 6.59) or by customer or customized for several other categories.

Options are available to drill down to a specific customer, to focus on concerning accounts, and to use the insight from the real-time SAP HANA database to act. As with accounts payable data, report links can be forwarded to individuals for follow-up, such as to sales people so they can call on and manage their customers if receivables are trending too high. The result is a highly informed and actionable accounts receivable function, driving improved cash flow and reducing company risk.

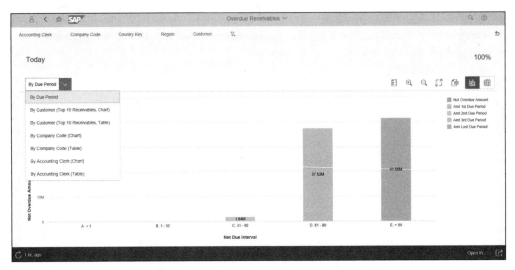

Figure 6.59 Overdue Receivables Graph

For areas like overdue receivables management, insight to action is one of the driving principles of SAP S/4HANA Cloud, but SAP takes operational efficiency one step (actually, several steps) further with machine learning technology. SAP Cash Application is a separately licensed, cloud-based solution that integrates natively with SAP S/4HANA Cloud. The application applies the power of neural networks to learn from payment matching actions taken by accounts receivable clerks. Once payments are matched to outstanding invoices, the data is passed to the machine learning system, which pays attention and begins to make scoring recommendations for which invoices to match to which payments. Future payments can then be sent to the machine learning system, which then proposes payment applications. By taking on the task of thinking through payment applications at the speed of light, companies with extensive payment volumes can use machine learning to improve the accounts receivable process exponentially.

Asset Accounting

Cash (from receivables) is one of the most important assets for a company—but it isn't the only asset. To manage fixed assets, SAP S/4HANA Cloud provides multiple scope items, the mainstay of which is asset accounting. This scope item starts with asset acquisition, which can be performed via a purchase order or independently. Asset master data retains the critical information about the asset (see Figure 6.60).

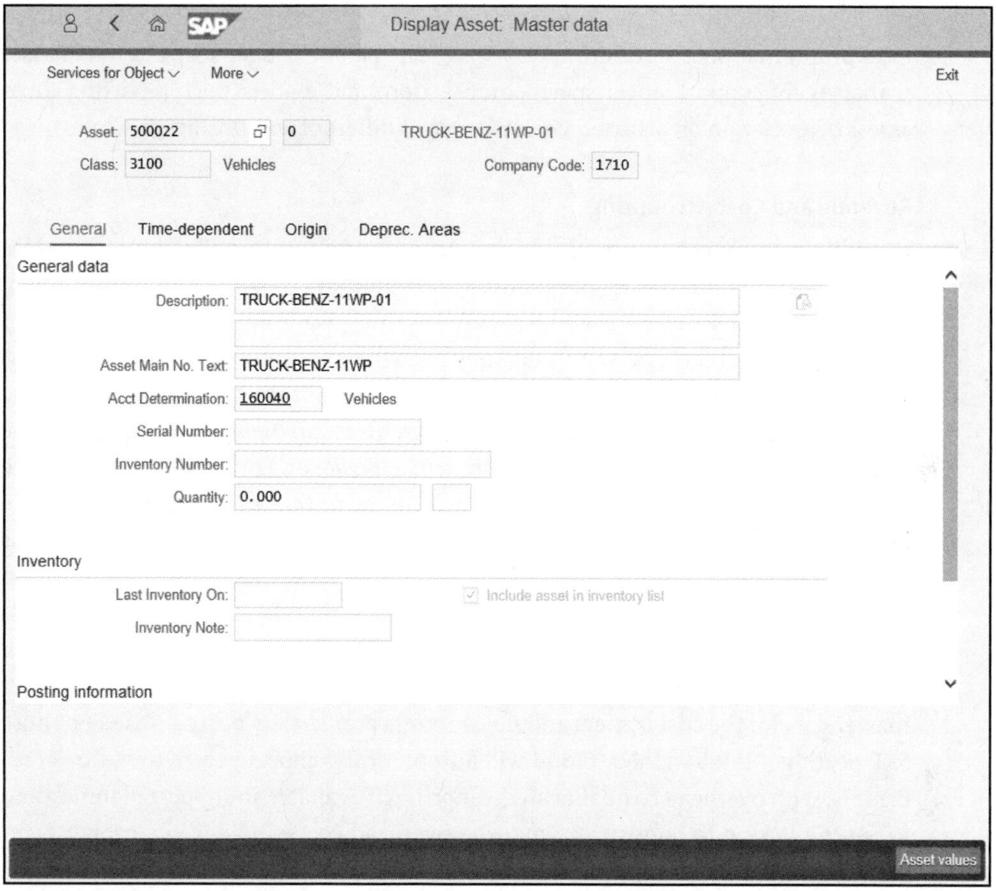

Figure 6.60 Asset Master Data

Master data for assets includes everything from simple descriptions to information about the seller and original value to depreciation details and more. Once acquired, assets' assigned values begin depreciating. The month-end closing process includes depreciation runs for fixed assets. Ultimately, the asset lifecycle ends with retirement or sale. SAP S/4HANA Cloud has provisions to account for both ways of disposing of an asset. Year-end asset accounting covers all asset acquisition, depreciation, and retirement.

Additional asset management scope items cover the accounting for assets under construction and accounting for assets on a parallel ledger. Parallel ledgers are accounting tools that allow specific valuations and closing preparations for a company according to the accounting principles of the group and other accounting principles, such as local or international accounting principles. The parallel ledger scope items in asset management support ledger-specific transactions and reports. Such reporting could assess depreciation on an asset with respect to a different accounting principle.

Revenue and Cost Accounting

In addition to payables, receivables, and assets, SAP S/4HANA Cloud also provides accounting functions to support additional revenue and cost items, as well as inventory. Overhead costs aren't always attributable to a specific cost center; they're often shared across cost centers. As a result, they need to be allocated to the applicable cost centers during period-end closing. A resource pool manager, for example, might be shared across multiple service organizations, in which his/her cost would need to be allocated to each. Not all cost centers are equal, however. For example, one service organization may require much more time from the resource pool manager than the others. As a result, it may not be desirable to allocate overhead costs equally across cost centers. Making manual allocations could be extremely time-consuming and error-prone, so SAP S/4HANA Cloud uses a concept called *statistical key figures* (SKFs) to enable automated allocations. An SKF can be any number that estimates use of overhead, such as department headcount, revenue, and so on. SKFs are defined in master data for the cost centers and the amounts periodically posted. Based on those SKF postings, SAP S/4HANA Cloud will automatically allocate costs to various cost centers. With overhead costs allocated, reporting is available to support planning and variance tracking to control and manage overhead costs. In addition, proper overhead allocation supports improved period-specific profitability analyses.

Inventory Accounting and Closing Operations

For inventory management, inventory valuations must be accounted for in accordance with applicable accounting principles and standards (such as GAAP or IFRS). The *inventory valuation for year-end closing* function supports establishing a valid inventory valuation method, accounting for overhead and valuation variants and reduction of the value based on inventory movement.

Everything comes together, as it must, with closing operations. With all business transactions captured in SAP S/4HANA Cloud and the application fully integrated across finance and operations, the closing process can be completed efficiently with accurate reporting. As discussed earlier, unique situations like event-based revenue recognition are resolved and accounted for within the closing process. In addition, as previously discussed, the system supports a parallel ledger to allow for accounting under two separate principles. When parallel ledgers are in use, the closing process accounts for both. The result is an efficient and timely process for closing the accounting books, allowing management to get the data needed to run the company and enabling the statutory reporting required to keep the regulators happy.

6.6.2 Statutory Reporting

With the continued globalization of business, statutory reporting is taking on an entirely new complexity and importance. Not all countries of the world are covered currently, but the SAP S/4HANA Cloud statutory framework provides the flexibility to enable legal reporting and monitor compliance uniformly across many countries. Where necessary, a statutory report design tool is available to create additional reports not already in the system.

Although statutory reporting is a necessary output of core finance, one of the more beneficial outputs after period-end close is cost and profitability analysis. The scope item hierarchy is as follows:

- *Profitability and cost analysis*, including the following scope items:
  - J55: Profitability and cost analysis
  - 1HB: Profit and loss data plan load from file
  - 1KU: Integration with SAP RealSpend and SAP Financial Statement Insights
- *Product cost management*, including the following scope item:
  - BEG: Standard cost calculation
- *Cost management*, including the following scope item:
  - BEV: Internal order—actual

Multiple analysis tools are provided to allow for interactive profitability evaluation in a data cube type of environment, as follows:

- **Market analysis**
  Segmenting a customer market allows for more tailored solutions. A common example of market segments is commercial versus residential. Market segmentation can be much more detailed and creative, however, based on many factors. Without profitability reporting by segment, companies can't evaluate if the segmentation strategy is truly successful and/or if resources should be shifted from one segment to another to maximize company profitability. The market segment

analysis report provides an interactive tool to view financial data by market segment (see Figure 6.61).

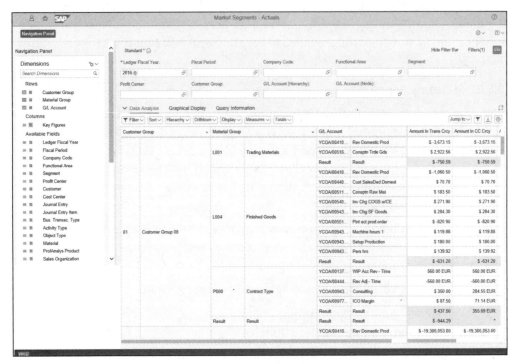

Figure 6.61 Market Segments Actuals Report

This report provides many capabilities for customization, such as adding or removing different **Dimensions**. For example, an additional **Fiscal Period** dimension could be added to view financial performance by market segment and by time period to identify any potential seasonality issues. In addition, filters can narrow reporting output, data can be sorted, and, if desired, data can be downloaded to a spreadsheet.

- **Product profitability**
  Like the market segment report, product profitability reporting is provided in the same multidimensional format. This report (see Figure 6.62) allows for evaluation of specific product lines, with the same flexibility for business intelligence drill down.

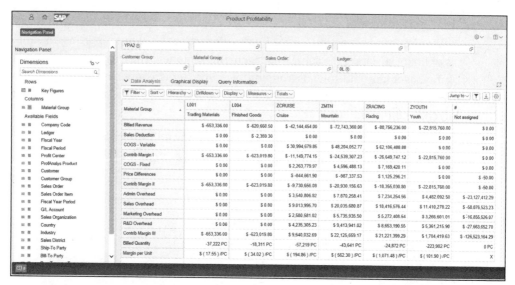

Figure 6.62 Product Profitability Report

- **Project profitability**

  For professional services companies or companies that sell services in addition to products, if the project services functionality of SAP S/4HANA Cloud is utilized, project profitability reporting is provided. Project profitability is an often-elusive analysis due to complexities with revenue recognition and varying team member rates, but this option makes the reporting effortless—and extremely flexible, as well.

- **Planned to actual**

  Variance between planned and actual performance can help a company improve its overall planning and resource allocation. To provide this reporting, plan data must be imported. Because SAP has a strong business planning tool, SAP Business Planning and Consolidation (SAP BPC), SAP S/4HANA Cloud provides a native integration to import plan data. In addition, SAP S/4HANA Cloud allows for the import of plan data from external spreadsheets if SAP BPC isn't being used.

  Internal projects can have a significant impact on overall profitability. When not managing such projects through the internal project management capability, their costs can still be tracked and accounted for via the *internal order—actual* scope item. Internal orders are created for each internal project, such as development of a new product or service. Cost items related to the project are posted to the internal order, allowing for proper cost allocation and profitability reporting.

6.6.3   Treasury and Financial Risk Management

Another important function for the finance department beyond reporting and analysis of financial data is the actual management of money. The treasury and financial risk management end-to-end grouping of scope items contains the functionality required for managing and integrating with banks for effective cash management. The scope item hierarchy is as follows:

- *Payments and bank communications*, including the following scope items:
  - 16R: Bank integration with SAP Financial Services Network
  - 1EG: Bank integration with file interface
- *Cash and liquidity management*, including the following scope items:
  - BFA: Bank account management—standard
  - J77: Bank account management—extended
  - BFB: Cash operations—standard
  - J78: Cash daily operation—extended
  - 19O: SAP Ariba—payment and discount management integration with finance

Payments and Bank Communications

Bank account management is provided at a standard or extended level. *Standard bank account management* lets you maintain and view bank master data. Controls are available for approval of any changes to the master data. *Extended bank account management* (available with SAP Cash Management, itself available via a separate licensing agreement) lets you review bank accounts on an annual basis and lets you review foreign bank account data and bank master data in general via various reports and fact sheets.

Cash and Liquidity Management

Bank account management is important for knowing where company cash is, but knowing the actual cash position for a company is required for ongoing operations. Like bank account management, cash management functionality is provided at standard and extended levels. Standard functionality provides immediate insight into general information about bank subaccounts, including cash availability (or liquidity) forecasts based on incoming and outgoing payments, as well as any plan data that has been entered. Extended functionality is provided with SAP Cash Management (separately licensed). This functionality includes the ability to view actual cash positions and transfer money between bank accounts to cover short-term liquidity needs.

Whether standard or extended, both cash management approaches are greatly enhanced with integration via SAP Financial Services Network or simple file integration. The latter provides electronic upload of bank statement data and download of payment information for subsequent upload to the bank. Integration with SAP Financial Services Network (separately licensed) provides an additional level of sophistication and automation. SAP Financial Services Network enables automatic connection with banks to send payment instructions and receive bank statements (and receive other bank account notifications).

6.6.4 Receivables Management

The final core finance functional category, covering collections processing, is often part of the overall accounts receivable functional area. SAP Best Practices, however, has it broken out as its own process. Collections issues are often due to a missed process from a customer, but they can also start from a customer dispute. Disputes can be entered directly from the Process Receivables app, where all outstanding invoices for a customer are listed and additional actions, like creating a customer promise to pay and documenting customer communications, can be handled (see Figure 6.63). Dispute cases are then opened and managed separately to help manage customer satisfaction while also managing cash flow.

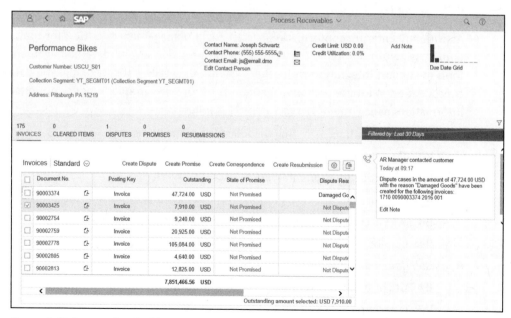

Figure 6.63 Process Receivables

As you can see, the core finance function covers all necessary financial management processes and reporting and provides additional support to make those processes efficient and continually improving.

6.7   HR Connectivity

Companies often say that their people are their most important asset. This is true in most organizations, but especially so in services businesses, which is a diverse grouping including professional services, education, government, not-for-profits, finance, healthcare, and more. To help manage people, human capital management (HCM) systems, like SAP SuccessFactors, have evolved to cover every aspect of recruiting, developing, and retaining employees. The HCM wheel has been invented and improved and taken to the cloud—and SAP wants to integrate with it, keeping SAP S/4HANA Cloud as the digital core. For companies that use SAP SuccessFactors, native integration is provided with Employee Central, enabling bidirectional and automated data exchange between the two systems. Integrated data includes employee master data, as well as cost center information.

6.8   Data Management

As with any enterprise information system, data management is critical for maintaining system integrity. SAP S/4HANA Cloud provides several data management tools to support integration with other systems, data security, data aging, and data consolidation. All these data management functions are grouped under enterprise information management. The hierarchy is as follows:

- *Basic data integration*, including the following scope items:
  - BH5: Data migration to SAP S/4HANA from file
  - 1JB: Social collaboration integration
  - 1M1: Concur—financial integration
  - 1B1: SAP SuccessFactors Employee Central—integration with SAP S/4HANA
  - 1FD: Employee integration—SAP S/4HANA enablement
- *Master data maintenance*, including the following scope items:
  - 1J7: Data protection and privacy
  - 1K8: Data aging

- 1KA: Information lifecycle management
- *Master data management*, including the following scope items:
  - 1N3: Consolidation—consolidate business
  - 1N5: Central mass processing—change product data
  - 1N7: Central mass processing—change business partner data
  - 1MZ: Master data quality—product master data

6.8.1   Basic Data Integration

Data migration tools provide file-based data migration capabilities for moving data from a legacy SAP or non-SAP system. The Migration Cockpit provides spreadsheet templates that define the data mapping into SAP S/4HANA Cloud. Once the spreadsheets are filled in, the Migration Cockpit runs validation checks to confirm the data is ready for migration. After the data is cleansed and ready, the upload can be run automatically from the cockpit.

With the concept of SAP S/4HANA Cloud as the digital core for a business, additional integration tools create a seamless experience between SAP S/4HANA Cloud and the following:

- SAP Jam social collaboration tool
- Concur Travel and Concur Expense
- SAP SuccessFactors Employee Central human capital management system
- Distributed manufacturing

In addition, prebuilt integration is provided for third-party sales force automation tools.

6.8.2   Master Data Maintenance

With a massive increase in digitized data, in combination with data intrusions, identity theft, ransom hacking, and more—not to mention legal requirements for data retention to prevent spoliation—maintaining data has become an ongoing necessity. With respect to data security, SAP S/4HANA Cloud doesn't provide compliance with data protection laws as a feature, but it does provide simplified blocking and deletion of personal data. In addition, with information lifecycle management, data retention rules can be created to manage the proper retention and destruction of data based on ILM policies that can be created for a specific company. The application of these rules can also be audited for ongoing tracking and the prevention of legal issues associated with the improper destruction of data. On the other side of the coin, however, is the requirement to manage data so that it doesn't form an overwhelming sea of old, irrelevant information that business users must swim through to reach what they need. Even with data being stored in the cloud, it can be optimal to periodically archive stale data that must be retained for legal purposes but is no longer relevant to ongoing business operations. To that end, through the data aging scope item, companies can archive such data to disk, maintaining data retention compliance while keeping the system navigable for business users.

6.8.3   Master Data Management

As businesses operate, master data can become overwhelming. With large sales and customer service teams, for example, a customer could inadvertently be entered as Acme Co., Acme Corp., Acme Corporation, Acme Cos., and so on—all as names for the same customer. At the same time, something like a business partner or product name change could lead to a massive effort to update master data created over time. SAP S/4HANA Cloud provides data management tools to address both data consolidation and mass data change. Currently, these tools are provided for both product and business partner data.

6.9   Functionality in New Releases

As SAP S/4HANA Cloud is on a quarterly innovation and release cycle (as was discussed in Chapter 5, Section 5.1), new functionality comes frequently. To give you a sense of the types of functionality that are added with new releases and the general scope of these updates, this section will provide a summary of the functionality that was added with release 1708. As you can see, this new functionality covers multiple functional areas. While we do expect future releases to have a similar breadth, we encourage you to check out SAP's roadmaps for information regarding specific functionality that is in the works.

Highlights from the 1708 release include the following:

- General functionality
  - SAP Cockpit: This app enables you to view all the extensible objects that correspond with a business context after you select an edition, solution scope, and one or more scope items.

- Finance
  - Treasury management: Treasury management allows you to be fully informed about your exposure to fluctuations in foreign currency rates using a combination of a real-time position analysis based on automatic cash flow forecasts and an integrated market data feed. You can also see what hedging you have in place to manage risks, so you always know exactly what your net exposure is.
  - Lease accounting: Lease contracts describe contractual agreements between two partners: the lessor and the lessee. This scope item helps you standardize and automate your lease-in and lease-out credit contract management activities, like creating and managing new contracts, setting helpful reminder rules and running reports that help you save time and effort and make more informed lease management decisions.

- Materials management and operations
  - Advanced variant configuration: With the enablement of advanced variant configuration, we can efficiently model the configurable product with a configurable BOM, so your business process can now handle highly individualized products in sales and manufacturing. This means you can now extend make-to-stock and make-to-order production with variant configuration.
  - Master recipe/routing management: During the process engineering phase, you design and continuously improve manufacturing equipment and production facilities. This process enables you to model the capabilities of the manufacturing equipment and to monitor its performance.
  - Demand driven replenishment: Demand driven replenishment helps you plan and manage supply chains efficiently based on customer demand. It helps create the basis for a reliable material flow by defining buffers at strategically important points and adjusting these buffers regularly.
  - Third-party warehouse management integration: This scope item enables the integration of physical warehouses operated by third-party warehouse management systems (WMS) to SAP S/4HANA Cloud.

- Professional services
  - Resource management: Direct staffing from the resource scheduling application now allows resource managers to create assignments for resource requests (project work package roles) to the best fitting resources. A dashboard of the graphical assignment board gives a clearer view of actual assignments to give the transparency you need on resource assignments—from a monthly, weekly,

and even down to the daily view. If a consultant, for instance, is booked to several projects at the same time, the assignment board makes this visible.

6.10   Summary

The functional depth and breadth of SAP S/4HANA Cloud is only touched on here, for two primary reasons. First, within the scope items covered here are myriad options for use, depending on configuration. How one company uses a scope item could be very different from another company's use; even within SAP Best Practices, there's room for tailoring the system to meet a specific company's needs. Second, because current applications are being enhanced and new scope items are being added every quarter, the functional capabilities of the system continue to expand. The point-in-time view in this book is intended to provide an overview of the available functionality and the way it's structured within SAP S/4HANA Cloud while knowing that new functionality is always just around the corner.

Business can be complex, but managing the information for a business doesn't need to be. SAP S/4HANA Cloud provides comprehensive functionality for the digital core while also providing key integrations for peripheral but necessary functions that are better accomplished via point applications (such as Concur, SAP Fieldglass, SAP Ariba, etc.). This end-to-end integration of data makes information management simple, allowing companies to focus on what's most important to them: their customers, their products, and their business processes. With its process-based orientation, SAP S/4HANA Cloud provides the ability to make running a business an exercise in continual business process improvement—the highest level of maturity in a capability maturity model.

This chapter included a few insights into the embedded analytical capabilities of SAP S/4HANA Cloud. The next chapter will go into much greater detail about these important capabilities and how they make the data within the system not only visible, but also actionable.

Chapter 7

Embedded Analytics: What Can SAP S/4HANA Cloud Teach You About Your Business?

Embedding analytic capabilities into an ERP system has been nothing but a dream due to the requirement to separate online data from reporting data. This separation was necessary to maintain online system performance, but SAP S/4HANA Cloud has removed this barrier and enabled real-time embedded analytics.

One of the most common complaints about legacy ERP systems is that data goes in, but value-adding information can't be extracted. Many companies address this issue by downloading data to Excel and creating countless shadow systems for viewing and analyzing the data (and sapping company productivity by turning business users into spreadsheet developers). Alternatively, or in addition to the Excel download dilemma, companies invest in costly external reporting systems. These systems and spreadsheets allow business users to view system data, but the data is most likely stale (i.e., not in real time) and creates the additional problem of having multiple sources of truth.

SAP S/4HANA Cloud takes full advantage of the SAP HANA in-memory database to provide embedded analytics and render these costly and inefficient practices unnecessary. This chapter will address embedded analytics capabilities with respect to the following preconfigured items:

- Tiles (Section 7.2)
- Graphical reports (Section 7.3)
- Overview apps (Section 7.4)
- Multidimensional analytics (Section 7.5)
- Customized queries (Section 7.6)

This chapter addresses the ability to create online reports and graphs within SAP S/4HANA Cloud, but paper reports are addressed instead in Chapter 5. Because these capabilities are all within the system, they allow for drill down and for immediate connection to relevant apps for acting on data. The result is single source of truth reporting and analytics that enable insight to action—all within one system. Before we get into details regarding SAP S/4HANA Cloud's embedded analytics capabilities, however, let's begin by taking a closer look at the SAP Fiori UX, which drives user interaction with SAP S/4HANA Cloud processes.

7.1   SAP Fiori UX Overview

SAP Fiori is designed to provide a clear interface and intuitive experience that helps cut down on the (often static, incomplete or outdated) shadow systems that users create to view, analyze, and collaborate on data.

SAP Fiori is the design language for all SAP products, including SAP S/4HANA Cloud. SAP Fiori 2.0 has been available for SAP S/4HANA since the 1610 release when it was applied to classic applications, which covers SAP GUI for HTML UIs as well as Web Dynpro for ABAP. SAP GUI for Windows also supports the SAP Fiori theme as of mid-2017. Customer-developed transactions also run with the SAP Fiori theme by default.

The SAP Fiori UX design principles are straightforward, but far-reaching. Compared to prior generations of UI, SAP Fiori is built to fulfill three objectives:

- Role-based simplification of business processes
- A shift from monolithic solutions to activity-based apps
- A philosophy intended to empower users with a clearer structure and easier orientation than standard ERP

SAP's goal with SAP Fiori is to provide faster and more direct access to relevant information and applications, and thus drive productivity. To provide a concrete example, Figure 7.1 shows the classic UI for changing a standard order. Figure 7.2 shows this same functionality in an SAP Fiori UI.

The SAP Fiori UX deliberately streamlines the UI to show only what is necessary based on the user's function. The streamlined approach to the UI is built around the idea of giving users a single entry point to the SAP system that they can customize based on their role and project needs. Users gain the relevant information they need from this single screen launchpad that brings together information from all relevant applications with live content such as up-to-date key performance indicators (KPIs) and insights so users can take action based on current information.

Figure 7.1 Change Standard Order: Classic UI

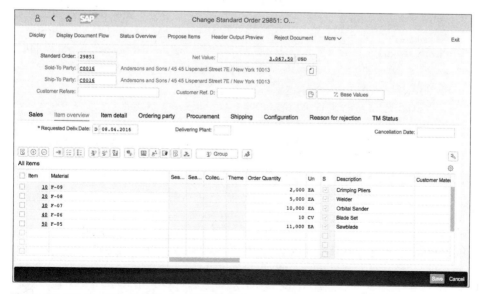

Figure 7.2 Change Standard Order: SAP Fiori UI

241

The screen enables users to drill down into lists, live reports, and business objects quickly. Taking a cue from consumer technology, notifications are structured similar to email or other popular messaging apps.

SAP currently provides three SAP Fiori elements; according the SAP roadmap, further SAP Fiori elements are planned. Following are the three currently available:

- **Overview page**

  The **Overview** page is designed to offer immediate domain-specific insight on what issues need attention from each particular user. The **Overview** page aggregates information from different applications from relevant business areas and provides a fast way for users to access the most important applications.

  Users can trigger quick actions such as extending a contract or changing a delivery date. Or, if users need to drill down further, they can enter details and explore business objects in depth. This UI streamlines the visual presentation of information by reducing the number of tiles that were formerly located in a group on the homepage and helps users to easily anticipate which items need the most attention.

  From the **Overview** page, users can also invoke the SAP CoPilot, an intelligent assistant supporting ad-hoc tasks in the context of their business activity.

Note

SAP CoPilot, which extends the SAP Fiori UX is being developed as an assistive, conversational UI that serves as a digital assistant. The very first version available with SAP S/4HANA Cloud 1705 focuses on productivity and collaborative features. According to the SAP roadmap, future releases of SAP CoPilot will support users through natural language interaction, i.e. it will be addressable via text or speech and will be powered by machine learning algorithms, turning it into the intelligent assistant for the enterprise user.

SAP CoPilot is an extension of the SAP Fiori UX philosophy in that it provides business context awareness and emphasizes fast resolution of tasks to drive efficiency. A new capability for ERP, machine learning, is part of the SAP CoPilot foundation, which enables the system to improve the way it serves each user and learn from their particular needs and habits.

Integrated with SAP S/4HANA Cloud 1705, the SAP CoPilot has a variety of functions: it helps users collect notes, screenshots, and objects for reference; it facilitates collaboration with team members; and it allows users to take action based on business context. SAP technology roadmaps for SAP CoPilot plan for regular launch of enhanced features that integrate machine learning to provide additional functionality to resolve issues faster, recommend and facilitate actions within business contexts,

---

collaborate with colleagues in new ways based on context and user relationships, and even introduce the use of biometric information to complete tasks such as submitting approvals. SAP is planning on using the SAP S/4HANA Cloud quarterly update cycle to push out new features based on the quickly evolving fields of artificial intelligence and machine learning.

- **List report**

  The list report (see Figure 7.3) allows users to filter huge amounts of data down to a number that they can more easily interpret and manipulate. It provides predefined variants the user can choose from, and flexibility to create their own variants and ad-hoc queries. The visualization and complexity of the filtering adjusts depending on the necessary type of filtering.

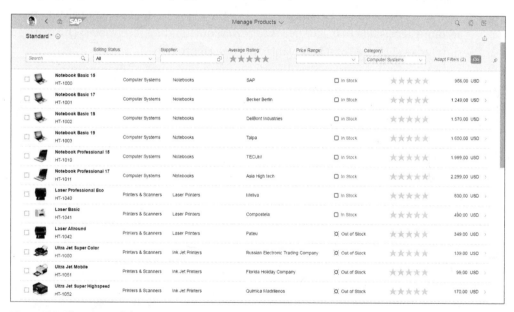

Figure 7.3 Elements of the List Report

- **Object page**

  The **Object** page shows all facets of a single business object—a view on all facets of one object instance in one place. This enables users to gain access to business objects for the purpose of creating, editing, and viewing them in an easy-to-consume way. Visualizations of data are determined by the type of information. A core feature of each **Object** page is intuitive data visualizations that facilitate easy comprehension and embedded analytics to turn data into business insights.

7.2   Tiles

The entry point to SAP S/4HANA Cloud is the SAP Fiori launchpad. Its importance as a gateway to apps goes without saying—but tiles are much more than just entry points for specific applications. Tiles can be set up to provide dashboard-style metrics for critical operational data. Beyond just showing metrics, tiles can be set up with limits and then color-coded to help drive attention to where it's needed most. As a result, tiles and their usage become a very useful analytical tool. The following sections will cover two methods for creating tiles.

7.2.1   SAP Smart Business Tiles

There are two ways to create tiles. For a business user, user-specific SAP Smart Business tiles can be created easily on the fly with a few clicks. For example, assume an accounts receivable manager needs to review outstanding receivables. The manager simply can click the **Total Receivables** tile (see Figure 7.4).

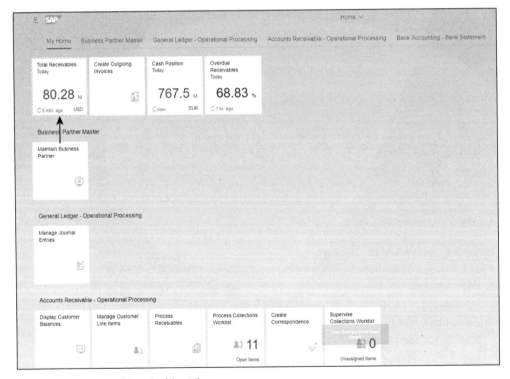

Figure 7.4 Total Receivables Tile

A chart of total receivables sorted **By Due Period** will be displayed (see Figure 7.5).

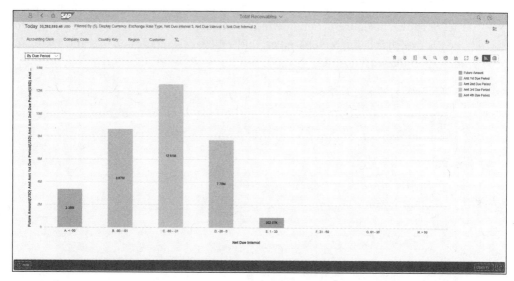

Figure 7.5 Total Receivables Chart

If the manager prefers to focus on a specific account, he or she can filter results by using the **Filter** button shown in Figure 7.5 to select a specific customer of interest. A new chart is then generated, as shown in Figure 7.6.

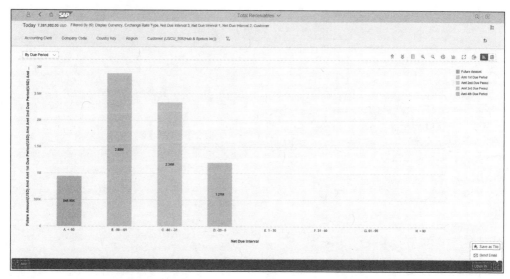

Figure 7.6 Filtered Receivables Chart

Because this information is of interest to the manager, she or he might choose to click the **Action** icon located at the lower right of the window and save this graph as a tile. As shown in Figure 7.7, a new window will appear, asking for a subtitle name for the tile (which is being built based on the **Total Receivables** main tile) and asking for range boundaries if desired.

Figure 7.7 Saving SAP Smart Business Tile

The new tile will appear in the group of the master tile it's based on, as shown in Figure 7.8.

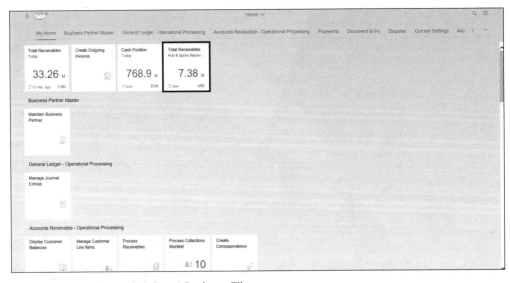

Figure 7.8 New SAP Smart Business Tile

The new tile is automatically updated with the revised total receivables amount for the selected customer.

New tiles like this can be created for graphics and to point to specific apps with pre-loaded, filtered data. Ad hoc tiles like these can serve a short-term purpose by directing attention to a critical issue. In this case, the business user can easily remove the tile once the need for it is over.

7.2.2 Custom Tiles

Custom tile development begins with key performance indicators (KPIs). KPIs can be specific to a company's operations or a common industry metric. The Create KPI app (see Figure 7.9) provides an entry point and allows you to perform the following actions:

- Assigning a name to the KPI
- Providing a goal type for the KPI (e.g., establishing if a higher number is better than a lower number or vice versa, or noting if the number needs to be within a specified range)

Figure 7.9 Create KPI

- Defining data source details from the system, based on Core Data Services (CDS) views and OData services
- Saving and activating the new KPI

The analytics specialist role is required to manage KPIs.

Once created, KPIs can't be edited. However, they can be copied and modified should business needs dictate via the KPI Workspace (see Figure 7.10).

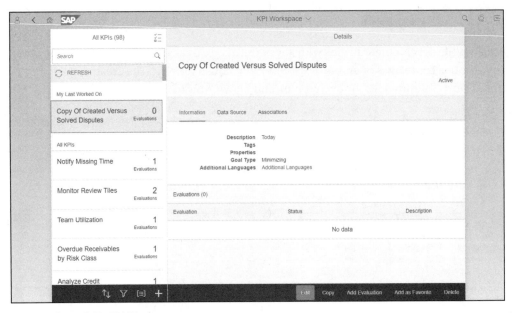

Figure 7.10 KPI Workspace

Once a KPI is created, an evaluation must be created. An *evaluation* is a combination of parameters, filter settings, input parameters, thresholds, targets, and trends that are applied to a KPI. The evaluation defines what information about the KPI is visible to the user. In addition, it's possible to define target and threshold values (e.g., target, warning, and critical levels of a KPI that would indicate whether some action is required by the business). Fixed values or measures can be used for the threshold values. For warning and critical thresholds, a percentage of a measure also can be used.

When creating an evaluation, it's possible to choose an additional set of measures. Additional measures can be used to create a comparison tile and to define targets and thresholds. A warning, for example, can be triggered when the KPI reaches a certain percentage of another measure.

With the KPI and evaluation(s) in place, it's now possible to create a tile using the Create Tile app. The first step in creating the tile is to select the evaluation that was created (as shown in Figure 7.11).

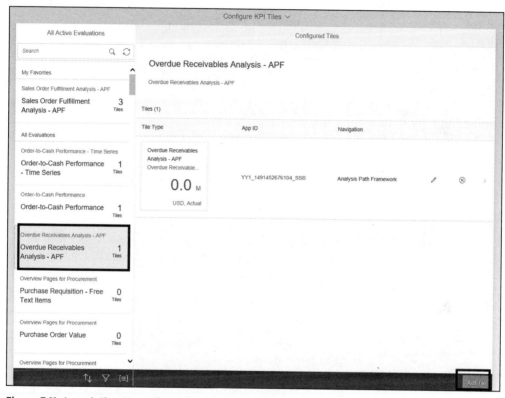

Figure 7.11 Associating New Tile with Evaluation and KPI

This step creates the association of the new tile with the KPI and associated evaluation. From there, the **Add Tile** button can be used to create the tile (as shown in Figure 7.12). Beyond just creating a visualization of the KPI, this app also allows for configuring a drilldown navigation path to an application for exploring the KPI or its implications in more detail.

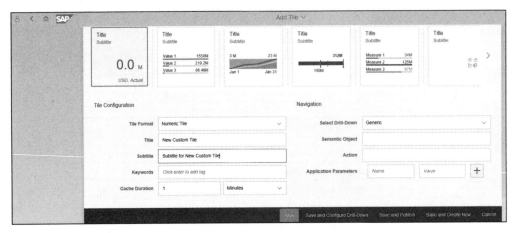

Figure 7.12 Create Tile

As Figure 7.12 shows, there are multiple tile formats to choose from, as listed in Table 7.1.

Tile Type	Description
Numeric	The aggregate value of the KPI is presented in a number format. If thresholds are defined, color-coding will indicate which threshold category the number is in.
Comparison	A dimension (e.g., vendor or customer) is selected, and the top KPI values across that dimension are presented.
Trend	Based on a provided time dimension, the KPI data is presented as a trend over that time.
Actual versus target	Data is presented as a graphical chart that compares the KPI to defined targets and/or thresholds.
Multiple measure comparison	Two or three different measures can be displayed. Options include the KPI and a threshold measure, or if multiple measures were defined in the evaluation, those could be displayed.
Dual	This tile is a double-wide tile with any KPIs on the left side and a mini chart on the right.
Blank	This tile is like the numeric tile, but without a number. It's used to drill down into an app.

Table 7.1 Tile Formats

Once created, the tile will be available for business users to add to their SAP Fiori launchpads and use. Tile security and availability is based on the catalog the tile is assigned to (and the business roles that include that catalog).

Figure 7.13 shows an example of how KPI tiles can be used to provide a dashboard. The boxed tiles are the standard KPI tiles for a receivables manager.

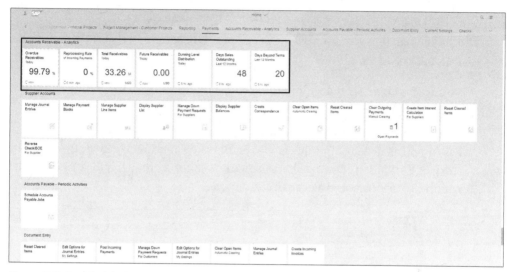

Figure 7.13 Receivables Manager KPI Tiles

7.3   Standard Graphical Reports

KPIs, visible through tiles, are extremely useful for taking the pulse of the business. Often, however, it's necessary to view more detailed information; for example, it's one thing to know how many order issues there are, but it's another to know the number of issues by type or by customer. Such data certainly can help clarify the nature of an issue, but if the data is only provided in a tabular or spreadsheet view, sorting through it to reach a conclusion may take an inordinate amount of time. Worse, a number could be missed or misinterpreted, leading to an invalid conclusion. As a result, graphical representation of data becomes very useful for quick and accurate analysis.

Rather than requiring users to download data to Excel and create graphics, SAP S/4HANA Cloud provides extensive graphical reporting capabilities. A partial list of graph types includes the following:

- Horizontal bar chart
- Vertical column chart
- Line chart
- Pie chart
- Doughnut chart
- Heat map
- Bubble chart
- Bullet chart

- Vertical bullet chart
- Stacked bar chart
- Stacked column chart
- 100 percent stacked bar chart
- 100 percent stacked column chart
- Waterfall chart
- Horizontal waterfall chart

No one chart is better than another; each type represents data differently and allows for different conclusions.

In addition, by using the analysis path capability within SAP S/4HANA Cloud, business users can develop multiple graphs on the same data quickly to see the complete story of a situation. The pie chart in Figure 7.14, for example, indicates that sales volume is fairly balanced across all customers.

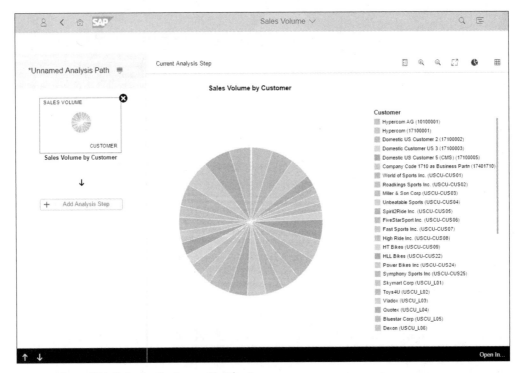

Figure 7.14 Sales by Customer Pie Chart

Significant differences across customers hide in this picture, however, due to the scale of the numbers and the volume of customers. Changing to a bar chart, as shown in Figure 7.15, makes it much easier to quickly identify the highest-revenue customer at a glance. It also helps to better identify customer revenue concentration.

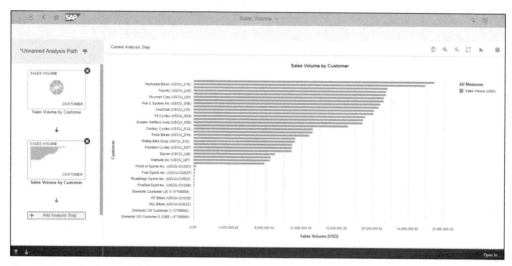

Figure 7.15 Sales by Customer Bar Chart

Viewing by customer is helpful, but an analyst may want to see the best-selling products. Another new graph, as shown in Figure 7.16, can be added easily to support viewing sales by product.

Still, this graph doesn't show which products are growing in sales relative to last year. A fourth graph (see Figure 7.17) can be added with a few simple clicks to provide this comparative view.

This analysis path functionality is available across multiple functions (orders, purchasing, etc.), and additional analysis paths can be created. The possibilities are virtually endless—but the truly impressive aspect of all this is that it's all produced with real-time data, all from within the SAP S/4HANA Cloud application. No downloads to Excel required, nor any additional expense for a reporting tool.

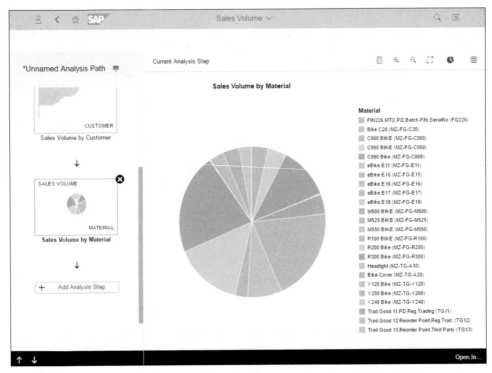

Figure 7.16 Sales by Product

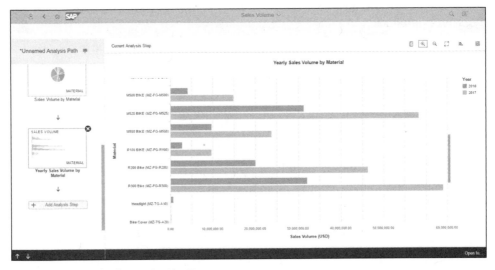

Figure 7.17 Sales by Product by Year

7.4   Standard Overview Apps

Somewhere in between tiles and graphical reports lie overview apps. These apps provide multiple related graphical reports all at once, giving an end-to-end process manager an overview of an entire process. The graphs are sized down into *cards*, which can be hidden or rearranged by dragging and dropping. In addition, clicking a card lets you drill in and open a full report. Examples of the Purchasing Overview and Order to Cash Overview apps were shown in Chapter 6. Figure 7.18 shows how the Procurement Overview app can be filtered and cards moved around to provide a tailored experience.

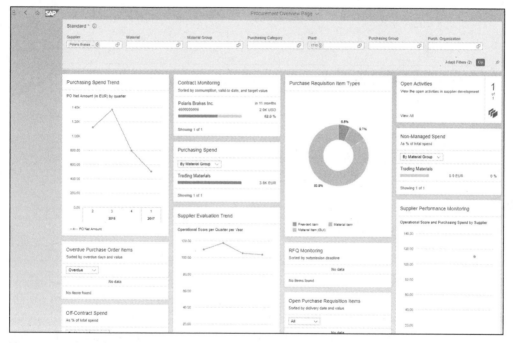

Figure 7.18 Filtered and Modified Purchasing Overview Page

As you can see, this **Procurement Overview Page** provides much different information than the KPI summaries. The idea is to provide summary information that's more detailed than a KPI but still gives a picture of the end-to-end process. Because metrics are only good if they can be acted upon, each of the charts allows for drilling down, from insight to action. For example, when you click the **Contract Monitoring** card, the Manage Purchase Contracts app is opened with a list of purchasing contracts (see Figure 7.19).

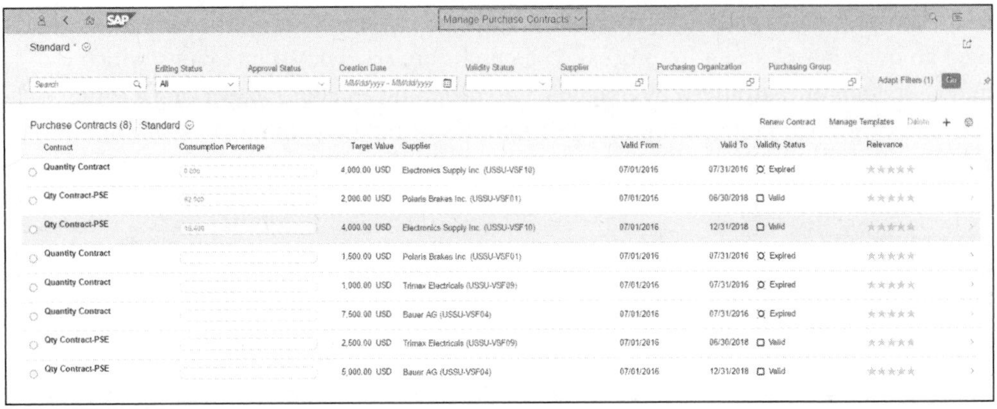

Figure 7.19 Drilling Down from Overview Page to Detail

From this point, click any contract to take further action; thus, the promise of insight to action is realized.

As of version 1705, end-to-end overview apps are provided for procure-to-pay and order-to-cash. Other overview apps can be created with tailored cards.

7.5 Multidimensional Analytics

In addition to graphical analysis, a major rationale behind downloading data to Excel or another external reporting tool is the requirement for multidimensional analysis. Slicing and dicing data across multiple dimensions can provide significant insight into operations. Examples for this type of analysis are limitless, bounded only by the business user's imagination and the data dimensions available, such as the following:

- Sales by store by month
- Sales by store by product
- Sales by product by salesperson
- Travel expenses by type by employee by month

Tools such as Excel pivot tables provide this capability, but once data is downloaded to Excel it's out-of-date, creating multiple versions of the truth. As discussed earlier, insight without action has very limited value.

Because the SAP HANA database allows for real-time data inquiry, SAP S/4HANA Cloud can provide multidimensional data analysis as a built-in function. Beyond this capability, however, is the user interface, as shown in Figure 7.20 for the Sales Volume app.

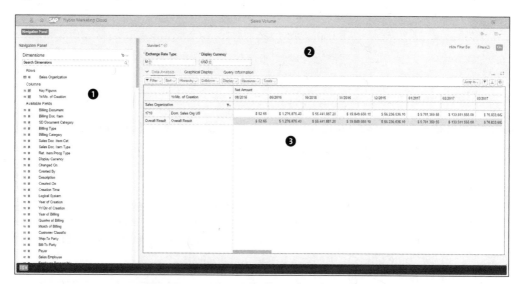

Figure 7.20 Sales Volume Multidimensional Analysis

As shown, the screen is split into three sections:

❶ **Navigation panel**

On the left is the navigation panel. This section provides all the dimension options available for this analysis. The dimensions are determined by a SAP Best Practices CDS view (discussed in further detail in Section 7.6). Adding or removing dimensions from the analysis is as easy as clicking the horizontal or vertical bar to the left of a data element name. Figure 7.21 shows the view after adding a new customer dimension.

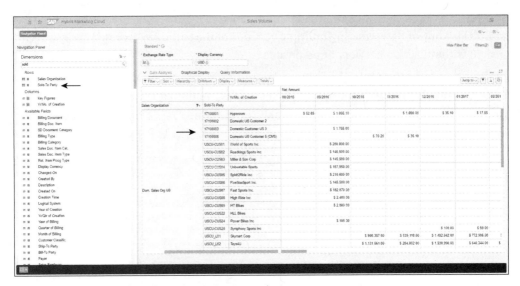

Figure 7.21 Adding New Dimension to Analysis

❷ Filters

The top section allows the user to filter the results. Standard filters will default to the initial view, but additional filters can be added by the user. In addition, if specific filters are used often, a variant can be saved for quicker access. Figure 7.22 shows some filters in use for a cost center analysis.

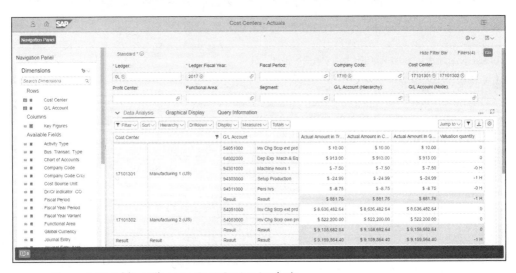

Figure 7.22 Adding Filters to Cost Center Analysis

In this case, the results are filtered to the manufacturing cost centers for the US operating company.

❸ Data

The third section provides the data results. Figure 7.20, Figure 7.21, and Figure 7.22 provide several examples of the data displays. The highlighted rows are *summary rows*, which can be hidden if desired. Additional options are provided for further customizing the analysis with filters, sorting, and more. One option is to change the view type to a graphical display; Figure 7.23 shows a graphical display from the profit and loss (P&L) analysis.

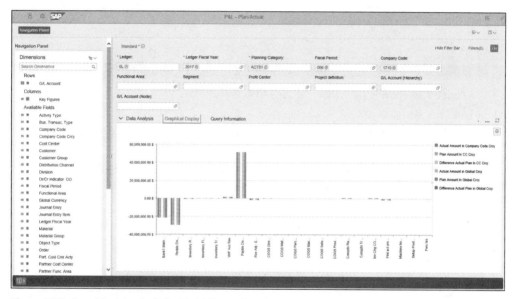

Figure 7.23 Graphical Analysis in Multidimensional View

The graphical analysis will require variables to be limited to two dimensions. In addition to viewing data graphically and across multiple dimensions, this section allows for jumping back into the applications that manage the data, thus enabling insight to action (as shown in Figure 7.24). After clicking the **Jump To** button, the user is shown a list of logical options based on the open analysis. In Figure 7.24, while viewing cost center data, the user can access cost center management applications as well as G/L and cost line item management applications.

Figure 7.24 Moving from Viewing Data to Acting on Data

As you can see, the multidimensional analysis tool provides comprehensive capabilities not only for exploring and interrogating data but also for using newfound knowledge to act on that data. Users nevertheless may still want to download the data to Excel—and that capability is provided as well, at the click of a button.

7.6   Customized Queries

With the dozens of SAP Best Practices views and supporting graphics and analytics tools, there may be no need for any customized reporting. Different businesses, however, will have different needs and may require reporting that isn't preconfigured in SAP Best Practices. For this purpose, SAP S/4HANA Cloud provides query design tools to develop tailored queries from SAP Best Practices data views and to develop custom views when the SAP Best Practices views don't provide the necessary data for a query, without affecting the quarterly upgrade process.

Central to queries is the concept of a *virtual data model* or CDS view. This view provides a semantic layer on top of the physical database, hiding technical details and providing user-friendly and understandable names. The data is still the live, real-time data in the SAP HANA database; it's just provided in a virtual view that's easier to use. Thousands of views are available in the system, as indicated in Figure 7.25.

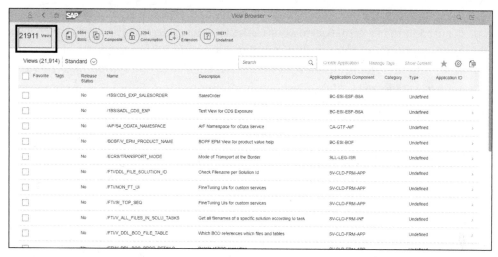

Figure 7.25 Available CDS Views

With this many views, it's necessary to filter down to what's needed for a specific query. Usable business terms like "sales" or "inventory" can be entered as search criteria and the views filtered down. After selecting and clicking a view, details such as the columns in the view are shown. Figure 7.26 shows an example of a material view.

C_HISTMATERIALSMALFUNCMANAGE Historic Materials

Application Component: PM
Description: Plant Maintenance
Tags:

Manage Tags

DEFINITION   ANNOTATION   CROSS REFERENCE

Column Name	Data Element	Description	Data Type	Length	
TECHNICALOBJECT	EAMS_TECH_OBJ_CONV	Technical Object Identifier	CHAR	40	>
TECHOBJISEQUIPORFUNCNLLOC	EAMS_TEC_OBJ_TYPE_VALUE	Technical Object Type	CHAR	20	>
MATERIAL	MATNR	Material Number	CHAR	40	>
STORAGELOCATION	LGORT_D	Storage Location	CHAR	4	>
PLANT	WERKS_D	Plant	CHAR	4	>
MATERIALNAME	MAKTX	Material Description	CHAR	40	>
RCRRCOFMATLUSAGEINTECHOBJ			DEC	10	>
MATERIALTYPE	MTART	Material Type	CHAR	4	>
MATERIALGROUP	MATKL	Material Group	CHAR	9	>

Figure 7.26 View Details

261

From this view, the user can explore all details of the view, including where and how it's used in the system. Backing out to the view list, selecting the view also enables menu items to open the multidimensional analytics viewer to see the data in the view. With these tools, an analytics specialist is enabled to find appropriate CDS views and create tailored queries to meet business user needs.

Figure 7.27 Creating Custom Query

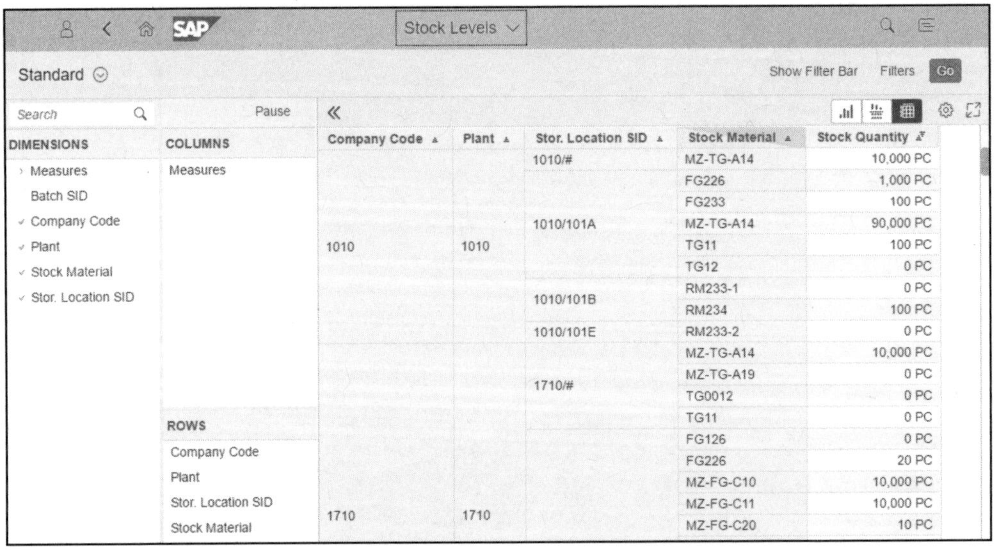

Figure 7.28 Preview of Custom Query

As mentioned earlier, if the data needed for a query isn't provided in one of the SAP Best Practices queries, a custom query can be created. In the example shown in Figure 7.27, a new view named **YY1_StockLevels** is being created.

When creating a view, specific fields can be selected, the view designed, and filters added. The view can then be previewed, as shown in Figure 7.28.

The query can be displayed as data or as a graph, like the graph shown in Figure 7.29.

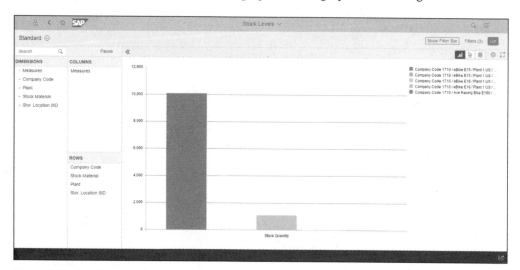

Figure 7.29 Creating Graphical Query

7.7   Summary

This chapter provided an overview of the embedded analytics capabilities within SAP S/4HANA Cloud. From high-level KPIs, readily displayed via tiles on the SAP Fiori launchpad, to detailed and customized queries that can be displayed in multidimensional formats or graphically, the analytics capabilities are virtually endless. All these capabilities are provided within the application using real-time data, providing the additional power of taking action directly upon review of the data. Further, because all the data is within the application, there's a single source of truth, promoting improved communications and better decision-making throughout an organization.

The next chapter discusses the ability to extend SAP S/4HANA Cloud to provide even greater capabilities.

PART III

Next Steps

In Part II, we looked within the four metaphorical walls of SAP S/4HANA Cloud. We discussed SAP S/4HANA Cloud's product functionality in depth by business process stream and workflow, including embedded analytics.

In Part III, we begin to look past the walls of SAP S/4HANA Cloud. We'll explore beyond core SAP S/4HANA Cloud functionality and look at expanding its reach through extensibility within the application and adding complementary applications, via either integration or custom development. Integrated applications can come from within the SAP world (e.g., SAP SuccessFactors, SAP BusinessObjects Cloud, SAP Hybris, etc.) or from the larger IT application world (e.g., third-party payroll software such as ADP, project management software, or other legacy applications). Custom-developed applications, built using SAP Cloud Platform, can provide functionality not covered by SAP or third parties while still providing a user experience consistent with SAP S/4HANA Cloud. Critical in this discussion of extending the application is the promise that these extensions won't remove a business from the SAP S/4HANA Cloud update path, allowing the company to continue to take advantage of all the new functionality and technology that will be continually released by SAP. By bolstering SAP S/4HANA Cloud with other complementary functions provided by external applications, the utility of SAP S/4HANA Cloud grows exponentially, enabling it to cover a broad canvas of business functions while maintaining a strong SAP digital core.

Chapter 8

Integrations: Can You Connect SAP S/4HANA Cloud with Other Applications?

With SAP S/4HANA Cloud's strong digital core as the foundation, the ability to extend its strength via integration multiplies the functionality and capabilities of the SAP S/4HANA Cloud value to the customer.
—Mike Foley, vice president, Cloud ERP

The depth and richness of core SAP S/4HANA Cloud provide the primary building blocks needed for most businesses looking to implement a holistic business framework. In fact, for many organizations, core SAP S/4HANA Cloud can and will cover all business needs. This scenario holds true for two primary and common SAP S/4HANA Cloud use case scenarios:

1. **Growth-stage businesses**

   This use case centers on early-stage businesses that are of some scale (~$10m in annual revenue/turnover and above) and looking to implement a more robust IT backend system that handles more than financials. These business are looking to remove barriers to fast growth and are working with aggressive strategies to enter greenfield markets or disrupt incumbents in existing markets. For these organizations, scalability is essential.

2. **Two-tiered ERP systems**

   This use case centers on organizations that most likely have already implemented larger enterprise software packages such as SAP ERP or on-premise SAP S/4HANA and are looking to deploy a lightweight and faster-to-deploy ERP system quickly for their less-complicated, potentially remote business units who still need core ERP functionality.

Figure 8.1 depicts the two-tiered scenario.

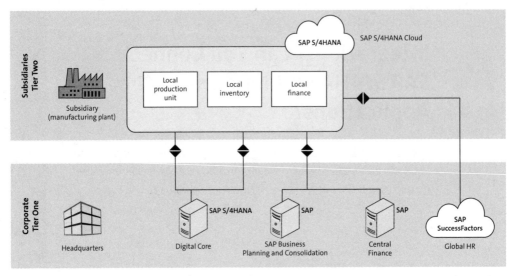

Figure 8.1 Common Scenarios in Which SAP S/4HANA Cloud Functionality Doesn't Need to be Extended

However, organizations looking to expand SAP S/4HANA Cloud functionality by integrating with other applications can do so. Fortunately, there are several kinds of connections available between SAP S/4HANA Cloud and external applications.

The following sections highlight some of the main methods currently available for SAP S/4HANA Cloud integration. The various types of integration with SAP S/4HANA Cloud are tremendously important to the product's ability to effectively expand core SAP S/4HANA Cloud functionality. This chapter will explore how the integration feature within the SAP S/4HANA Cloud world can provide the additional benefit of functionality expansion. The integration options including built-in (generally SAP-to-SAP) and custom integrations (usually unique to a specific customer) will be discussed in detail. The following subsections highlight the most common and valuable extensibility opportunities for this new ERP SaaS platform.

8.1   Built-in Integrations

SAP S/4HANA Cloud is designed to be able to natively integrate with various SAP applications and products to extend its functionality. Specifically, SAP S/4HANA Cloud is purposely constructed so that other SAP applications can be leveraged not only to drive further business value in non-core-ERP business functions, but also to drive additional SAP software consumption.

Based on the greater SAP product portfolio design (aligned with its acquisition strategy), SAP has developed a more holistic style of business function framework with distinct products determined by commercial area. The following list highlights the other cloud-based applications with which SAP S/4HANA Cloud is typically integrated along with the business value you can expect to gain from these out-of-the-box integrations:

- **Concur**
  SAP's travel management software platform can be integrated with both SAP and non-SAP applications. Core functions often leveraged by organizations include expense management and business travel booking. Organizations have an incentive to integrate Concur because it combines a spend management tool with SAP business applications so financial teams can more easily and accurately manage expenses and gain a complete view of their finances.

  Concur is designed to reduce costs by standardizing and streamlining travel and expense management throughout the enterprise. Finance teams can process employee T&E quickly for faster payments. Controllers get end-to-end visibility into spending with automated data transfer from SAP S/4HANA Cloud to Concur. Business users have an incentive for uptake because it streamlines trip planning and the administrative overhead of filing expense reports. Teams can also quickly and efficiently identify and correct financial posting issues.

  Integration with SAP S/4HANA Cloud enables users to export cost objects such as cost centers, internal orders, and WBS elements; import expense reports and cash advances ready for posting; and export posting confirmations.

- **SAP SuccessFactors**
  SAP's HCM software platform includes functions related to payroll, learning, recruiting, employee management, onboarding, and other core HR processes.

  SAP SuccessFactors Employee Central, designed to be an organization's core cloud-based HR system, is the system of record for all HR data. Integration with SAP S/4HANA Cloud means systems can share data on workers (employee data, contingent worker data, employment data, etc.), corporate structure (enterprise structure and reporting lines), and HR-related financial data (company code and cost center information) among other aspects of continual HR management.

  Broadly speaking, SAP SuccessFactors Employee Central is designed for three audiences. HR leaders gain tools to advise business managers on business-driven people strategies. Business leaders can better translate strategy into operational success by automating end-to-end processes across administrative and business functions. Workers gain easy-to-use tools for self-service, continuous improvement, and social collaboration. Integration with SAP S/4HANA Cloud strengthens a company's ability to serve all three audiences with better data and a more comprehensive experience.

- **SAP Ariba**

  SAP's procurement, contracting and sourcing solution is actually two platforms in one: SAP Ariba Sourcing and the Ariba Network. Ariba Network enables buyers to manage the entire procurement process from source to settlement, while controlling spending, finding new savings, and building stronger supply chains. SAP Ariba Sourcing helps businesses find qualified suppliers, accelerate sourcing cycles, and create higher-value agreements. Integrated with SAP S/4HANA Cloud's operational procurement and related finance processes, this solution helps organizations interact with trading partners more strategically, especially when users follow the SAP Activate implementation methodology and its industry best practices.

  SAP Ariba is open to all systems and all types of goods and services. Through integration with SAP S/4HANA Cloud, you can access SAP Ariba's core functionality, including operational sourcing, self-service, both direct and indirect material procurement, services procurement, and payment/discount management. Users can digitize and automate procurement/finance processes with the application's built-in functionality. Ultimately, users integrating with SAP S/4HANA Cloud should be able to realize projects faster, with predictable outcomes, and at a lower cost.

- **SAP Hybris**

  This multifunction CRM and e-commerce platform allows organizations to manage marketing and sales functions. Typical SAP S/4HANA Cloud integration scenarios with SAP Hybris include CRM cloud functionality, such as SAP Hybris Cloud for Customer. The business functionality brings sales, customer service, and social CRM together in a single cloud-based system.

  A typical flow of information for companies that integrate (and therefore replicate accounts, contacts, and materials from SAP S/4HANA Cloud to SAP Hybris Cloud for Customer) is for users to create a new sales opportunity from data in SAP Hybris Cloud for Customer and then create a quote with pricing and a follow-on sales order that originates in the SAP S/4HANA Cloud system. Once the sales order is in the SAP S/4HANA system, the sales order ID is sent back to SAP Hybris Cloud for Customer. This seamless data sharing reduces TCO by leveraging information you already store in your digital core system, and by using SAP S/4HANA Cloud to manage processes after sales order creation.

- **SAP Analytics Cloud**

  This application provides analytics, business intelligence, data visualization, and re-porting above and beyond the embedded analytics that are part of SAP S/4HANA Cloud. This product expands upon what SAP S/4HANA Cloud provides and is a common integration option for organizations looking to expand analytics functions.

  SAP Analytics Cloud is a unified analytics platform delivering integrated business intelligence (BI), planning, and predictive capabilities, and provides a very strong compliment to SAP S/4HANA Cloud for BI and financial planning. Strong BI and visualization capabilities, along with live connectivity, augment native SAP S/4HANA Cloud analytics for both planning and non-planning reporting use cases.

  SAP Analytics Cloud has enriched acquisition and live reporting, along with forth-coming financial planning enhancements. It supplements native SAP S/4HANA Cloud capabilities with rich analytics and visualization capabilities. Tighter inte-gration and support for a broader range of planning and reporting scenarios are planned for future releases.

- **SAP Fieldglass**

  SAP's contingent workforce application is leveraged by organizations for managing external nonemployee talent. Companies typically leverage this solution if they want to maintain a vendor management system (VMS). Integration with S/4HANA Cloud extends a company's contingent labor hiring and management processes to enhance and automate their flexible workforce management and services pro-curement programs.

  SAP Fieldglass is designed to manage high volumes of users and transactions to meet the needs of the largest of organizations. It can scale for growth with high availability, redundancy and security. Integration brings additional benefits to SAP S/4HANA Cloud users, including the ability to digitize processing of invoices for external staff. Companies can automate postings by transferring master data (cost centers, internal orders, organizational data such as plants and purchasing organizations, etc.) from SAP S/4HANA Cloud to SAP Fieldglass. The pre-config-ured integration with SAP Fieldglass means SAP S/4HANA Cloud users can opti-mize their workforce both short term by speeding staff augmentation and long-term by sustaining the right workforce mix for flexibility and business results.

Figure 8.2 highlights the current, built-in, SAP-to-SAP integrations available for SAP S/4HANA Cloud.

8

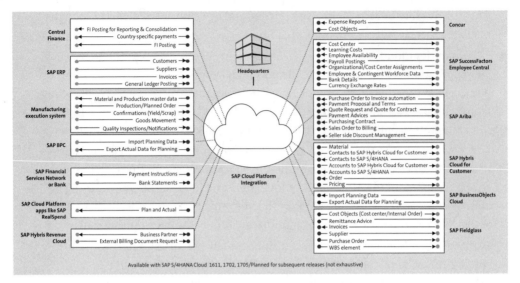

Figure 8.2 SAP S/4HANA Cloud SAP-to-SAP Built-in Integrations

These SAP-delivered, preconfigured, SAP S/4HANA Cloud to other SAP product integrations are available out of the box using internal configuration methods for application-to-application connectivity.

The configuration for these integrations does require a bit of technical knowledge, including infrastructure, passwords/usernames, connectivity data, and so on, but it doesn't require extensive technical expertise. SAP provides a wealth of step-by-step integration instructions for how to configure SAP-to-SAP product connectivity. One excellent resource for step-by-step SAP S/4HANA to external SAP product integration is the SAP API Business Hub, which provides a wealth of integration how-to resources exist. The website and corresponding knowledge can be found at *https:// api.sap.com/#/shell/integration*.

Behind the Curtain: SAP S/4HANA Cloud Integration Strategy

Integration with other, non-SAP S/4HANA Cloud products is a current and future method for expanding greater customer functionality; however, it's possible that SAP S/4HANA Cloud will continue to expand upon its internal business processes to begin to capture more features. Thus, some integration with external, non-SAP S/4HANA Cloud applications in the future may no longer be needed. This most likely will include even market vertical business processes not being positioned in the near-term roadmap. Therefore, customer-created custom (SAP Cloud Platform-based) application functionality to fill this gap therefore may no longer be required. SAP functionality currently handled via other SAP products (such as SAP SuccessFactors and SAP Ariba) will never be included in SAP S/4HANA Cloud; however, customer-specific, custom-created application functionality may be included in future SAP S/4HANA Cloud releases.

To make these prepackaged integrations easier to implement, SAP provides a wealth of documentation, including an ever-growing library of prebuilt integrations. These prebuilt integrations break down even further to include artifacts, descriptions, process flows, and additional helpful documentation. For example, in Figure 8.3, SAP depicts the out-of-the-box SAP S/4HANA Cloud to SAP SuccessFactors integration specific to the data exchange related to employee and cost center allocation.

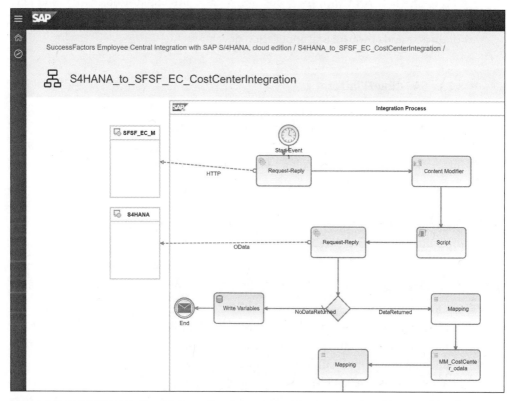

Figure 8.3 SAP S/4HANA Cloud Integration Scenario and Documentation for Prepackaged Integration

8.2   Custom Integrations

The method by which SAP S/4HANA Cloud enables integration with other applications is via an application program interface (API). APIs are packets of structured code within the data container as well as the method by which one sending system handles the processing of that information and transfer to the receiving system.

As part of its intelligent design, SAP S/4HANA Cloud provides three distinct methods of API connectivity:

1. Web-based technology APIs, such as OData, REST, and SOAP

2. More traditional SAP APIs, such as BAPIs and IDocs

3. CDS views, which can be exposed as OData services

The next sections provide insight into SAP S/4HANA's model regarding the integration of SAP S/4HANA with more custom, related SAP applications. SAP Cloud Platform and its corresponding development platforms provide a robust environment for diverse and powerful SAP application development.

8.2.1   SAP Cloud Platform

To make the SAP S/4HANA Cloud application integration structured and seamless, SAP has constructed a process and framework with which to deploy integrations easily. The platform in which to develop, test, deploy, and support SAP S/4HANA Cloud integrations is known as SAP Cloud Platform.

SAP Cloud Platform is an SAP open PaaS that enables developers to develop custom applications for SAP S/4HANA Cloud integration. SAP Cloud Platform provides tremendous flexibility for what and how SAP Cloud Platform apps are created, leveraging industry-standard development environments such as Cloud Foundry and Neo.

SAP Cloud Platform includes multiple options for SAP S/4HANA Cloud-related application development. The two primary development environments are as follows:

1. **Cloud Foundry**
   Open source and based on open standards, Cloud Foundry provides choices for technologies, runtimes, and services when using SAP Cloud Platform, thereby allowing for great flexibility in your development process. Cloud Foundry also allows for native SAP HANA development with SAP HANA XSA. SAP recommends that you use the Cloud Foundry environment to develop 12-factor and/or

microservices-based applications, for services for applications using non-Java run-times, and for Internet of things (IoT) and machine-learning scenarios.

2. **Neo**

Neo is a feature-rich and easy-to-use development environment that allows you to develop Java, SAP HANA XS, and HTML5 applications. SAP recommends that you use the Neo environment to develop HTML5 and complex Java applications.

SAP Cloud Platform provides multiple options for the development of applications based on the specific needs of the given application. Ranging from development platforms to specific industry standards, this suite of toolsets provides a robust framework for the rapid design, development, and deployment of SAP S/4HANA Cloud applications. The following is a list of some of the more frequently used tools:

- **Cloud Cockpit**
  Central SAP hub for managing activities specific to your SAP Cloud Platform sub-account and accessing the key information related to your SAP Cloud Platform application.

- **SAP Web IDE**
  This toolset is an integrated development environment (IDE) in which multiple application developers and users can work together collaboratively to construct SAPUI5 applications. SAP Web IDE enables development teams to prototype, develop, and implement SAP Cloud Platform applications quickly.

- **Cloud Connector**
  The Cloud Connector exists as the link between SAP Cloud Platform on-demand applications and on-premise systems.

- **SDK for Java development**
  The software development kit (SDK) for Java-based programming contains all components needed to work within the SAP Cloud Platform for Java application development.

- **SDK for iOS**
  This SDK is much like the Java development SDK, but the focus is on Apple's mobile operating system, iOS.

The beauty of SAP Cloud Platform is its self-contained nature. Within SAP Cloud Platform, all the necessary components, tools, services, and deployment capabilities are available for application construction specifically within the SAP Cloud Platform Cockpit. As shown in Figure 8.4, the SAP Cloud Platform Cockpit creates the necessary framework for SAP application development.

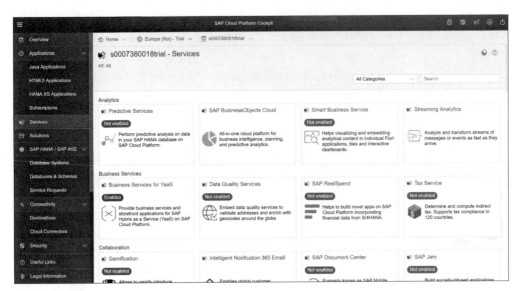

Figure 8.4 SAP Cloud Platform Cockpit

8.2.2   Development Process and Components

When developing custom integrations for SAP S/4HANA Cloud applications, the development process, and its various components, it's important to first identify which types of applications your organization needs to develop.

The following are the three types of scenarios available for SAP Cloud Platform development:

1. **New cloud applications**
    This scenario is a rapid, lightweight method for the deployment of custom SAP S/4HANA Cloud applications, whether focused on cloud-first SAP deployments or not. Most likely, this scenario would be utilized for an SAP S/4HANA Cloud implementation that doesn't follow a two-tiered SAP S/4HANA Cloud approach.

2. **Extend on-premise applications**
    This scenario is most likely leveraged for the two-tiered on-premise SAP S/4HANA to SAP S/4HANA Cloud scenario. As the name suggests, this scenario extends a company's on-premise SAP ERP solution via cloud applications. Specific to the two-tiered SAP S/4HANA Cloud model, this scenario can apply when the combined two-tier holistic functionality requires additional customer-required functionality and deployment via an SAP cloud application.

3. **Extend cloud**

   Like the new cloud application scenario, this model is utilized when deploying SAP S/4HANA Cloud via an SAP Cloud Platform application beyond core SAP S/4HANA Cloud functionality. This could be either through new SAP Cloud Platform application construction or integration with another application, such as SAP SuccessFactors. In either situation, SAP S/4HANA Cloud exists as the core through cloud extension.

Figure 8.5 illustrates all three scenarios and how SAP Cloud Platform can extend SAP S/4HANA Cloud functionality.

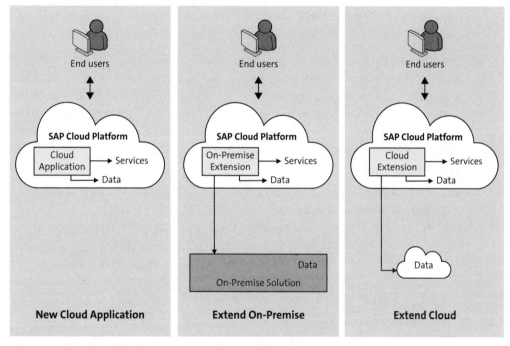

Figure 8.5 SAP Cloud Platform Extension Scenarios

The following sections highlight the positives and negatives associated with the development and corresponding development process associated with the construction of SAP S/4HANA Cloud integration. Some of these considerations include long-term SAP S/4HANA Cloud application support costs.

Internal Development Pros and Cons

There are multiple choices for how an organization wishes to deploy SAP Cloud Platform applications within an SAP S/4HANA Cloud landscape. One solution is to develop the application in-house or internally.

If a company has the internal capabilities and/or the desire to internalize this skillset, this option is most definitely a viable one. The advantages of internally developing SAP Cloud Platform applications are the same as those of internalizing any other technical skillset (including in-house knowledge, leveraging internal business process functional knowledge, potential cost savings, etc.). However, one strong argument against internalizing this development process resides in the potential complexity of the given application(s), as well as the rapidly changing technologies within the SAP Cloud Platform world with additional services and the like.

The other development option is to partner with an SAP Cloud Platform consultant. Again, the argument for leveraging a dedicated SAP development expert is to outsource technical services to organizations that specialize in this type of work. As this technology continues to become more common, at least within the greater SAP ecosystem, the options for strong partners continue to grow. Likewise, cost continues to decline, which always exists as a major factor in any customer-vendor relationship, regardless of software.

Behind the Curtain: Who Am I?

Many organizations struggle with the question of how much SAP expertise to internalize. Some organizations believe strongly in internalizing a great deal of SAP knowledge, whereas others believe equally as strongly in focusing on their core business, rather than being an SAP consulting shop. Larger organizations are afforded with more options based on resources; for smaller organizations, those options simply are not available. Regardless of whether a company possesses the luxury of choice, it seems that more organizations are selecting options somewhere in the middle. More specifically, companies are choosing to internalize more business-focused resources and partnering with an SAP consultant for the more technical activities. Furthermore, as SAP S/4HANA Cloud begins to be deployed within smaller organizations (start-ups, family businesses, etc.) in which resources are generally scarcer, the option to internalize SAP expertise simply isn't there. For those companies not deploying SAP S/4HANA Cloud within a two-tiered landscape, these SAP S/4HANA Cloud shops run leaner. This is something to think about when looking at SAP S/4HANA Cloud as a core ERP platform and the costs associated with long-term support.

Development Process

The method by which to develop an SAP Cloud Platform application requires a book of its own. However, the following section provides a high-level overview of the steps and required toolsets needed for application development.

> **Note**
>
> If you're interested in learning more, a wealth of instructions, tutorials, and information exists from SAP PRESS and from other valuable SAP resources, such as SAP Open-Course, SAP Community, and so on.

Figure 8.6 shows the high-level flow of the development process for the deployment of an SAP Cloud Platform application. The figure depicts scenarios from both trial and productive development processes.

For the purposes of this discussion, let's assume that you're in a productive scenario. (If you're exploring this functionality within a trial scenario, the process is easier, and your objective most likely will be simply to create a proof-of-concept application.) As such, the development process is broken into three primary steps: application infrastructure set-up, application deployment, and application monitoring. Let's breakdown at a high level the three primary components of the SAP Cloud Platform application lifecycle:

1. **Application infrastructure setup**

   The activities associated with this first step can be a bit technical. These activities require the initial software purchase and the allocation of resources needed for application development.

   – Within this first step of application infrastructure setup, you needs to create the development user setup, allowing your (or your partner's) developers to access SAP Cloud Platform.

   – The next major step within the SAP Cloud Platform application infrastructure setup is to select the environment in which to develop: Neo or Cloud Foundry. Section 8.2.1 speaks in greater detail about which platform to leverage in a given situation.

   – Finally, the final action within the application infrastructure setup in this SAP Cloud Platform lifecycle stage is security administration. The security configuration required differs depending upon which environment or platform (i.e., Neo or Cloud Foundry) is selected, but conceptually the requirements are the same: Provision SAP Cloud Platform developers across the appropriate data-bases with the necessary access, along with any potential SAP Single Sign-On functionality.

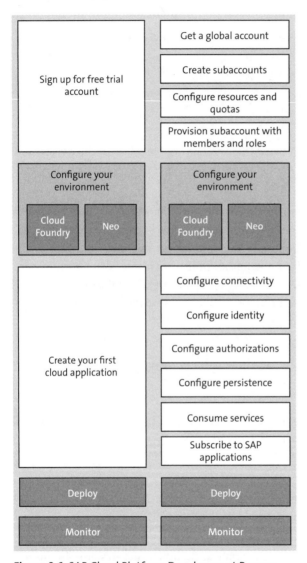

Figure 8.6 SAP Cloud Platform Development Process

2. **Application deployment**

   Within this step, you design, develop, test, and deploy the SAP Cloud Platform application. The activities at a conceptual level are the same independent of environment; however, the technical tactical activities do differ depending upon the specific environment of choice, whether within an SAP S/4HANA Cloud landscape or other cloud development platforms.

   Table 8.1 highlights the two different paths associated with the high-level differences between the deployment of SAP Cloud Platform applications within the Neo and Cloud Foundry platforms.

Cloud Foundry	Neo
Develop, deploy, and manage applications	Develop applications
Develop and deploy SAP HANA XSA applications	Operate applications
Application logging	Multitarget applications

Table 8.1 Two SAP Cloud Platform Application Development Paths: Cloud Foundry or Neo

   This phase within the process is where the magic happens. Specifically, this process is the most active for the SAP Cloud Platform developers, beginning with the ideation of the app and ending with deployment to a productive state.

   The development lifecycle for this phase is typically an iterative process or Agile development process. SAP's new development process is known as SAP Activate. With short sprints and focused, results-driven iterations, SAP Activate is meant to create quick outcomes that produce success or failure indications for quick pivoting. SAP Activate often is used for SAP Cloud Platform application development.

3. **Application monitoring**

   The final stage within SAP Cloud Platform deployment is application monitoring. The activities within this stage include the upkeep of the application, including application logging, break/fix activities, increased functionality, and other production support responsibilities.

8.2.3   APIs

Another major exciting puzzle piece within the greater SAP S/4HANA Cloud world is the use of APIs.

Whether for IT in general, SAP, SAP S/4HANA Cloud, or other, the usage of APIs enables interfacing between different applications. Specific to the SAP S/4HANA Cloud space, APIs facilitate the transfer of data or information from SAP S/4HANA Cloud through SAP Cloud Platform to another business-relevant application. The use of APIs lets SAP S/4HANA Cloud extend its business functionality by leveraging other application functionality richness.

The wealth of SAP-provided APIs is tremendous. To continue to make SAP S/4HANA Cloud more accessible, less complex, and more plug and play in nature, SAP has created an SAP API Business Hub filled with many pages of content, available online at *https://api.sap.com/*.

Within the SAP API Business Hub, SAP breaks down the APIs available for integration between systems, business services, and SAP-to-SAP integration capabilities (as described earlier). Figure 8.7 highlights the primary functions and features within the SAP API Business Hub.

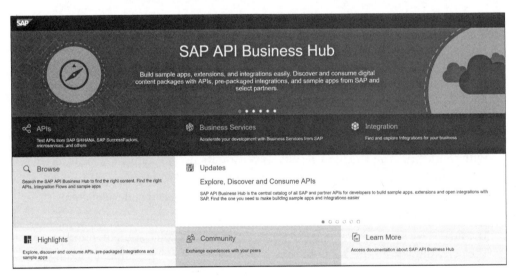

Figure 8.7 SAP API Business Hub

Digging a bit deeper, within the SAP S/4HANA Cloud-specific API pages at *https://api. sap.com/#/shell/discover/contentpackage/SAPS4HANACloud*, specific SAP S/4HANA Cloud documentation for pertinent APIs is available. Figure 8.88 depicts the current list of SAP S/4HANA Cloud-specific APIs available at the time of writing.

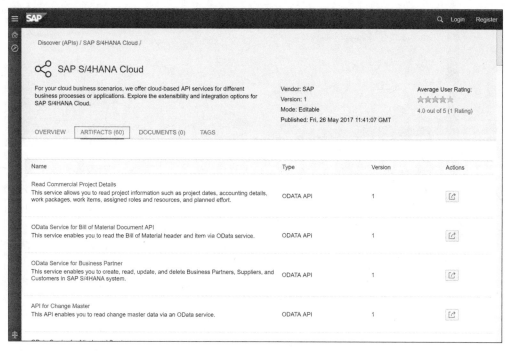

Figure 8.8 SAP S/4HANA Cloud API Catalog

For a bit more understanding of how an SAP S/4HANA Cloud API works in the real world, let's take a real-life example and break down the logic, application, and process specifically for the creation of a sales order, as follows:

- **Business case**
  SAP S/4HANA Cloud acts as the central application within a landscape for capturing all business activities. Within this business scenario, an external system creates a limited number of sales orders outside of SAP S/4HANA Cloud.

- **Technical application**
  Within the SAP API Business Hub, an SAP S/4HANA Cloud API exists that allows for the consumption of an external sales order via an out-of-the-box API. The required components of the sales order, including sales order header and item level information, are available for the external third-party sales order creation application.

  Figure 8.9 shows how the SAP API Business Hub provides explicit documentation on specific sales order API services (such as *A Sales Order Get*), along with the ability to generate code (Figure 8.10) across a variety of common coding languages.

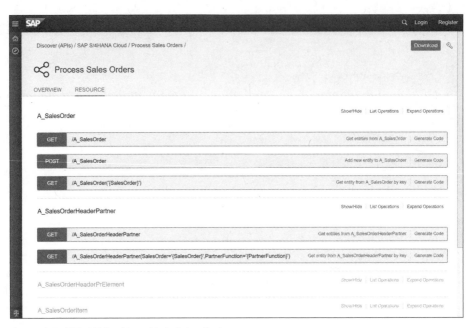

Figure 8.9 SAP API Business Hub Sales Order

Figure 8.10 SAP API Business Hub Sales Order Services: Generate Code Functionality

As you can see, SAP is attempting to make the extension of SAP S/4HANA Cloud functionality more robust and easier to consume to cast a wider net for end user (and company) adoption. This API list is constantly evolving and provides the SAP ecosystem with a real-time, up-to-date catalog.

8.2.4   Electronic Data Interchange

Another common integration scenario widely used within SAP S/4HANA Cloud is Electronic Data Interchange (EDI). EDI is frequently leveraged as a communication vehicle between SAP S/4HANA Cloud and third-party systems that use EDI industry-standard transactions, such as business partner communication. Using APIs pivoting off SAP Cloud Platform, SAP S/4HANA Cloud can exchange business data, such as purchase order creation and shipping notifications. EDI is an older communication method that predates more flexible and cutting-edge middleware technologies, such as SAP Cloud Platform. Still, it's been a predecessor for future generations of communication standards, providing a common language and framework for both system-to-system data exchange and industry standards for business data definitions (e.g., the common transaction EDI 856: Shipping notifications). Figure 8.11 provides another high-level depiction of how SAP S/4HANA Cloud leverages API's for EDI transactions.

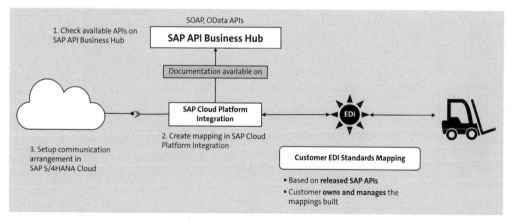

Figure 8.11 SAP S/4HANA Cloud EDI to API Exchange

8.3   Summary

As you've seen in this and earlier chapters, SAP is positioning SAP S/4HANA Cloud as the digital core for organizations looking towards a cloud-first ERP approach. Via extensibility and integration, SAP S/4HANA Cloud can expand upon its core business processes through the use of SAP-provided APIs and custom integration.

SAP-provided frameworks such as SAP Cloud Platform provide an infrastructure, a development platform, a common language, and a community that allow organizations to constantly evolve as needed for successful SAP S/4HANA Cloud deployment.

In the next chapter, we'll look at additional methods for SAP S/4HANA Cloud personalization, enhancing an organization's and user's experience without modifying the product. In-app extensibility provides robust personalization capabilities, allowing you to make the SAP S/4HANA Cloud experience unique without code modification—a core tenet of the SAP S/4HANA Cloud philosophy.

Chapter 9

Extensibility: How Can You Personalize SAP S/4HANA Cloud?

Customization has become a negative term when associated with ERP solutions. It implies cost and timeline overruns, and creation of a viscous application that can't take advantage of vendor upgrades readily. SAP S/4HANA Cloud can't be customized, but it can be extended to provide functionality beyond what's standard without impacting upgradeability.

Although ERP systems provide end-to-end functionality across a broad array of businesses, individual organizations will often require additional functionality that's unique to their operations. This requirement often leads to excessive customization, which in turn removes a company from the standard upgrade path. The result is an unwieldy system that's costly to maintain, difficult (at best) to integrate with other best practices applications, and unable to support new technologies that can drive further business productivity. Companies are left with a quandary: Do they not fully support the business but keep the system maintainable and costs reasonable, or do they leave the upgrade path via customizations to support the business while taking on significant maintenance costs that may exceed the value the customization brings to the business? Worse yet, the latter choice may ultimately prevent the business from being able to adapt to changes in technology and the marketplace.

In designing SAP S/4HANA Cloud, SAP looked to solve this dilemma by providing the flexibility needed to develop customized functionality while allowing companies to stay on the upgrade schedule and take advantage of emerging technologies like machine learning and digital assistants. Because this functionality can't change the inner workings of the application, it is not considered customization. Instead, the term extensibility is used to indicate the core solution is being extended, not changed.

SAP S/4HANA Cloud users can personalize the application through two kinds of extensions:

1. *In-app extensions:* Customization of fields and business rules without coding

2. *Side-by-side extensions:* Built on SAP's Cloud Platform, providing full-fledged applications designed with the same look and feel as the SAP S/4HANA Cloud application itself

This chapter will take an in-depth look at in-app extensibility and provide an overview of side-by-side extensibility, exploring the virtually limitless potential to enhance functionality and fill any gap. We will also briefly touch upon customer-developed extensions that can be created using the SAP S/4HANA Cloud software development kit (SDK).

9.1   In-App Extensibility

In-app extensibility lets you tailor components of SAP S/4HANA Cloud within the application—without customizing the software. Such extensibility can include business configuration, UI/form/report layout adoption, customizing fields, adding objects and logic, and more.

The following sections cover who can create in-app extensions, how to determine what applications can be extended, and the various types of in-app extension capabilities (from editing fields to programming logic and more).

9.1.1   In-App Extensibility Authorization

For lighter changes, such as changing the name of a field or relocating a group of fields on a screen, properly authorized business users can complete the extensions relatively easily. More extensive changes, like adding new business logic or new data tables, generally require a more technical team member. In either case, these changes are pervasive through the system, affecting all users. As such, the ability to make changes is secured. Making extensibility changes requires the extensibility business catalog (SAP_CORE_BC_EXT) to be assigned to a business role assigned to the specified team member. For this reason, it may be useful to create a business role just for extensibility, then assign that role to qualified business users or technical support specialists.

9.1.2   Locating Extensible Apps

Before we get too far, it's important to note that not all SAP S/4HANA Cloud apps are extensible. Only apps that are built on SAPUI5 are extensible. An example of a SAPUI5 app is shown in Figure 9.1.

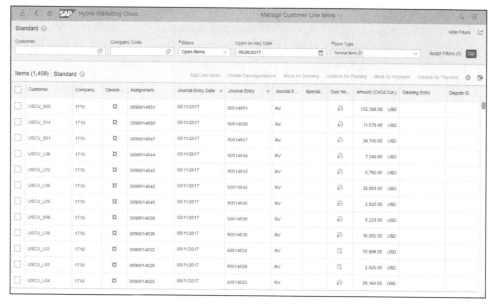

Figure 9.1 SAPUI5 User Interface

By comparison, an app built in SAP GUI is shown in Figure 9.2.

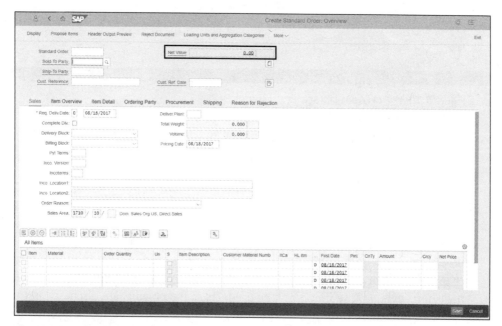

Figure 9.2 SAP GUI User Interface

Note that the URL for this app contains the text *sap-ui-tech-hint=GUI* at the end. There are a couple of other ways to tell if an app is an SAPUI5 extensible app or not. In general, when opening an SAP GUI app, a new tab will open, whereas an SAPUI5 app will open in the current tab. Also, when in doubt, you can search the SAP Fiori apps library for an app, as shown in Figure 9.3.

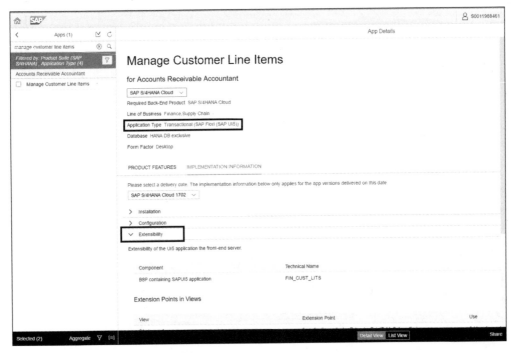

Figure 9.3 SAP Fiori Apps Library

The library will confirm the nature of the app and provide additional technical information if desired. With extensibility capability confirmed, the team can move forward.

9.1.3   Changing, Adding, and Deleting Fields and Groups on a Screen

Apps come preconfigured with screen fields that are deemed necessary based on SAP Best Practices. These fields may suffice for a company's needs, or they may need to be changed to match company vernacular, have company-specific fields added, or have fields removed because they won't be used. These in-app edits are discussed in the following sections.

Changing Fields

Updating fields and field groupings can be performed within the app itself. Figure 9.4 shows the standard **Create Customer Project** screen.

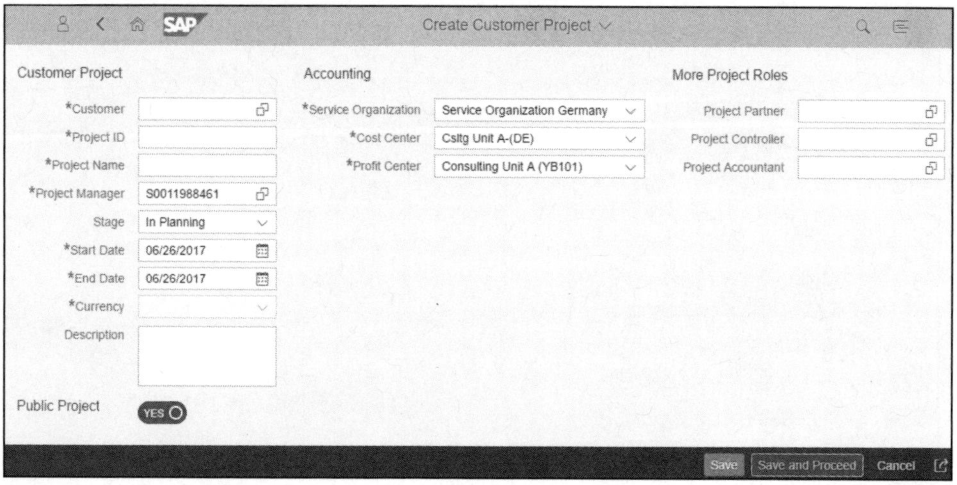

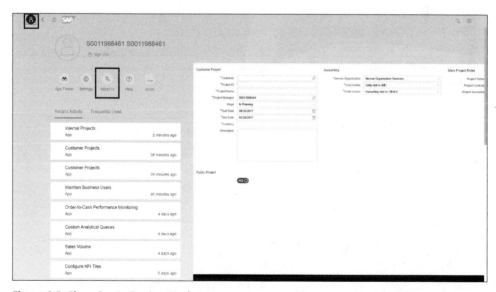

Figure 9.4 Create Customer Project

Click the user icon in the top-left corner for options, then change to design mode by clicking the **Adapt IU** icon, as shown in Figure 9.5.

Figure 9.5 Changing to Design Mode

In design mode, changing the look and fields is an extremely user-friendly experience. Right-click a field to access a menu with options to edit that field or create a new field, as shown in Figure 9.6.

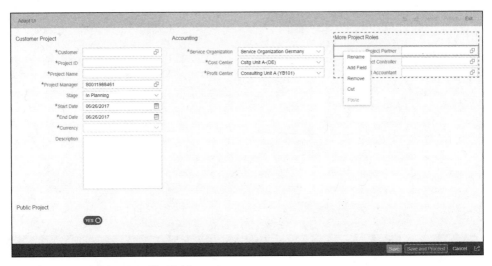

Figure 9.6 Editing Specific Field

Renaming a field is as simple as typing over the existing name. Groups of fields can also be renamed. Move fields (or groups) via the **Cut** and **Paste** menu items or via drag and drop. Figure 9.7 shows the screen after the **More Project Roles** group was renamed to **Project Governance** and moved to the middle section of the screen.

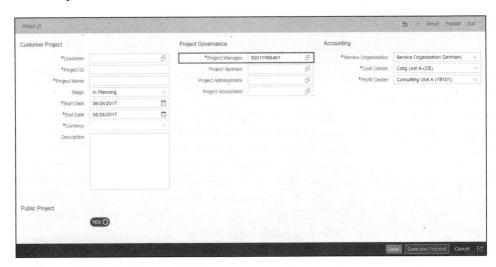

Figure 9.7 Moving Groups of Fields

Adding Fields

Adding a group consists of just typing in the new group name, but adding fields requires a few more steps. Figure 9.8 shows the window that displays when adding a field. The list provided shows both standard fields enabled for this screen and any custom fields that have been created and enabled for this screen. In this example, the **Estimated Cost** field is standard and available, so it will be selected. Two additional fields, **Estimated Effort** and **Estimated Duration**, will need to be created so that they can be selected.

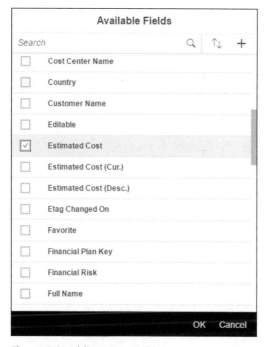

Figure 9.8 Adding New Field

Click the plus sign (**+**) in the top-right corner of the pop-up window to see a list of created **Custom Fields** (as shown in Figure 9.9).

If the desired field hasn't been created, click the plus sign again to open the detail screen for adding a field (see Figure 9.10).

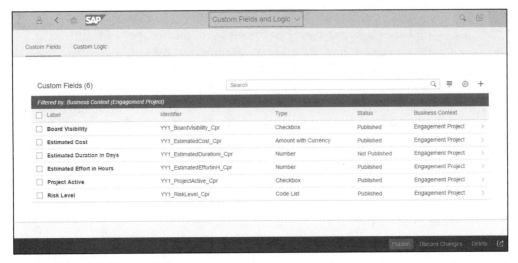

Figure 9.9 Custom Fields List

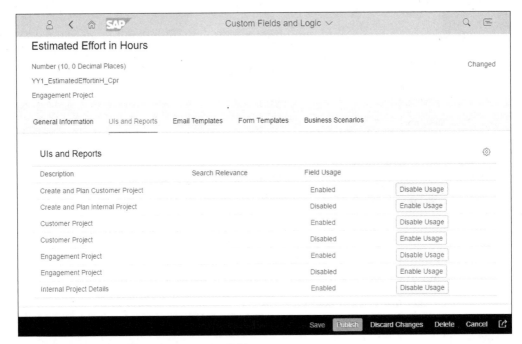

Figure 9.10 Adding New Custom Field

As you can see, there are tabs for general information about the field and for enabling the field for specific uses on screens, reports, email templates, and forms.

Now that the fields are created, they can be selected and placed on the screen and the new UI published. The finished product is shown in Figure 9.11.

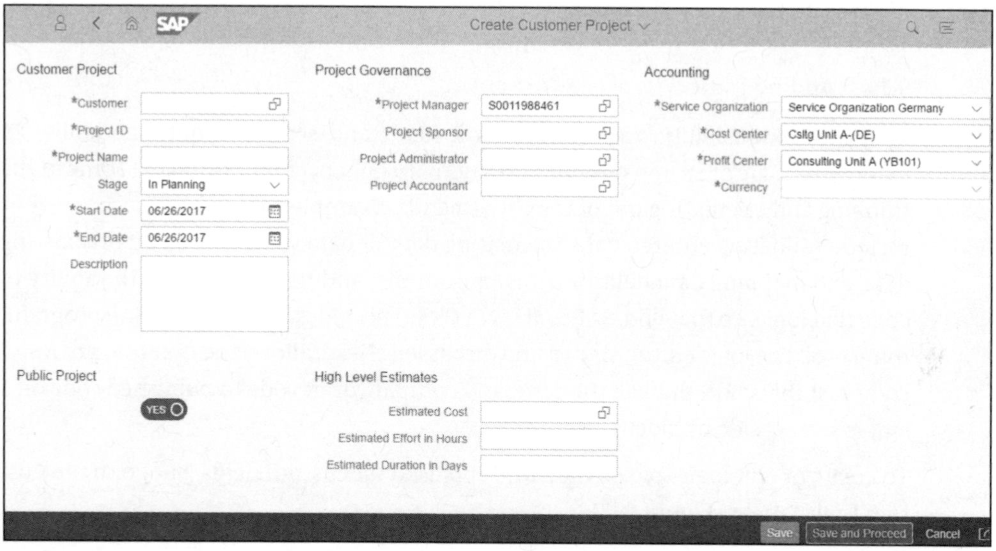

Figure 9.11 Create Customer Project Screen with Changes

It's important to note that this new UI will be what all users of the app see. In some apps, you can customize options such as filter criteria for a specific user; however, in-app extensibility changes apply to all users.

Deleting Fields

The process for deleting fields is like that for adding or renaming fields. The field edit menu list (from right-clicking a field in design mode; see Figure 9.6) also provides an option to remove a field. Removing a field from the app doesn't remove it from the system database, but it does remove it from the screen, clearing the way for additional fields or decluttering the screen by removing fields that won't be used. Removing such fields is considered a best practice to help minimize confusion and training time.

Undoing Changes

It's helpful to know that changes can always be undone and the UI set back to its original state (even after publishing). Back in Figure 9.6, in the top-right corner of the screen, you can see a **Reset** button. Clicking it will return the entire user interface to the original version delivered. The ability to tailor SAP Fiori screens can be an exceedingly powerful tool. With that power comes responsibility—but, with the ability to reset the UI, also forgiveness.

9.1.4 Adding Logic

In-app UI extensibility doesn't stop with fields and screen layout. The ability to extend the logic of an app provides productivity enhancement by taking some of the thinking and calculating out of the user's hands. Examples of useful logic extensions include validating entered data, calculating default data values based on preexisting data, and mapping data fields within applications. Adding logic implies the ability to code that logic. To that end, SAP S/4HANA Cloud provides a restricted ABAP programming tool. The logic editor, shown and discussed ahead, allows the user to write ABAP code, test that code, publish the code, and compare draft code to published code on a single screen, side by side.

To create or edit logic, access the same app used for custom fields, but go to the **Custom Logic** tab (see Figure 9.12).

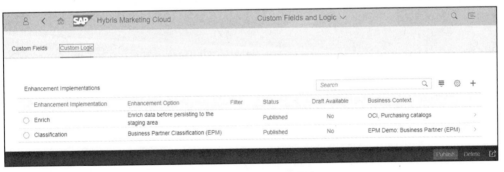

Figure 9.12 Custom Fields and Logic, Custom Logic Tab

When creating or modifying custom logic, open the editor shown in Figure 9.13. Upon initial view, the editor will show the logic that has been published to date. In the example shown in Figure 9.13, the sample logic is using the businesspartner field to determine a customer's rank field.

Figure 9.14 shows how a developer can test the logic by entering a value in the variable **businesspartner** field (above the logic), then clicking the **Test** button at the bottom right of the screen.

Figure 9.13 Custom Logic Editor

Figure 9.14 Testing New Logic

To edit the logic, click the **Create Draft** button. Figure 9.15 shows the split screen, with the **Published Logic** on one side and the **Draft Logic** next to it to allow for comparison. In this example, the rankings are reversed in the draft version; the test must be rerun. The test results show that the rank changes from **1** to **3**, even though the business-partner value remained the same.

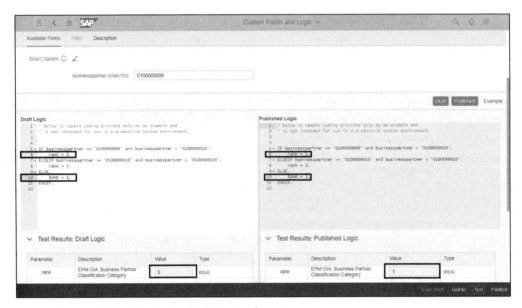

Figure 9.15 Developing and Testing Draft Logic

If this result was desired, the change could be published and the logic made available to UIs and other applications.

As this example shows, the editing tool provides a simplified interface for developing and testing code. The technical details of the underlying technology are hidden, indicating that they can't be manipulated or changed, which helps enable continued upgradeability, as well as security and data consistency. The following practices aren't allowed:

- Any DB operation, except selects from released views
- Spawning new tasks
- Dynamic programming
- Code generation

For applications that require this type of logic, a side-by-side extension (see Section 9.2) is required.

9.1.5 Adding Business Objects

Until this point in the chapter, in-app extensions have used existing UIs and tables in the database. In some cases, an entirely new database and UI may be required. Depending on the complexity, an in-app extension can still be used. The starting point is the **Custom Business Objects** tile within the extensibility catalog. Figure 9.16 shows the Custom Business Objects app and the **New Custom Business Object** pop-up.

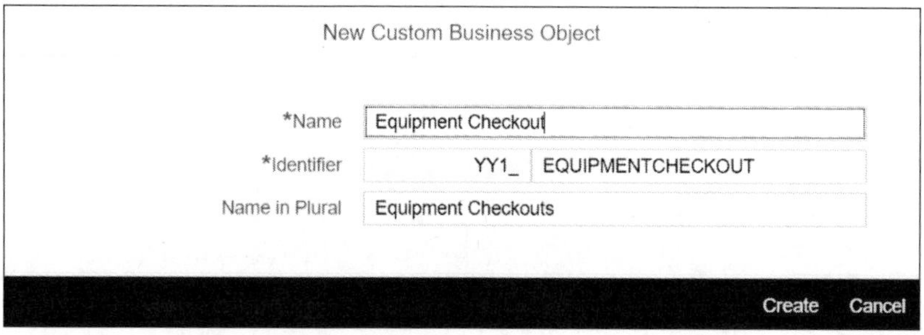

Figure 9.16 Creating New Business Object

For this basic example, a new business object is being created to support a project equipment checkout function. Once the business object is named and created, details are provided that will address how the new business object will be used. Figure 9.17 shows the options for allowing the business object to be used in a UI.

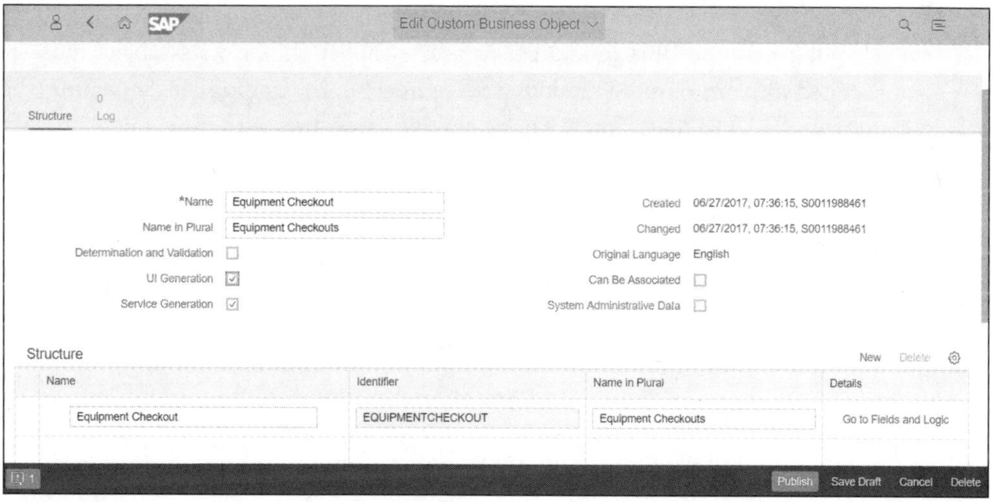

Figure 9.17 Custom Business Object Definition Detail

By enabling **UI Generation**, when the business object is completed and published, an SAP Fiori UI will automatically be generated. To complete the definition of the business object, however, fields and logic first must be added, as shown in Figure 9.18.

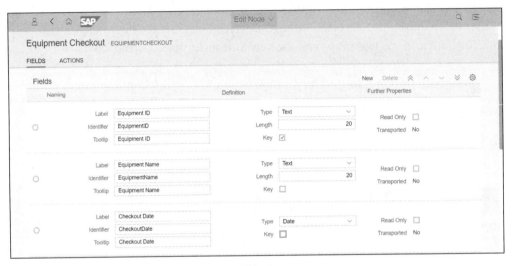

Figure 9.18 Adding Fields to Business Objects

Predetermined field types help ease the creation process. Once the fields have been added, logic can also be added (as discussed in Section 9.1.4). At this point, the business object is created and ready to be published.

Once published, the UI is generated. To access the UI, the business object must be associated with one or more catalogs (see Figure 9.19). The catalog will determine who has access to the UI (based on the business role associated with the catalog) and will also determine which grouping to place the tile in.

In this case, the business object is supporting the customer project management function, so it will be added to the **Project Management—Customer Projects** catalog. Figure 9.20 shows the new tile in the associated group.

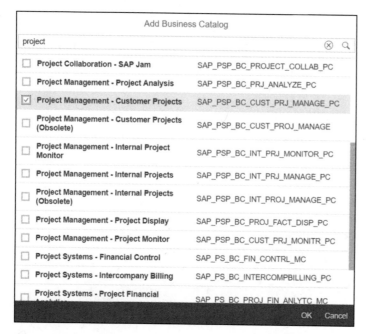

Figure 9.19 Associating Business Objects with Catalogs

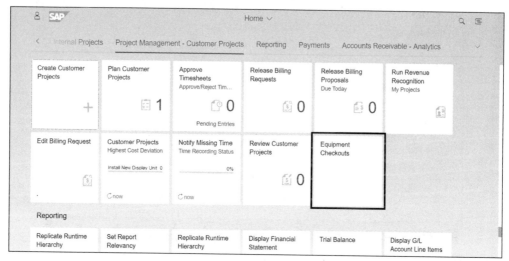

Figure 9.20 Addition of New UI Tile

After clicking on the tile, the new UI is displayed (see Figure 9.21).

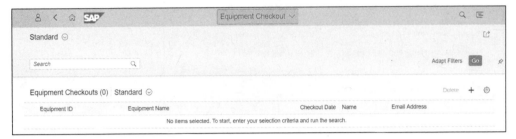

Figure 9.21 New Equipment Checkout UI

The added fields are shown, and the table is ready to accept new data. Following the standard SAP Fiori concepts, a new data row can be added by clicking the plus (+) sign. This action opens the new record UI shown in Figure 9.22.

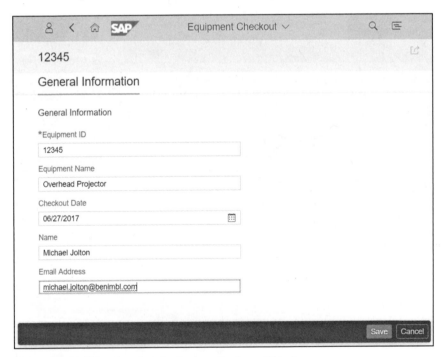

Figure 9.22 Adding New Row to Custom Business Object

As discussed in Section 9.1.3, the SAP Fiori UI can be changed as desired as well, allowing you to complete the extension.

9.1.6   Adding CDS Views

Chapter 7 discussed the ability to create custom queries from existing CDS views. Because CDS views are virtual views of data, should one of the existing CDS views not meet the needs for a query, new CDS views can be created via in-app extensibility. The process for creating a CDS view starts with the Custom CDS Views app, found within the extensibility app group. The initial screen, shown in Figure 9.23, lets you review each of the data sources to see which ones contain the fields to support the CDS view.

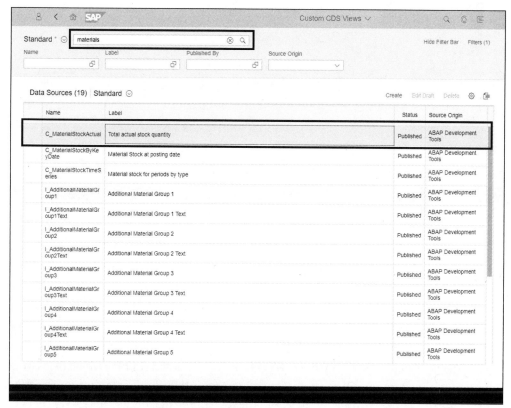

Figure 9.23 Potential Data Sources for Custom CDS View

For this example, the new CDS view will be based on fields related to material and stock. Click a data source to see its specific fields and their characteristics, as shown in Figure 9.24.

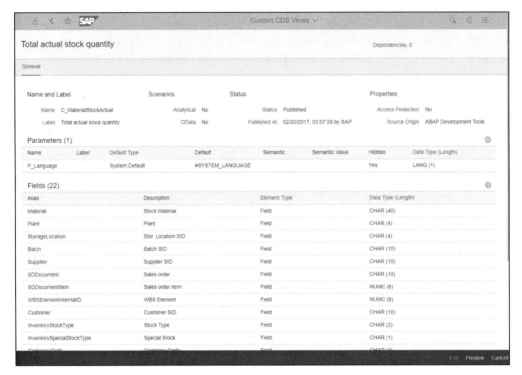

Figure 9.24 Data Source Fields

After you've determined the required data sources, select the **Create** option (shown in the top-right corner of Figure 9.23). Figure 9.25 shows a new CDS view being created. The process for creating the CDS view starts with specifying general information, such the name of the view, which will always be prefixed with *YY1_* to indicate that it's a custom CDS view. Also select the scenarios in which the CDS view will be used, for reporting or use by an app. Finally, specify the data sources.

The next step in setting up the new CDS view involves determining which fields from the data source(s) will be used. Figure 9.26 shows the simple interface for selecting data source fields (from the left side of the screen) and making any necessary changes to the **Field Type**, **Alias**, or **Label** (on the right side of the screen).

Field properties, parameters, and filters for the new view are set up in a similar fashion. Once complete, the new CDS view can be published for use in reports, apps, or other extensions.

Figure 9.25 Setting General Information for New CDS View

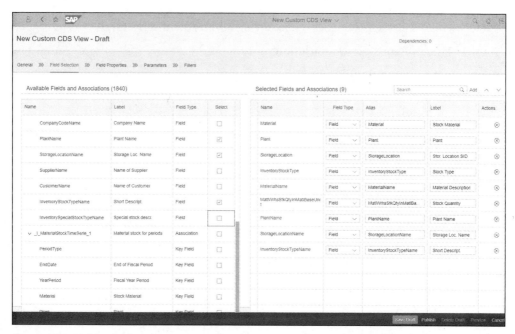

Figure 9.26 Field Selection for Custom CDS View

From changing UI layouts to customizing fields and logic to adding new database tables and UIs, in-app extensibility clearly provides tremendous flexibility to tailor SAP S/4HANA Cloud to meet individual company needs. Moreover, this tailoring doesn't create any customization code—or "Z code," as some old-school SAP developers may call it. As a result, though any extensions should be tested after upgrades, they shouldn't be affected and won't affect the ability to accept a new upgrade.

9.2   Side-by-Side Extensions Using SAP Cloud Platform

When in-app extensibility doesn't meet your business needs, you can build side-by-side extensions. The goal of these types of extensions is to add sophisticated business logic with the same SAP Fiori look and feel found throughout SAP S/4HANA Cloud, while maintaining separation from the program to prevent affecting upgradability.

Use of SAP Cloud Platform is critical to implementing side-by-side extensions. This PaaS tool is a fully fledged development platform that can support building completely new solutions with a loose coupling to SAP backend systems (to not affect upgradeability).

SAP Cloud Platform includes the following development services:

1. Infrastructure services, including:
   - Cloud operations
   - Data backup
   - Compliance
   - Service-level agreements

2. SAP HANA database services, including:
   - In-memory analytics
   - Text search
   - Planning
   - Predictive and stored procedures

3. Application services, including:
   - SAP Cloud Platform Portal
   - Security
   - Document, administration, and development tools

4. Integration services

With these services, SAP Cloud Platform is the default choice for building side-by-side extensions. Developers can use Java, HTML5, or native SAP HANA extended application services combined with the underlying open API layer.

Note that once applications are built and tested in the quality (Q) environment, they must be exported as a part of a software collection and then imported into the production (P) environment. This two-step process requires the two apps highlighted in Figure 9.27.

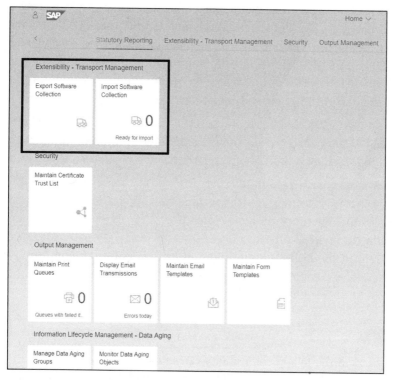

Figure 9.27 Transport Management Apps for Side-by-Side Extensions

Both apps are available in both the Q and P systems, but note that the export must originate from the Q environment, and then the import must be originate from the P environment. Any changes to the extensions must follow this same process; in other words, the extensions can't be changed in the P environment.

Although side-by-side extensions provide maximum flexibility for development, because of their loose coupling, their ability to influence the internal transactional process behavior of SAP S/4HANA Cloud is limited. This limitation is one of the reasons in-app extensibility capabilities are provided. With both approaches available, SAP S/4HANA Cloud can be extended almost without limit, yet never be removed from the upgrade path.

9.3   Customer-Developed Extensions via SAP S/4HANA Cloud SDK

The SAP S/4HANA Cloud software development kit (SDK), currently in beta release, enables users to quickly develop their own application(s) extending SAP S/4HANA by providing all the necessary libraries and project templates. With the SDK, SAP is aiming to provide an attractive development environment that enables you to efficiently develop extensions for SAP S/4HANA on SAP Cloud Platform, while ensuring that you can easily adhere to established SAP S/4HANA quality standards with regard to performance, resource consumption, and operations.

The SAP S/4HANA Cloud SDK contains tools for setting up the connection with both SAP S/4HANA and SAP S/4HANA Cloud. Components support communication with SAP S/4HANA using standard protocols such as OData.

The SDK provides a layer of abstractions for such platform features as logging, multi-tenancy, SAP S/4HANA connectivity, as well as important application features such as caching management, latency, and fault tolerance. These extensions can even be leveraged into commercial offerings for businesses facing similar challenges. More information on the SDK for user-driven extensibility is online at *https://www.sap.com/developer/topics/s4hana-cloud-sdk.html.*

9.4   Summary

This chapter presented the in-app extensibility capabilities and an overview of the side-by-side extensibility approach. The ability to create extensions without customizing the core SAP S/4HANA Cloud software can truly free a company to develop capabilities that are core to business differentiation but don't add undue overhead or costs to manage. Thus, when the developers ask where their jobs go with SAP S/4HANA Cloud being a preconfigured, uncustomizable application, the answer is that they don't necessarily go anywhere—but they *do* get better. Developers get to focus on real added value for the business, rather than maintaining the same old code just to keep the lights on.

The next and final chapter provides a summary of this book and SAP S/4HANA Cloud.

Chapter 10

Roadmap:
Where Do We Go from Here?

The SAP S/4HANA Cloud roadmap is constantly evolving with its quarterly innovation cycles. With the amount of energy SAP is investing in this game-changing product, SAP S/4HANA Cloud is poised to disrupt the SaaS ERP market like no other product before. Exciting times indeed.

—Jason Hardy, vice president, Cloud ERP

In the previous chapter, we explored how SAP S/4HANA Cloud can be extended through integration. External integration expands SAP S/4HANA Cloud's existing reach and provides an additional opportunity for customers to leverage SAP SaaS ERP in ways that help them better operate their businesses.

Although we predict that the integration function always will be a primary component of the SAP S/4HANA Cloud model, the SAP S/4HANA Cloud roadmap and its increasing functionality expansion will most likely eliminate some of the need for customer-specific extensions. Simply put, as core SAP S/4HANA Cloud functionality expands, additional extensibility contracts.

Currently, SAP S/4HANA Cloud provides a set of solid building blocks that allow organizations to construct an SAP S/4HANA Cloud digital core, either standalone or as the hub of a greater business functionality framework through additional extensions. Figure 10.1 illustrates SAP S/4HANA Cloud's vision of its ecosystem.

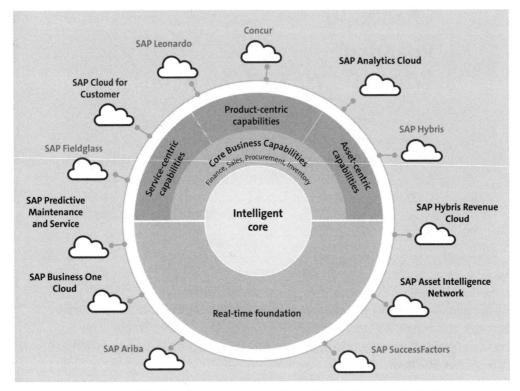

Figure 10.1 SAP S/4HANA Cloud, Expansion of Functionality from Its Digital Core

In this chapter, we'll explore the SAP S/4HANA Cloud roadmap, discussing what current plans exist for increased functionality by function and the innovation cycle concept and corresponding consumption model. Then, most importantly, we'll provide real-time online references you can use to always remain up-to-date on the latest and greatest roadmap plans.

10.1   Current Roadmap

Since its general release to the public, SAP S/4HANA Cloud has been constantly evolving to capture as much core enterprise management functionality as possible. The challenge of SAP S/4HANA Cloud was to balance between two extremes: speed to market and meaningful business value.

This was apparent in many of the early sales cycles, in which SAP S/4HANA Cloud didn't hit the bull's-eye of an organization's true business needs. Organizations were open to and intrigued by SAP S/4HANA Cloud as a potential ERP solution, but the functionality wasn't yet developed sufficiently, so SAP S/4HANA Cloud often was eliminated as a potential and viable candidate for a customer's ERP platform. Therefore, the SAP S/4HANA Cloud roadmap became crucial to the adoption of SAP S/4HANA Cloud as a solution.

The SAP S/4HANA Cloud roadmap helps customers determine the solution's applicability for any given need their organization may have. Beyond the existing functionality, many customers will decide whether SAP S/4HANA Cloud is a viable solution based upon the near-term SAP S/4HANA Cloud roadmap. In the following subsections, we discuss the importance of the roadmap and what organizations can expect as part of the evolution of SAP's flagship ERP SaaS solution.

10.1.1   The Importance of the Roadmap

The SAP ERP product roadmap as a concept has always played an important role within the SAP world. All those involved in the SAP ecosystem, whether customer, partner, competitor, or even SAP itself, needed to understand and be interested in new innovations SAP was planning to deliver as part of an upcoming release.

However, for many years, the SAP customer base was simply optimizing its SAP investment as opposed to focusing on innovation. With the introduction of SAP HANA as a platform and SAP S/4HANA as a major ERP version release, this all changed.

On-premise SAP S/4HANA and now SAP S/4HANA Cloud aren't simply newer versions of SAP ERP: They're complete reimaginings of SAP ERP. Thus, the roadmap for both products is important, because the products are being developed as we speak.

A new, dedicated, and reenergized focus has emerged for what new functionality will be introduced when. Business decisions, including product adoption and selection, are being based on what functionality currently exists within SAP S/4HANA Cloud and, for functionality gaps that customers truly need filled now, when it will be in the roadmap. As you can see, the development team can never move fast enough for the market; the market is hungry for functionality now that might be coming soon, in a year, or never. The good news is that the SAP S/4HANA Cloud innovation cycle and its new functionality is released quarterly. Figure 10.2 shows the current SAP S/4HANA Cloud roadmap and the corresponding timing of the quarterly releases.

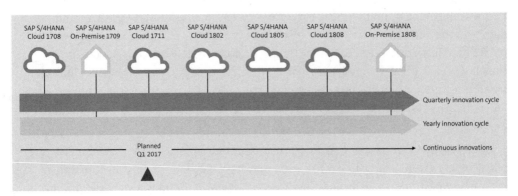

Figure 10.2 SAP S/4HANA Cloud Quarterly Release Cycles

10.1.2   Upcoming Functionalities

For the current SAP S/4HANA Cloud roadmap, the various features and functions being developed are unique to the functionality and evolving at differing degrees of rapid innovation; however, the following are several of the highlights by line of business (LOB) and business process scheduled for the upcoming planned release in August 2017:

- *Core ERP functionality, sourcing and procurement,* which can be divided into the following categories:
  - *Operational procurement:* Check item price in the catalog; perform simple services; make mass item changes in requisitioning; flexible workflow for purchase orders
  - *Sourcing and contract management:* Compare supplier quotations; mass changes to purchasing contracts; centrally manage and archive legal content in SAP S/4HANA; create and manage templates for legal transactions; ease requesting legal content for employees
  - *Invoice and payables management:* Flexible workflow for supplier invoices; simplified vendor management through integration with solutions from OpenText
  - *Purchasing analytics:* Predictive analytics for contract consumption; embedded analytics in SAP Fiori apps
- *Core functionality, sales,* with the following category:
  - *Intercompany scenarios:* Intercompany debit memo processing; intercompany credit memo processing

- *Core functionality, asset management*, which can be divided into the following categories:
  - Breakdown analysis for enterprise asset management for SAP S/4HANA Cloud
  - SAP Fiori apps for finding technical objects and maintenance execution data in SAP S/4HANA Cloud
  - Report and Repair Malfunction SAP Fiori app for SAP S/4HANA Cloud enhancements
- *Core functionality, research and development*, which can be divided into the following categories:
  - *Core product lifecycle management:* SAP S/4HANA, enhanced change records with release 1708; maintain configurable BOMs; BOM comparison service for consumption by external applications; recipe development in SAP S/4HANA Cloud; product lifecycle management content search; simplified document management in the cloud with draft 2.0; recipe finder; new change record support
  - *Manufacturing engineering:* Handover of EBOM to manufacturing
  - *Advanced variant configuration:* Enhancement of classification reuse UI component; new state-of-the-art configuration engine supporting single-level venture capital models; SAP Fiori simulation environment for BOMs; integration of new configurator with the sales order and product master, supporting the make-to-order process
  - *Enterprise portfolio and project management:* Project brief for stakeholder management; project financial reporting enhancements
- *Core functionality, manufacturing*, which can be divided into the following categories:
  - *Inventory management and batch management:* Overview page to support the inventory manager and plant manager in daily business by presenting selected and relevant key performance indicators (KPIs) and charts at a glance; inventory KPI analysis with respective follow-up actions for slow-moving materials; process and usability improvements to post; scrapping activity for quality inspection stock
  - *Available to promise:* Copy function for product allocation data; enable field extensibility; enable customer-specific definition of the visualized business impact, displaying shortage situations in the Release for Delivery app; logistics execution/delivery management; integrate decentral third-party warehouse management systems using classical interfaces

10

- *Production planning and operations (demand-driven manufacturing):* Manage safety stock and the reorder point for demand-driven replenishment; monitor stock status and stock levels of demand-driven materials; automated replenishment for demand-driven materials
- *Production planning and operations (manufacturing execution system integration):* Integrate local manufacturing execution systems with the digital core via classical interfaces
- *Quality management (quality inspection):* Provide analytical information, such as defects and quality score, for different roles; enable stock transfers and quantity splits during usage decision-making
- *Quality management (complaint management):* Monitoring defects, including worklist and graphics

- *Core functionality, finance,* which can be divided into the following categories:
  - *Accounting:* Internal tax calculation according to US sales tax requirements; managing material prices and inventory valuation; adoption of Germany's Accounting Directive Implementation Act (BilRUG)
  - *Business reporting:* Improved analytical content; how-to tutorials for customer-specific reports
  - *Planning:* Derivation of profit centers on data entry
  - *Revenue recognition:* Additional scenarios for sell from stock
  - *Financial shared services:* Enable shared services to support financial processes
  - *Payments:* Integration with SWIFT network to support multibank connectivity
  - *Cash management:* Integration with credit risk analyzer for treasury; multistep workflow in bank account management (BAM); integration of promise-to-pay; replace cash management account by bank account type; integration with payment order
  - *Treasury and risk management:* Foreign currency risk management and accounting; debt and investment management and accounting
  - *Consolidation:* Improved reporting capabilities
  - *Real estate:* Contract management and leasing based on flexible real estate management (RE-FX); IFRS 16 and US-GAAP 842 lease accounting
  - *Integration with business networks:* SAP SuccessFactors Employee Central Payroll integration
  - *Integration with SAP Analytics Cloud:* Automated transfer of master and transactional data into SAP Analytics Cloud

- *SAP Cloud Platform (use for real estate):* Enablement of customer and partner extensibility

- *SAP Cloud Platform (use for treasury):* Foreign currency and further market rates as a service

- *SAP Cloud Platform (SAP Financial Statement Insights):* Actual versus plan comparison; SAP S/4HANA Cloud for customer payments (integration of dispute management and extensibility); SAP digital payments add-on (support further payment service providers and integration scenarios for credit cards); SAP S/4HANA Cloud for credit integration (integration of further credit agencies)

- *Core functionality, human resources*, which can be divided into the following categories:

  - Integration of SAP SuccessFactors Employee Central Payroll with SAP S/4HANA Cloud

  - Support employee country transfers and the global assignment process in the time sheet and in dependent applications

  - Replication of currency exchange rates from SAP S/4HANA Cloud to SAP SuccessFactors Employee Central

  - Enable a report to give line managers greater insight into the utilization of team members

  - Enablement of additional accounting objects, such as WBS elements for activity-based time recording

  - Release CDS views for use in SAP Cloud Platform

- *Professional services functionality*, which can be divided into the following categories:

  - *Services automation:* Project services, resource requests, resource scheduling, and enhanced reporting

  - *Resource management:* Resource management—graphical overview of assignments; resource management—assignment creation

As you can see, the constant new functionality being rolled out by line of business and business process functionality is prolific—and the preceding list is only for the upcoming 1708 release. SAP's investment into SAP S/4HANA Cloud is tremendous, as is SAP's commitment to rapidly adding continuous innovation to round out the product.

10.2   Recent Innovations and How They Might Affect the Roadmap

With SAP S/4HANA Cloud being relatively new software, improvements to the product are being introduced at an uncharacteristically breakneck speed. Much of the customer adoption is founded on a complete functionality match; likewise, many of the SAP S/4HANA Cloud decisions taking place are based on new functionality to be released according to the near-term roadmap. Thus, the roadmap is of paramount importance for user adoption—and even for the ultimate success of on-premise SAP S/4HANA and SAP S/4HANA Cloud.

Recent innovations—such as core ERP functionality additions, enhanced business processes, new ways to position SAP S/4HANA as a framework, and a push towards pioneering functionality, including integration with artificial intelligence, machine learning, and more—are impacting the roadmap in exciting ways. Figure 10.3 depicts how SAP is positioning SAP S/4HANA Cloud as the digital core for cloud innovation.

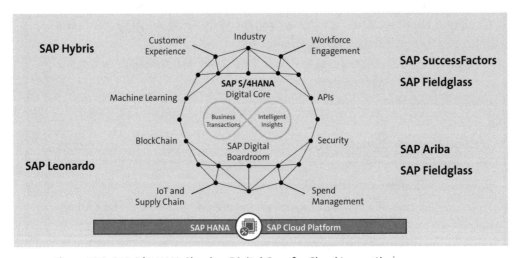

Figure 10.3 SAP S/4HANA Cloud as Digital Core for Cloud Innovation

The following sections discuss some of the roadmap innovations affecting SAP S/4HANA Cloud and how organizations can reap the benefits of new SAP S/4HANA Cloud functionality. The two primary innovation components highlight major factors within the SAP S/4HANA Cloud roadmap. Master data and extensibility are fundamental not only to the overall success of SAP S/4HANA Cloud customer implementations but to the cost to implement, as well. These key factors are discussed in further detail in the following sections.

10.2.1   Master Data

Master data is a major issue in any SAP initiative, especially within the ERP world. Within the SAP S/4HANA Cloud world, the topics of data, data conversion, and master data are all equally as important.

As discussed in Chapter 4, Section 4.4, one of the ways that SAP S/4HANA Cloud implementations limit scope and associated cost is by eliminating the expense associated with data conversion. This often-tedious and sometimes complex activity of data cleansing and data conversion is being looked at by the SAP S/4HANA Cloud product team, including ways to simplify the overall data component of implementations.

Understanding the importance of master data, SAP S/4HANA Cloud is addressing this need via a series of innovations. The following are several of the upcoming SAP S/4HANA Cloud master data innovations coming to life shortly:

1. Business partner and product maintenance

2. Business partner and product integration

3. Master data mass processing

4. Master data consolidation

5. Master data governance

10.2.2   Extensibility

Arguably, the greatest area of SAP S/4HANA Cloud innovation opportunity resides within extensibility functions, because they essentially extend SAP S/4HANA Cloud's capabilities. SAP S/4HANA Cloud will never possess the superset of all needed business process (and technical) functionality for all the possible customers. Thus, the way to fill all possible functionality gaps is to open SAP S/4HANA Cloud via hooks into outside applications. This is performed via extensibility.

By leveraging extensibility capabilities, SAP S/4HANA Cloud can act as a digital core or platform in which all business transactions can persist. These hooks act as a gateway or portal into SAP S/4HANA Cloud for access to its functions and data. More information on extensibility can be found in Chapter 9.

The exponential growth opportunity for SAP S/4HANA Cloud functionality via extensibility is tremendous. As such, SAP S/4HANA Cloud is continuing to grow innovation specific to this topic. The following are several of the upcoming SAP S/4HANA Cloud extensibility innovations being released soon:

- An extensibility cockpit as a central repository for SAP S/4HANA Cloud's extensibility capabilities
- Ability to create new UIs using the SAP Web IDE
- An SAP S/4HANA Cloud SDK to support building applications for SAP S/4HANA Cloud
- Ability to view replication of SAP S/4HANA Cloud data to SAP Cloud Platform for building applications
- Supporting field extensibility of nonvisible SAP standard fields in custom forms and queries

---

Behind the Curtain: SAP S/4HANA Cloud Becoming Creative

With the relative newness of SAP S/4HANA Cloud as a product and the fluidity in its positioning, SAP is becoming creative with how SAP S/4HANA Cloud can be deployed within some more complex scenarios. This is primarily driven by the currently missing pieces of functionality that customers are requesting. SAP is looking to close the perceived functionality gap through some very creative solutions. This may or may not be the future of how SAP is looking to position SAP S/4HANA Cloud in the long term, but it's happening now.

One very common example we're seeing in the marketplace positions SAP S/4HANA Cloud as the primary ERP platform and user experience for the customer, then complements SAP S/4HANA Cloud with non-SAP S/4HANA Cloud functionality. This non-SAP S/4HANA Cloud functionality may come from another SAP product or may be SAP Cloud Platform customer-specific functionality.

Here's a more extreme example: To replatform a global manufacturing company, SAP proposed presenting the company with a single SAP S/4HANA Cloud instance integrated with an SAP HANA Enterprise Cloud-hosted on-premise SAP S/4HANA instance, complementing the missing functionality required by the customer (and missing from SAP S/4HANA Cloud). In essence, SAP is using SAP S/4HANA Cloud and on-premise SAP S/4HANA in tandem, showing customers a single entry point into the SAP world via SAP S/4HANA Cloud.

This creative SAP S/4HANA Cloud positioning could potentially change the way SAP pivots to more complex, formerly on-premise SAP solutions.

10.3   Where to Find Roadmap Updates

With such a rapidly changing product focused on speed to market and continuous product enhancement, without question the best method of remaining up-to-date in real time is to receive updates from one of the following sources:

1. Directly from SAP online
2. From an organization's dedicated SAP account executive
3. From an SAP S/4HANA Cloud lighthouse partner

With the assistance and wealth of knowledge from any one of these trusted channels, all pertinent product functionality, innovation, capabilities, limitations, use cases, and roadmaps should be immediately available for a customer's needs.

Specific to SAP's online presence related to roadmaps and corresponding innovation, the following links should be bookmarked by all those interested in SAP S/4HANA Cloud's latest and greatest:

- **SAP Innovation Discovery**
  This website provides a real-time and constantly up-to-date innovation library across multiple products, including SAP S/4HANA Cloud and other SAP products. One of the benefits of this website is that a user can customize the innovation feed to show products highlighted based on interest and/or customer platform.

  This website can be found at *http://bit.ly/2xzxMBx*. Note: This website requires an SAP user ID and password.

- **SAP S/4HANA Cloud roadmap**
  This website links to the most recent SAP S/4HANA Cloud roadmap published. This presentation—typically a PDF—discusses the upcoming releases, starting with the current release and forecasting out typically through another three releases (or three quarters). Within the SAP S/4HANA Cloud roadmap document, highlights show what new innovation is to be released and when.

  This website can be found at *http://bit.ly/2wNZhKg*. Note: This website requires an SAP user ID and password.

10.4   Summary: What a Long, Strange Trip It's Been

As the saying goes, you have to know where you came from to know where you're going. In the previous nine chapters, we dug deep into the foundation of SAP S/4HANA

Cloud and its various components, focusing a great deal on its functionality. In this chapter, we focused on SAP S/4HANA Cloud's ever-evolving product and its future, represented by the SAP S/4HANA Cloud roadmap. Understanding the importance of the SAP S/4HANA Cloud roadmap and having the resources to always find the roadmap in real time provides insight into where SAP S/4HANA Cloud is going.

Next, we will wrap up the book by highlighting the most important concepts behind S/4HANA Cloud. With so much information and content behind SAP's latest groundbreaking SaaS ERP, we will provide a recap and refresher for one last review.

Conclusion

Deep in the financial district in the epicenter of the investment world, a small room within the New York Stock Exchange stood as the backdrop for the 2017 SAP Capital Markets Day. The entire SAP SE executive board, including SAP CEO Bill McDermott, and Jennifer Morgan, president of SAP North, were in attendance for another important SAP S/4HANA Cloud announcement.

The day was meant to highlight many of SAP's recent innovations and its future outlook, but no product raised more excitement than SAP S/4HANA Cloud. It's true that SAP S/4HANA Cloud's existence was announced only 21 months earlier at SAPPHIRE 2015—but the product's true celebration party was now.

Darren Roos, the newly anointed SAP S/4HANA Cloud president, was on hand to showcase its elevated relevance in the world. He announced: "Decades ago, SAP invented and became the leader in first-generation ERP. Later, we were early to build first-generation cloud ERP along with other new cloud vendors. While many cloud ERP vendors remain on this early architecture, SAP did not stop there, and invested in innovating the next generation of cloud ERP. SAP S/4HANA Cloud encompasses the latest architecture and technology innovations, along with SAP's proven set of business management expertise to usher in a true new generation of intelligent ERP in the cloud."

SAP is positioning SAP S/4HANA Cloud as a primary software product within its portfolio. As we've explored in this book, SAP S/4HANA Cloud continues to evolve and increase its reach, both in functionality and use case areas, and both wide and deep. We believe that SAP S/4HANA Cloud will not only begin to replace other SAP midmarket ERP products, such as SAP Business ByDesign and SAP Business One, but also will begin to expand north into the large enterprise space (Fortune 1000) as a major complement to on-premise SAP ERP offerings such as on-premise SAP S/4HANA. Too much energy, investment, buzz, and executive leadership is being deployed to think otherwise.

Within this book, we explored the basic tenants of SAP S/4HANA Cloud. Throughout Part I, we defined the basics of SAP S/4HANA Cloud, including answering the question "What is S/4HANA Cloud?" in Chapter 1 and reviewing fundamental cloud-based ERP basics such as the concepts of SaaS, IaaS, and PaaS.

In perhaps arguably the most important chapter of the book, Chapter 2 detailed the use cases for deploying SAP S/4HANA Cloud, including the two common and distinct scenarios of the two-tiered federated SAP ERP landscape and the single SAP S/4HANA Cloud ERP installation as an organization's SAP ERP choice. We continued to discuss additional important deployment factors, such as implementation requirements from a delivery perspective (Chapter 3) and SAP S/4HANA Cloud investment needs, such as software, implementation, and long-term production support costs (Chapter 4). Chapter 5 rounded out Part I with things to think about regarding post-go-live SAP S/4HANA Cloud support requirements.

Part II focused more on the what of SAP S/4HANA Cloud, probing deep into its product functionality. Chapter 6 was another crucial cornerstone chapter of the book, in which we detailed SAP S/4HANA Cloud's module and corresponding business process functionality. In essence, this chapter illustrates a key decision-making factor for whether SAP S/4HANA Cloud is the right solution for your organization. Chapter 7 dug into the analytics functions of S/4HANA Cloud's embedded business intelligence capabilities. Rounding out Part II, Chapter 8 explored integrations and how built-in integrations and custom integrations have the ability to add to SAP S/4HANA Cloud's core functionality through customer enhancement.

Finally, in Part III, we explored how an organization can extend SAP S/4HANA Cloud as a digital core with extensibility options. Chapter 8 focused on integrations, and Chapter 9 covered extensibility, including in-app and side-by-side extensibility. Both features enhance SAP S/4HANA Cloud by filling in those gaps the product doesn't fill in its core form. Leveraging the extension concept increases SAP S/4HANA Cloud's reach and functionality, which truly increases the application of the SAP S/4HANA Cloud platform as a digital core. Finally, Chapter 10 presented a look into the future, contemplating where SAP S/4HANA Cloud is going. Although predicting the future is impossible, especially with this ever-evolving product, this chapter did provide a glance into SAP's documented future innovation plans based on published roadmaps. Without question, however, the greatest value of this chapter can be found in the resources and websites provided. These real-time SAP links provide current information on SAP S/4HANA Cloud's new innovations and future functionality.

In fact, to prove this very point, during the writing of this book we experienced the fluidity of SAP S/4HANA Cloud firsthand. When we began writing the book, SAP S/4HANA Cloud had established "editions" focused on specific features such as finance, professional services, and so on. Soon after writing a full chapter on editions, the concept changed, and we had to rewrite several sections to align our book with the new SAP S/4HANA Cloud changes!

Key Takeaways

This book covered a great deal of content and several new concepts. To reinforce the book's most salient points, we've compiled the following list of the most important takeaways from our perspective:

- **Building the business case is paramount.**
  SAP S/4HANA Cloud as an ERP platform isn't for every organization. If you're reading this, then there's a high probability that your organization is exploring SAP S/4HANA Cloud. Thus, being able to effectively articulate the business case for yourself and your leadership is a first fundamental step. If the balance between pre-configured SAP Best Practices and more limited functionality/configuration on the one hand and lower overall IT costs on the other resonates, then SAP S/4HANA Cloud could be the right solution. However, if your organization requires extensive customer-specific configuration and/or customization, on-premise SAP S/4HANA most likely is the better choice.

- **Extensibility is a key method for digital core extension.**
  SAP S/4HANA Cloud provides a digital core for cloud-first landscapes. With a host of extensibility options available, such as in-app extensibility, side-by-side extensibility, APIs, and SAP Cloud Platform, the opportunities to link other applications (both SAP and non-SAP), build customer-specific SAP Cloud Platform applications, and increase an organization's business process scope all exist as excellent methods for expanding SAP S/4HANA Cloud's functionality. Extensibility is an excellent solution for expanding SAP S/4HANA Cloud's reach via integration with other apps.

- **Accelerators and SAP Best Practices ease SAP S/4HANA Cloud deployment.**
  Like no other ERP product before it, SAP S/4HANA Cloud doesn't just promote the usage of industry best practices or accelerated methodology; its design is based on it. Because SAP S/4HANA Cloud has limited end user configuration to a major extent, implementing it is truly driven by and on the back of accelerators in the form of delivered preconfigured functionality. These accelerators not only are tremendous cost savings implementation mechanisms but also ensure users deploy ERP in a proven, SAP Best Practices way. Furthermore, SAP S/4HANA Cloud is meant to be delivered via SAP Activate. SAP Activate's implementation approach is founded in the fit-to-standard methodology, stressing (imploring!) that SAP S/4HANA Cloud should be implemented as an out-of-the-box solution.

- **SAP S/4HANA Cloud is an economical choice for ERP.**
  SAP is pushing cloud hard in product, practice, and messaging. In a major move,

SAP S/4HANA Cloud has been created to present SAP's first true SaaS ERP offering built for the primary purpose of driving cloud-based ERP. As such, the economics factors of SAP S/4HANA Cloud, from monthly user subscription pricing through rapid implementation and lean long-term production costs, are very competitively priced. For those familiar with on-premise SAP pricing, the new SAP S/4HANA Cloud cost structure is not only refreshing but eye-opening.

- **SAP S/4HANA Cloud is always evolving.**
  This message has been reinforced throughout the pages of this book, over and over. As a relatively new SAP innovation, SAP S/4HANA Cloud is continuing to grow in breadth and depth. In fact, the quarterly innovation cycle in which new functionality is added to the product says it all. Thus, it's imperative to understand what resources exist to help you remain abreast of what new functionality is available and when. Fortunately and strategically, SAP has created a wealth of knowledge sources available for the SAP S/4HANA Cloud user community, including release info, how-tos, and extensibility insight. Staying close to these resources provides an organization with the opportunity to maximize its SAP S/4HANA Cloud investment.

The new world of SAP S/4HANA Cloud is exciting. Although the analogy of building a car while you're driving it doesn't necessarily apply to SAP S/4HANA Cloud, the product is constantly evolving, and information in the greater marketplace is scarce, frankly.

SAP S/4HANA Cloud is the future. This is not marketing. This is not salesmanship.

Just like SAP bet the farm on the concept of and commitment to SAP HANA in 2010 (which has paid off), it's now investing an equal amount of resources into what SAP S/4HANA Cloud is and its impact on the greater ERP SaaS market. We believe that the promise of this product platform is real and will continue to grow in adoption, importance, and functionality within the greater ERP space.

We wish you the best of luck on your SAP S/4HANA Cloud journey!

The Authors

Michael Jolton is the vice president of service delivery at NIMBL, an award-winning Denver-based SAP consulting firm and the leader of its SAP S/4HANA Cloud practice. Throughout his career, Michael has helped clients develop and implement ERP strategies, and he's now applying those experiences to help clients evaluate and implement SAP S/4HANA Cloud. Michael received his MBA in Finance from the University of Wisconsin-Madison and his BA in Economics from Lawrence University.

Yosh Eisbart is the CEO and cofounder of NIMBL. Yosh has helped NIMBL grow into one of North America's most respected SAP technology firms; it's received local and national awards and serves both Fortune 1000 companies and midmarket firms. Most importantly, Yosh is a proud husband and the father of four amazing children.

About NIMBL

Based in Colorado, NIMBL is an award-winning SAP consultancy and recognized thought leader servicing both midmarket firms and Fortune 1000 companies. NIMBL provides consulting services for SAP business transformation (on-premise SAP S/4HANA, SAP S/4HANA Cloud, functional/business process, analytics, etc.) and SAP technical knowledge (SAP HANA, development, SAP Cloud Platform, user experience, testing, SAP Solution Manager, upgrades/migrations, integration, test data migration services [TDMS], etc.), as well as US-based remote SAP application management services.

As one of a handful of trained and experienced SAP S/4HANA Cloud implementation partners, NIMBL (*www.benimbl.com*) is passionate about this exciting product. NIMBL is committed to being an SAP S/4HANA Cloud expert that's always ahead of the industry. On your journey, if you have questions regarding the product, its use cases, objective perspectives of the solution, pricing questions, or anything else, it would be our pleasure to act as a trusted SAP resource. With only a handful of SAP S/4HANA Cloud Lighthouse Partners available globally, NIMBL is positioned as a go-to SAP S/4HANA Cloud source, now and for the future.

To learn more about NIMBL, please email us at *jack@benimbl.com* or visit us at *be-nimbl.com*.

Index

80/20 rule 168

A

Accelerated customer returns 207
Accelerated plan-to-product 178
Accounting and closing operations 218
Accounting Directive Implementation Act
    (BilRUG) 314
Accounts payable 174, 220
Accounts payable accountant 221
Accounts payable process 159
Accounts receivable 224
Adobe Lifecycle Designer 105
Advanced available-to-promise (AATP)
    functionality 188
Advanced variant configuration 237
Analysis path 208, 253
Analysis scope items 213
Analytics 118
Analyze Outbound Delivery Logs app 200
Annual maintenance costs 113, 115
App Finder 141
Application management services
    (AMS) 41, 143
Application monitoring 281
Application program interfaces
    (APIs) 274, 281
Approval thresholds 158
Approve Purchase Order app 167
Approver IDs 222
Ariba Network 270
    purchase order collaboration 165
Ariba Network configuration 159
ASAP 60, 86
Asset accounting 226
Asset management 313
Asset master data 226
Automated payments 222

B

Backorder processing 189
Bank account management (BAM) 314
Bank-lockbox-Vertex 101
Bar chart 253
Basic data integration 235
Basic production planning 179
Basic production processing 182
Basic shipping 169
Batch management 164
Batch number 164
Billing block 199
Blueprinting workshops 119
Built-in integrations 268
Business analysts 43
Business framework 71
Business group scope items 82
Business intelligence (BI) 271
Business objects 299
Business practice-driven model 59
Business Process Model and Notation (BPMN)
    2.0 format 85
    2.0 modeler 85
Business roles 98
Business value 57

C

Cards 177, 255
Cash and liquidity management 232
CDS views 248, 260, 274, 303–304
Change acceptance cycle 127
Chart of accounts 100, 218
Charts 245
    filtering 245
Checkbook management 221
Claims, returns, and refund
    management 206
Classification and segmentation 151, 154
Cloud Cockpit 275
Cloud Connector 275

Cloud extension model 114
  advantages 114
Cloud Foundry 274, 281
Cloud Print Manager 137
Collective billing 200
Communication phases
  new release awareness 128
  postrelease support 131
  prerelease review/testing 129
  user enablement 129
Communication plan 131
Concur 269
Concur Expense 217
Confirm Production Order Operation
  app 187
Consignment-based sales 203
Contingent labor 174
Contingent workforce 54
Contract-to-cash 215
Core finance 218
Corporate venturing 75
Corrective maintenance 190
Cost center analysis 258
Cost estimation 119
Create Activity app 154
Create Customer Projects app 211
Create KPI app 247
Create Outbound Delivery without Order
  Reference app 200
Create PIR app 180
Create Purchase Order Advanced app 172
Create Supplier Invoice app 165
Create Tile app 140, 249
Credit and collections 218
Credit memos 206
Creditworthiness data 224
Custom Business Objects app 299
Custom CDS Views app 303
Custom code 118
Custom functionality 122
Custom integrations 274
  developing 276
Custom reports 139
Custom tiles 247
Customer project management 211
Customer projects scope item 214

Customer returns 207
Customer use cases 49
Customization 60, 64
Customized queries 260
  creating 263

D

Data conversion 117
Data management 234
Data migration 99
Debit memos 206
Demand driven replenishment 237
Demand forecast 179
Dependencies 211
Deploy phase 106
Deployment 75
Direct costs 111
Discover phase 87, 89
Discover work package 211
Discrete manufacturing 178
Display Subcontracting Stocks by
  Supplier app 167
Down payments 199

E

Edit Tile app 140
Editions 83
Electronic Data Interchange (EDI) 285
Embedded analytics 239
Emergency maintenance 191
Employee business role 94
Enabling new releases 134
End user support 121, 143
End-to-end business process flows 149
End-to-end process 36
End-to-end process orientation 149
Engineering bill of materials (EBOM) 192
ERP bake-off 116
ERP deployment 62
ERP in the cloud 50
ERP product portfolio 28
ERP systems 59
Evaluations 248
Event-based revenue recognition 216

Excel 239, 257
   SAP Activate 91
Expert configuration 37, 219
Explore phase 87, 95, 104
Extend cloud 277
Extend on-premise applications 276
Extended bank account management 232
Extensibility 31, 68, 116, 287, 317
   apps 288
   business catalog 288
   support 43
   usage 122
External integration 309

F

Federated manufacturing model 67
   factors 68
Fit-to-standard 62–63, 116, 119
   analysis 95
   exercises 120
   workshops 96–97
Free goods processing 202
Free of charge delivery 200
Freight costs 198
Full-time equivalent (FTE) 109
Functionality fit 53

G

G/L accounts 104
Gartner study 50
General ledger scope items 220
GL Account Master Data app 101
Goods receipt 168
Graph types 251
Graphical query 263
Graphical reports 251
Growth-stage businesses 267

H

Holding company model 70, 72
   benefits 71
Hot fixes 103
HR connectivity 234

I

IFRS 16 314
Implementation 79
   costs 71, 119
   timeline 29
In-app extensibility 43, 117
   adding business objects 299
   adding CDS views 303
   adding fields 293
   adding logic 296
   authorization 288
   changing fields 291
   deleting fields 295
In-app extensions 287
Incident report 136
Indirect materials 157
Industry-specific functionality 30
Infrastructure as a service (IaaS) 40
Install Additional Software app 105
Integration 76, 267
   management 143
   strategy 272
Intelligent cloud ERP 28
Intercompany processing for project
   services 216
Internal development 278
Internal order—actual scope item 231
International businesses 52
Intrastat processing 81, 207
Inventory accounting and closing
   operations 228
Inventory management 168, 190, 313
Inventory valuation for year-end
   closing 228
Invoice and payables management 173, 312
Invoice automation 174
Invoice collaboration 173
Invoice processing 174
IT Spend 51

K

Kanban 178, 189
Key performance indicators (KPIs) 126, 139,
   240, 247, 313
KPI Workspace app 139, 248

L

Lease accounting 237
Legacy data migration 106
Legacy ERP systems 239
Liquidity 232
Localization 77
Logic editor 296–297

M

Machine learning 39
Machine learning system 226
Maintain Business Partner app 220
Maintain Business Roles app 141
Maintain Form Templates app 138
Maintenance 125
Maintenance management 190
Maintenance strategy 191
Maintenance windows 133
Maintenance, repair, and operations [MRO]
    support materials 157
Make-to-order 178, 186
Make-to-stock 178, 183
Make-to-stock process manufacturing
    functionality 184
Make-to-stock repetitive manufacturing ... 186
Manage Materials Coverage app 182
Manage Production Operations app ... 187
Manage Purchase Contracts app 256
Manage Purchase Requisitions app 162, 167
Manage Questionnaire:Evaluation app 153
Manage Sales Quotations app 196
Manage Sales without Charge app 200
Manage Sources of Supply app 151
Manage Stock app 170
Manage Test Processes app 135
Manage Your Application app 84
Manage Your Solution app 99–100, 102, 158
Manufacturing resource planning
    (MRP II) 178
Market analysis reporting 229
Master data 317
Master data maintenance 235
Master data management 236
Material requirements planning (MRP) 237

Materials planner 180
Materials requirements planning
    (MRP) 158, 178
Mergers and acquisitions 72, 74
Migration 77
Migration Cockpit 109, 235
Monitor Product Availability app 188
Monitor Production Orders app 183
MRP run 180
Multidimensional analysis 256, 260
Multitenant 38
My Learning app 94

N

Neo 275, 281
New cloud applications 276
Nontransportable data 107

O

OData 308
Ongoing maintenance 125
OpenText 165
Operational contract management 166
Operational procurement 312
Operational purchasing 150, 156
Optical character recognition (OCR)
    engine 165
Order and contracts management 194
Order-to-cash 193, 208
    scope items 193
Order-to-Cash Overview app 208
Organizational structure change 101
Output Parameter Determination app 163
Outsourced IT 54
Overdue receivables management 226
Overview apps 255

P

Pallet 206
Parallel ledgers 227, 229
Pareto principle 168
Payments and bank communications 232
Pick, pack, and ship process 198

Pie chart 252
Planned independent requirements
(PIRs) 180
Planned to actual reporting 231
Platform as a service (PaaS) 40
Post Goods Movement app 170
Post Goods Receipt app 163
Prebuilt integrations 273
Preconfigured ERP 55
Preconfigured processes 35
Predetermined field types 300
Prepare phase 90
Preventative maintenance 191
Pricing structure 29
Process flows 85
Process manufacturing 178
Process Receivables app 233
Procurement analytics 175
Procurement manager 153
Procurement master data 150
Procurement Overview app 177, 255
Procure-to-pay 150
Product controls 179
Product functionality 147
Product lifecycle management 313
Product profitability reporting 230
Production (P) system 88, 107, 134, 307
Production cutover 107
Production system provisioning 102
Profit and loss (P&L) analysis 259
Proforma invoice 200
Project control and product development . 192
Project management 210
Project organization (org) chart 91
Project profitability reporting 231
Project scope 109
Project services 210
Project team 109
Purchase contracts 166
Purchase control functionality 166
Purchase of direct materials scope item 168
Purchase order collaboration 165
Purchase order processing 160
Purchase requisition 162
Purchaser business role 161
Purchasing analytics 312

Q

Quality (Q) system 88, 107, 134, 143, 307
provisioning 100
Quality engineer 169, 173
Quality management 187, 314
Quality management in stock handling 173
Quality technician 169
Quarterly release cycle 55
Quarterly release management 126
user communication 127
Questionnaires 153
QuickBooks 113
Quote automation 159

R

Realize phase 102
Rebates 203
Receivables management 233
Release for Delivery app 313
Repetitive manufacturing 178, 186
Report development 136
Request questionnaire 101
Requirements processing 157
Resource management 237
Resource manager 213
Return on investment (ROI) 49
Returnables processing scope item 206
Revenue and cost accounting 228
Rework processes 187
Roadmap 319
Run phase 108

S

SaaS ERP 28, 77, 116, 309
Sales monitoring and analytics 208
Sales of nonstock item with order-specific
procurement 201
Sales Order Fulfillment app 204
Sales order fulfillment monitoring 204
Sales order management and
processing 195
Sales order processing with customer
down payment 199

Sales quotation 196
Sales Volume app 257
SAP Activate 60, 79, 86, 91, 119, 270, 281
   guided configuration tools 61
   integration support 61
   lifecycle 87
   methodology approach 61
   realize phase 137
   tips 108
SAP Analytics Cloud 116, 271
SAP API Business Hub 272, 282–283
SAP App Center 32
SAP Ariba 156, 270
   quote automation 159
SAP Ariba integration 174
SAP Ariba Sourcing 167, 270
SAP Best Practices 29, 36, 55–57, 60, 73, 79,
   119, 126, 137, 260
   apps 290
   content 83
   navigating 80
   process flows 186
SAP Best Practices Explorer 56, 80, 137
SAP Best Practices workflow 162
SAP Business All-in-One 31
SAP Business ByDesign 28
SAP Business One 28
SAP Business Planning and Consolidation
   (SAP BPC) 231
SAP Business Suite powered by
   SAP HANA 34
SAP Cash Application 226
SAP Cash Management 232
SAP Cloud Identity 92
SAP Cloud Platform 31, 33, 40, 43, 46, 51,
   116, 144, 274, 306, 315
   deployment 278
   development 279
   development services 306
   extension 277
   lifecycle 279
SAP Cloud Platform Cockpit 275
SAP Cloud Platform Identity
   Authentication 92
SAP Cloud Print Manager 105
SAP Cockpit 236

SAP CoPilot 28, 242
SAP ERP 53, 311
SAP Fieldglass 174, 271
SAP Financial Services Network 222, 233
SAP Financial Statement Insights 315
SAP Fiori 240
   list report 243
   Object page 243
   Overview page 242
   UX 240
SAP Fiori 2.0 240
SAP Fiori apps 313
SAP Fiori apps library 290
SAP Fiori elements 242
SAP Fiori launchpad 143, 222, 225, 244, 251
SAP Fiori UI 300, 302
SAP Governance, Risk, and Compliance 98
SAP GUI 240
SAP GUI app 289
SAP HANA 39
SAP HANA database 257
SAP HANA Enterprise Cloud 34
SAP HANA in-memory database 239
SAP HANA XSA 274
SAP Help Portal 93
SAP Hybris 43, 270
SAP Hybris Cloud for Customer 270
SAP Innovation Discovery 319
SAP Jam methodologies hub 94
SAP Learning Hub 94
SAP Leonardo 39
SAP production support model 42
SAP S/4HANA 29, 311
   cost saving opportunities 51
SAP S/4HANA Cloud 287, 308
   1705 242
   1708 .... 313, 315
   add-ons 113
   analytics 118
   benefits 51
   best practices configuration 81
   bolt-ons 116
   business processes 35
   code line 31, 40
   configuration 37
   costs 111

SAP S/4HANA Cloud (Cont.)
    countries and languages 77
    customers 49
    ecosystem 309
    fact sheet 29
    for start-ups 73
    functional overview 148
    implementation 79
    implementation cost components 115
    implementation estimate template 120
    infrastructure 41
    innovation cycle 30, 311
    innovations 316
    integration 267
    lighthouse partner program 118
    M&A 75
    maintenance 125
    overview 27
    product functionality 147
    quarterly release cycles 312
    roadmap 66, 309–310, 312
    SAP Ariba Sourcing integration 167
    software development kit
        (SDK) 32, 288, 308
    support 41
    upcoming functionalities 312
    upgrade calendar 133
SAP S/4HANA Cloud AMS 122
    provider 123
SAP S/4HANA Cloud API 283
SAP S/4HANA Cloud Migration Cockpit 99
SAP Single Sign-On functionality 280
SAP Smart Business tiles 244, 246
SAP SuccessFactors 234, 269
SAP SuccessFactors Employee
    Central 234, 269
SAP support staff 55
SAP Web IDE 275
SAPPHIRE 59
SAP-to-SAP integrations 271
SAPUI5 app 288
Scheduling agreements in
    procurement 160
Scheduling deliveries 161
Scope item groups 82
Scope items 82, 135
    activation 136

Scrapping stock 170
SDK for iOS 275
SDK for Java development 275
Self-service configuration UIs (SSCUIs) 37
Serial number management 164
Side-by-side extensibility 45, 69, 117
Side-by-side extensions 288, 306
Software as a service (SaaS) 38
Solution scope 36
Source assignment 167
Sourcing and contract management 312
Sprints 88
Stage Materials for Production app 183
Standard bank account management 232
Starter system 87, 92
Start-ups 72
Statistical key figures (SKFs) 228
Statutory reporting 229
Subcontracting 166, 189
Subscription price structure 112
Subscription timeframes 113
Subsidiary process flow 69
Summary rows 259
Supplier activity management 154
Supplier classification and
    segmentation 154
Supplier evaluation 151–152
Supplier invoice 165
Supplier Invoices List app 222
Supplier management 151

T

T&E 269
Taxonomies 152
Team requirements 108
    timelines 109
Technical group scope items 82
Test plans 100, 105
Test scripts 84, 135
    overview table 84
    procedures table 84
Third party options 201
Third-party warehouse management
    integration 237
Tiered pricing 113

Tile customization 139
Tiles 244
    formats 250
Time and expense management 216
Timesheet entry 216
Total cost of ownership (TCO) 30
Transfer Stock app 171
    in-plant 171
Treasury and financial risk
    management 232
Treasury management 237
Trial system 87, 89
Two-tiered ERP 33, 64, 267
    argument 65
    maturity levels 66
    scenarios 33
Two-tiered manufacturing headquarters 69

U

United Nations Standard Products and
    Services Code (UNSPSC) 159
Upgrade cycles 55
Upgrade process 134
User attitudes 130
User experience 89
User interface (UI) adaptation 43

User training 117
Utilization analysis 213

V

Variant configuration 313
Vendor invoice creation 165
Vendor invoices 222
Vendor management system (VMS) 271
Venture capital 73
Vertex 101
Virtual data model 260

W

Whitelisted APIs 45
Wholesaler 203
Work breakdown structure (WBS) 192
Work items 211

Y

Year-end asset accounting 227

Z

Z code 306

- Learn what SAP S/4HANA offers your company for financials and logistics

- Get the scoop on SAP S/4HANA deployment options, implementation, extensibility, and more

- Reference customer case studies to see how other companies are transforming their businesses

Bardhan, Baumgartl, Chaadaev, Choi, Dudgeon, Lahiri, Meijerink, Worsley-Tonks

SAP S/4HANA

An Introduction

Moving your business to SAP S/4HANA or wondering if it's right for you? From finance to logistics, from on-premise to cloud implementations, and from industry solutions to reporting, see what SAP S/4HANA can offer! Understand its architecture, adoption scenarios, and how SAP Activate can expedite your transformation. Learn about all-new functionality for warehousing, manufacturing, procurement, and more. Up to date for release 1709!

approx. 550 pages, 2nd edition, avail. 11/2017
E-Book: $59.99 | **Print:** $69.95 | **Bundle:** $79.99

www.sap-press.com/4499

- Learn what SAP S/4HANA offers for supply chain management: manufacturing, warehousing, procurement, and beyond

- Explore embedded analytics and key SAP Fiori applications for supply chain processes

- Preview your migration to SAP S/4HANA

Bhattacharjee, Monti, Perel, Vazquez

Logistics with SAP S/4HANA

An Introduction

Welcome to logistics in a digital world. From procurement to production and everything in between, see how SAP S/4HANA transforms your SAP Logistics landscape. Examine each supply chain line of business in SAP S/4HANA: sales order management, manufacturing, inventory management, plant maintenance, and more. Discover key innovations such as MRP Live and embedded SAP EWM. Explore the future of logistics with SAP!

approx. 500 pages, avail. 11/2017
E-Book: $59.99 | **Print:** $69.95 | **Bundle:** $79.99

www.sap-press.com/4485

Interested in reading more?

Please visit our website for all new book
and e-book releases from SAP PRESS.

www.sap-press.com